LESSONS 1-60

GREGG
College Keyboarding & Document Processing
for Windows™
8th Edition

Scot Ober, Ph.D.
Professor, Department of Business Education
and Office Administration
Ball State University
Muncie, Indiana

Robert N. Hanson, Ed.D.
Professor Emeritus, Department of Office Systems
and Business Education
Northern Michigan University
Marquette, Michigan

Jack E. Johnson, Ph.D.
Director of Business Education
Department of Management
and Business Systems
State University of West Georgia
Carrollton, Georgia

Arlene Rice, M.A.
Professor, Office
Administration Department
Los Angeles City College
Los Angeles, California

Robert P. Poland, Ph.D.
Professor Emeritus, Business
and Distributive Education
Michigan State University
East Lansing, Michigan

Albert D. Rossetti, Ed.D.
Professor, Information
and Decision Sciences Department
School of Business
Montclair State University
Montclair, New Jersey

GLENCOE
McGraw-Hill

New York, New York   Columbus, Ohio   Woodland Hills, California   Peoria, Illinois

REVIEWERS

Ms. Dianne S. Campbell
Athens Technical Institute
Athens, Georgia

Dr. Marsha Gadzera
Northshore Community College
Danvers, Massachusetts

Dr. William J. Dross
Columbus State Community College
Columbus, Ohio

Mrs. Marilyn Satterwhite
Danville Area Community College
Danville, Illinois

Ms. Sherry Young
Kingwood College
Kingwood, Texas

Photo Credits Cover: Aaron Haupt, Stephen Johnson, Photone library; R-2, Aaron Haupt; 1, 39, 94, Jeff Bates: SB-1, Glencoe file.

Library of Congress Cataloging-in-Publication Data

College keyboarding and document processing for Windows, lessons 1-60
    /Scot Ober . . . [et al.] .--8th ed.
        p.   cm.
    Includes index.
    ISBN 0-02-803161-X
        1. Electronic data processing--Keyboarding--Study and teaching.
2. WordPerfect for Windows (Computer file)--Study and teaching.
3. Microsoft Word for Windows--Study and teaching. I. Ober, Scot,
Date
QA76.9.K48C645   1996
652.5' 5365--dc20   95-48921
                                                 CIP

Glencoe/McGraw-Hill
A Division of The McGraw·Hill Companies

**Gregg College Keyboarding and Document Processing for Windows, Eighth Edition,
Lessons 1-60**

Send all inquiries to:
Glencoe/McGraw-Hill
8787 Orion Place
Columbus, OH 43240

13 14 15 16 17 - 00

ISBN 0-02-803161-X

Contents

PART ONE

The Alphabet, Number, and Symbol Keys

PART TWO

Letters, Memos, Tables, and Reports

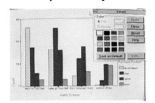

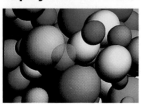

Preface

Gregg College Keyboarding & Document Processing for Windows, 8th Edition, is a multicomponent instructional program designed to give the student and the instructor a high degree of flexibility and a high degree of success in meeting their respective goals. To facilitate the choice and use of materials, the core components of this instructional system are available in either a kit format or a book format. *Keyboarding for Windows, 4th Edition,* is also available for the development of touch-typing skills for use in shorter computer keyboarding classes.

The Kit Format

Gregg College Keyboarding & Document Processing for Windows, 8th Edition, provides a complete kit of materials for both courses in the keyboarding curriculum generally offered by colleges. Each kit, which is briefly described below, contains a softcover textbook, a student data disk for use with the correlated software instructional program, and a student word processing manual.

Kit 1: Lessons 1-60 This kit provides the text, word processing manual, and software for the first course. Since this kit is designed for the beginning student, its major objectives are to develop touch control of the keyboard and proper typing techniques, build basic speed and accuracy, and provide practice in applying those basic skills to the formatting of letters, reports, tables, memos, and other kinds of personal and business communications.

Kit 2: Lessons 61-120. This kit provides the text and software for the second course. This course continues the development of basic typing skills and emphasizes the formatting of various kinds of business correspondence, reports, tables, electronic forms, and desktop publishing projects from unarranged and rough-draft sources.

The Book Format

For the convenience of those who wish to obtain the core instructional materials in separate volumes, *Gregg College Keyboarding & Document Processing for Windows, 8th Edition*, offers a textbook for the first course (*Gregg College Keyboarding & Document Processing for Windows, 8th Edition, Lessons 1-60*), for the second course (*Gregg College Document Processing for Windows, 8th Edition, Lessons 61-120*),

for a two-semester course (*Gregg College Keyboarding & Document Processing for Windows, 8th Edition, Lessons 1-120*), as well as for a third-semester course (*Gregg College Keyboarding & Document Processing for Windows, 8th Edition, Lessons 121-180*). In each instance, the content of these textbooks is identical with that of the corresponding textbooks in the kit format.

Supporting Materials

Gregg College Keyboarding & Document Processing for Windows, 8th Edition, includes the following additional components.

Instructional Materials. The special support materials provided for the instructor can be used with either the kits or the textbooks. Special instructor's editions of the textbooks (Lessons 1-60 and Lessons 61-120) contain annotated student pages. Solution keys for all of the formatting exercises in Lessons 1-180 are contained in separate booklets for different word processing programs used with this program. Separate instructor's notes booklets for different word processing programs contain specific suggestions for teaching the features of that program and contain lesson-by-lesson tips. A separate Instructor's Manual contains teaching and grading suggestions for the entire program. Finally, test booklets are available that contain masters of the objective and alternate document processing tests for each part.

Computer Software. IBM-compatible computer software is available for the entire program. The computer software provides a complete instructional system.

Acknowledgments

We wish to express our appreciation to all the instructors and students who have used the previous editions and who have contributed much to this 8th Edition.

Scot Ober	Robert Hanson
Jack Johnson	Arlene Rice
Robert Poland	Albert Rossetti

Introduction

A. STARTING A LESSON

Each lesson begins with the goals for the lesson. Read the goals carefully so that you understand the purpose of your practice. In the example at the left, the goals for the lesson are to type 29 wam (words a minute) on a 3-minute timing with no more than 5 errors and to format simple reports.

B. BUILDING STRAIGHT-COPY SKILL

Warmups: Beginning with Lesson 11, each lesson starts with a warmup paragraph that reviews alphabet, number, and symbol keys. Type the warmup paragraph twice.
Skillbuilding: The skillbuilding portion of each lesson includes a variety of drills to build both speed and accuracy. Instructions for completing the drills are always provided beside each activity.

Additional skillbuilding drills are included in the back of the textbook. These drills are used in various lessons and are available for extra practice.

C. MEASURING STRAIGHT-COPY SKILL

Straight-copy skill is measured in wam (words a minute). All timings are the exact length needed to meet the speed goal for the lesson. If you finish a timing before time is up, you have automatically reached your speed goal for the lesson.

Timings in Lessons 1-60 and Lessons 61-120 are of equal difficulty as measured by syllabic intensity (average number of syllables per word).

D. BUILDING FORMATTING AND DOCUMENT PROCESSING SKILL

Each new document format presented is illustrated and explained. A formatting reference manual is included in the front of the textbook for quick reference. Marginal notes are sometimes used to remind you of special directions.

Symbols are used on sample documents and within document processing activities to provide visual formatting reminders. For example, ↓3 ds means that you should set double spacing, then press Enter 3 times.

All word processing commands needed to format documents are explained and practiced in the word processing manual. A special "GO TO" icon (shown at the left) in the textbook alerts you to the need to refer to the manual. The document processing icon is used in the manual to remind you to complete the appropriate document processing exercises in the textbook.

E. CORRECTING ERRORS

As you learn to type, you will probably make some errors. To correct an error, press BACKSPACE (shown as ← on some keyboards) to delete the incorrect character. Then type the correct character.

If you notice an error on a different line, use the up, down, left, or right arrows to move the insertion point immediately to the left or right of the error. Press BACKSPACE to delete a character to the left of the insertion point or DEL to delete a character to the right of the insertion point.

F. TYPING TECHNIQUE

Correct position at the keyboard enables you to type with greater speed and accuracy and with less fatigue. When typing for a long period, rest your eyes occasionally by looking away from the screen. Change position, walk around, or stretch when your muscles feel tired.

If possible, adjust your workstation as follows:

Chair. Adjust the height so that your upper and lower legs form a 90-degree angle and your lower back is supported by the back of the chair.

Keyboard. Center your body opposite the J key, and lean forward slightly. Keep your forearms horizontal to the keyboard.

Screen. Position the monitor so that the top of the screen is just below eye level and about 18 to 26 inches away.

Text. Position your textbook or other copy on either side of the monitor as close to it vertically and horizontally as possible to minimize head and eye movement and to avoid neck strain.

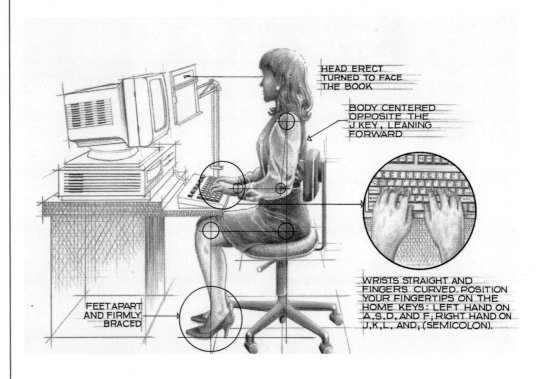

HEAD ERECT TURNED TO FACE THE BOOK

BODY CENTERED OPPOSITE THE J KEY, LEANING FORWARD

WRISTS STRAIGHT AND FINGERS CURVED. POSITION YOUR FINGERTIPS ON THE HOME KEYS: LEFT HAND ON A,S,D, AND F; RIGHT HAND ON J,K,L, AND, (SEMICOLON).

FEET APART AND FIRMLY BRACED

Reference Manual

MAJOR PARTS OF A MICROCOMPUTER SYSTEM

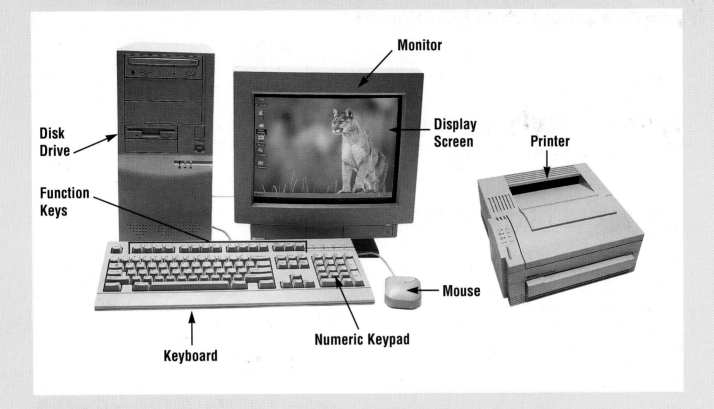

Monitor

Display Screen

Printer

Disk Drive

Function Keys

Mouse

Numeric Keypad

Keyboard

THE COMPUTER KEYBOARD

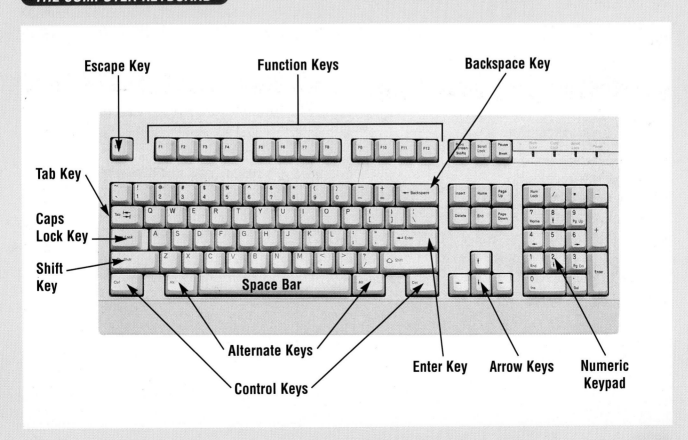

Escape Key

Function Keys

Backspace Key

Tab Key

Caps Lock Key

Shift Key

Space Bar

Alternate Keys

Enter Key

Arrow Keys

Numeric Keypad

Control Keys

Business letter in block style
(open punctuation)

Business letter in modified-block style
(standard punctuation)

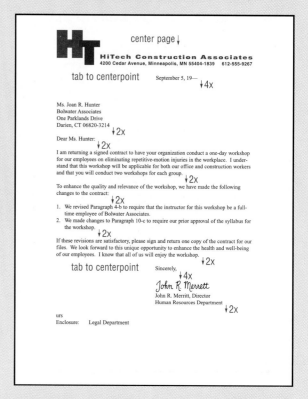

Business letter in simplified style

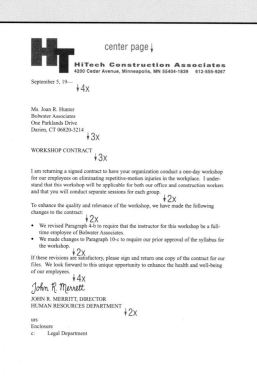

Personal-business letter
(modified-block style; indented paragraphs; standard punctuation)

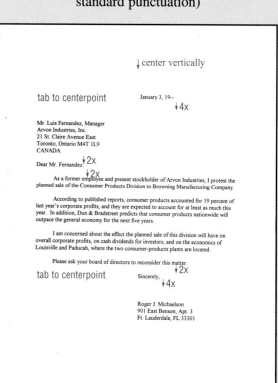

Business letter on executive stationery
(7¼″ × 10½″; 1-inch side margins)

center page↓
WELLINGTON INDUSTRIES
550 Thornail Street, Edison, NJ 08818   201-555-8000

July 18, 19— ↓4x

Mr. Rodney Eastwood
BBL Resources
52A Northern Ridge
Mt. Stuart, Tasmania 7000
AUSTRALIA ↓2x

Dear Rodney: ↓2x

I see no reason why we should continue to consider the locality around Geraldton for our new refinery. Even though the desirability of this site from an economic point of view is undeniable, there is insufficient housing readily available for those workers whom we would have to transfer. ↓2x

In trying to control urban growth, the city has been either turning down the building permits for new housing or placing so many restrictions on foreign investment as to make it too expensive to build.

Please continue to seek out other areas of exploration where we might form a joint partnership. ↓2x

Sincerely, ↓4x

Arlyn J. Bunch

Arlyn J. Bunch
Vice President for Operations ↓2x

urs
By fax

Business letter on half-page stationery
(5½″ × 8½″; 0.75-inch side margins)

center page↓
WELLINGTON INDUSTRIES
550 Thornail Street, Edison, NJ 08818   201-555-8000

July 18, 19— ↓4x

Mr. Rodney Eastwood
BBL Resources
52A Northern Ridge
Mt. Stuart, Tasmania 7000
AUSTRALIA ↓2x

Dear Rodney: ↓2x

I do not believe we should continue to consider Geraldton for our new refinery. There is insufficient housing for those workers whom we would have to transfer. In trying to control growth, the city has placed so many restrictions on foreign investment that it is too expensive to build.

Please continue to seek out other areas of exploration where we might form a joint partnership. ↓2x

Sincerely, ↓4x

Arlyn J. Bunch
Arlyn J. Bunch
Vice President for Operations ↓2x

urs

Business letter formatted for a window envelope

6x↓   **WELLINGTON INDUSTRIES**
550 Thornail Street, Edison, NJ 08818   201-555-8000

July 18, 19— ↓3x

Mr. Rodney Eastwood
BBL Resources
52A Northern Ridge
Mt. Stuart, Tasmania 7000
AUSTRALIA ↓3x

Dear Rodney: ↓2x

I see no reason why we should continue to consider the locality around Geraldton for our new refinery. Even though the desirability of this site from an economic point of view is undeniable, there is insufficient housing readily available for those workers whom we would have to transfer.

In trying to control urban growth, the city has been either turning down building permits for new housing or placing so many restrictions on foreign investment as to make it too expensive to build.

Please continue to seek out other areas of exploration where we might form a joint partnership. ↓2x

Sincerely, ↓4x

Arlyn J. Bunch

Arlyn J. Bunch
Vice President for Operations ↓2x

urs
Enclosure ↓2x
PS: I thought you might enjoy the enclosed article from a recent *Forbes* magazine on the latest misfortunes of one of your major competitors.

Memo

↓6x

MEMO TO: Nancy Price, Executive Vice President ↓2x

FROM: Arlyn J. Bunch, Operations ↓2x

DATE: July 18, 19— ↓2x

SUBJECT: New Refinery Site ↓2x

As you can see from the attached letter, I've informed BBL Resources that I see no reason why we should continue to consider the locality around Geraldton, Australia, for our new refinery. Even though the desirability of this site from an economic standpoint is undeniable, there is insufficient housing readily available for those workers whom we would have to transfer. As of July 1, the number of appropriate single-family houses listed for sale by real estate agents within a 25-mile radius of Geraldton was as follows: ↓2x

Castleton Homes	123
Belle Real Estate	5
Red Carpet	11
Geraldton Sales	9
TOTAL	148

↓2x

In addition, in trying to control urban growth, Geraldton has been either turning down building permits for new housing or placing so many restrictions on foreign investment as to make it too expensive for us to consider building housing ourselves.

Because of this deficiency of housing for our employees, we have no choice but to look elsewhere. ↓2x

urs
Attachment

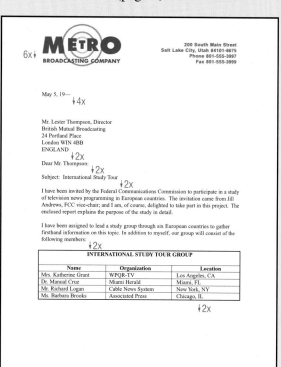

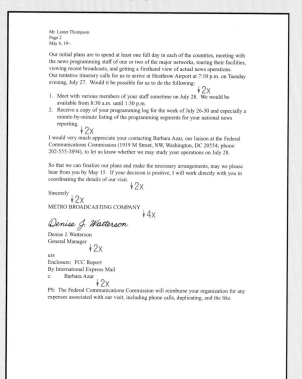

SPECIAL CORRESPONDENCE FEATURES

FOREIGN ADDRESS. Type the name of a foreign country in all capital letters on a line by itself.

SUBJECT LINE. If used, type a subject line in upper- and lowercase letters below the salutation, with 1 blank line above and below; the terms *Re:* or *In re:* may also be used.

TABLE. Leave 1 blank line above and below a table.

MULTI-PAGE LETTERS. Type the first page on letterhead stationery and the second page on matching plain stationery. On the second page, type the addressee's name, page number, and date as a header, blocked at the left margin. Leave 1 blank line after the page-2 header.

ENUMERATION. Create an enumeration by using the automatic numbering feature. Double-space a list that is part of the body of a double-spaced document. Single-space a list that is part of the body of a single-spaced document, but leave 1 blank line above and below the list.

COMPANY NAME IN CLOSING LINES. If included, type the company name in all capital letters below the complimentary closing, with 1 blank line above and 3 blank lines below it.

REFERENCE INITIALS. Type only the typist's initials (not the signer's) in lowercase letters a double space below the writer's name and/or title. (Optional: You may also include the computer filename; for example: *urs/SMITH.LET*).

ENCLOSURE NOTATION. Type an enclosure notation a single space below the reference initials if an item is enclosed with a letter. Use the term "Attachment" if an item is attached to a memo instead of enclosed in an envelope. Examples: *3 Enclosures, Enclosure: Contract, Attachment.*

DELIVERY NOTATION. Type a delivery notation a single space below the enclosure notation. Examples: *By Certified Mail, By Fax, By Federal Express.*

COPY NOTATION. Type a copy notation *(c:)* a single space below the delivery notation if someone other than the addressee is to receive a copy of the message.

POSTSCRIPT NOTATION. Type a postscript notation as the last item, preceded by 1 blank line. Indent the first line of the postscript if the paragraphs in the body are indented.

A standard large (No. 10) envelope is 9½ by 4⅛ inches. A standard small (No. 6¾) envelope is 6½ by 3⅝ inches. Although either address format shown below is acceptable, the format shown for the large envelope (all capital letters and no punctuation) is recommended by the U.S. Postal Service for mail that will be sorted by an electronic scanning device.

Window envelopes are often used in a word processing environment because of the difficulty of aligning envelopes correctly in some printers. A window envelope requires no formatting, since the letter is formatted and folded so that the inside address is visible through the window.

HiTech Construction Associates
4200 Cedar Avenue, Minneapolis, MN 55404-1839

MS JOAN R HUNTER
BOLWATER ASSOCIATES
ONE PARKLANDS DRIVE
DARIEN CT 06820-3214

Roger J. Michaelson
901 East Benson, Apt. 3
Ft. Lauderdale, FL 33301

Mr. Joseph G. Jenshak
17032 Stewart Avenue
Augusta, GA 30904

To fold a letter for a large envelope:
1. Place the letter *face up* and fold up the bottom third.
2. Fold the top third down to 0.5 inch from the bottom edge.
3. Insert the last crease into the envelope first, with the flap facing up.

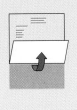

To fold a letter for a small envelope:
1. Place the letter *face up* and fold up the bottom half to 0.5 inch from the top.
2. Fold the right third over to the left.
3. Fold the left third over to 0.5 inch from the right edge.
4. Insert the last crease into the envelope first, with the flap facing up.

To fold a letter for a window envelope:
1. Place the letter *face down* with the letterhead at the top and fold the bottom third of the letter up.
2. Fold the top third down so that the address shows.
3. Insert the letter into the envelope so that the address shows through the window.

Outline

↓6x

THE FEASIBILITY OF IN-HOUSE MANUFACTURING

OF NAIL-POLISH LACQUERS ↓2x

↓2x

I. INTRODUCTION
↓2x
   A. Statement of the Problem
   B. Scope
   C. Procedures
   D. Organization of the Report ↓2x

II. FINDINGS

   A. Current Manufacturing Processes
      1. Contract Manufacturing
      2. In-House Manufacturing
   B. Market Differentiation
      1. Image Advertising
      2. Product Characteristics
      3. Manufacturing Control
   C. Advantages and Disadvantages

III. CONCLUSIONS

   A. Summary of Findings
   B. Conclusions and Recommendations

Title page

center page ↓

CONSOLIDATION OF THE PARTS WAREHOUSES AT ↓2x

SIOUX CITY AND CEDAR FALLS ↓2x

Maintaining Profitability in a Declining Market ↓12x

Prepared by ↓2x
Catherine Rogers-Busch
Chief Product Engineer
Helene Ponds and Associates ↓12x

December 3, 19—

Table of contents

↓6x

CONTENTS ↓2x

Unbound report

(first page)

↓3 DS

PREPARING FORMAL REPORTS ↓1x

Formatting Guidelines for Writers ↓1x

By Keith Stallings ↓1x

↓1x
Formatting formal reports is not a difficult task if you just take the time to study the technical aspects involved. This report discusses report headings, page numbers, reference citations, and the bibliography. ↓1x

HEADINGS ↓1x
The major heading in a report is the title. It should be centered and typed in all caps and bold approximately 2 inches from the top of the page. A subtitle or byline, if used, is typed in initial caps a double space below the title. The body of the report begins on the second line below the title or byline.

   Side Headings. A side heading (such as "PAGE NUMBERING" shown below) is typed at the left margin in all caps and bold, with a double space before and after it.

   Paragraph Headings. A paragraph heading is indented and typed in initial caps and bold a double space below the preceding paragraph. The paragraph heading is followed by a period and two spaces, with the text beginning on the same line.

PAGE NUMBERING

   Use the page numbering command of your word processing software to insert a page number at the top right of each page. Suppress the page number on the first page.

for the following reasons:

- Contrary to popular belief, modular homes are generally not less expensive than conventionally constructed homes.

- Zoning regulations and restrictive convenants often forbid the construction of modular homes especially in upscale areas.

The big advantage of modular homes is the speed with which they can be constructed.[2] Since the River Road development is not subject to time pressures, conventional construction methods were evaluated as the most appropriate for this

---
[1] Benjamin J. Ashley, "New Sales Versus Resales: Apples to Oranges?" *Real Estate Quarterly*, September 1995, p. 143.
[2] Jacqueline Miller, *Residential Real Estate: North Georgia Edition*, Georgia Real Estate Association, Atlanta, Georgia, 1995, pp. 216-224.

following reasons:

- Contrary to popular belief, modular homes are generally not less expensive than conventionally constructed homes.

- Zoning regulations and restrictive convenants often forbid the construction of modular homes especially in upscale areas.

The big advantage of modular homes is the speed with which they can be constructed.[2] Since the River Road development is not subject to time pressures, conventional construction methods were evaluated as the most appropriate for this submarket.

---
[1] Benjamin J. Ashley, "New Sales Versus Resales: Apples to Oranges?" *Real Estate Quarterly*, September 1995, p. 143.

[2] Jacqueline Miller, *Residential Real Estate: North Georgia Edition*, Georgia Real Estate Association, Atlanta, Georgia, 1995, pp. 216-224.

13

↓6x

BIBLIOGRAPHY
↓2x

Ashley, Benjamin J., "New Sales Versus Resales: Apples to Oranges?" *Real Estate Quarterly*, September 1994, pp. 143-149.
↓2x

Barrett, R. J., "Planning Your First Home," *The Long Island Herald*, September 13, 1993, pp. A3, A16.

Bullard, Mary Helen, *The Bullard Real Estate Report*, Bullard Consulting Group, Nyack, New York, 1995.

Heydenburg, Peter, and Rhonda Silver, "Restricting Covenants and the Law," *Journal of Real Estate Law*, Vol. 24, No. 3, Fall 1992, pp. 81-87.

Miller, Jacqueline, *Residential Real Estate: North Georgia Edition*, Georgia Real Estate Association, Atlanta, Georgia, 1995.

3

an option for this submarket because of the numerous developments of this type that already exist or are under construction in the area.

Modular homes, which have been partially constructed before being brought to the building site, were likewise rejected because:
↓1 DS

Contrary to popular belief, modular homes are generally not less expensive than conventionally constructed homes. Their biggest advantage, instead, is the speed with which they can be constructed. Their major disadvantage relates to the restrictions often placed on them by municipal zoning ordinances.
↓1 DS

Since the River Road development is not subject to time pressures, conventional construction methods were evaluated as the most appropriate for this submarket.

Most of the homes sold in Chestnut Log contain at least three bedrooms, but in the lowest price bracket most contain less than 1,600 square feet, as shown below.
↓1 DS

Selling Price	Number of Homes Listed	Days	Average Square Feet
Less than $90,000	55	145	1,571
$90,000-$109,000	29	81	1,917
$110,000-$129,999	7	105	2,094
$130,000-$149,999	8	85	2,291

↓1 DS
Because several planning experts have noted the importance of overall outside dimensions for first-time home buyers, the home plan selected for this submarket is only 37 feet wide, allowing it to be placed on a 67-foot-wide lot, with adequate footage on both sides.

Market research shows that smaller lots are more appealing because the landscaping needs are minimized. Reducing landscaping is a definite advantage

to whether hardware should be purchased or leased. Although many firms decide to purchase their own hardware, others have taken the route of time-sharing or remote processing whereby the costs of processing data can be shared with other users.

TRAINING OPERATORS

Many firms neglect this important phase of designing a computer system. It is not enough to offer a one-week training course in an applications package and then expect proficiency from a worker.[iii] Training must occur over time to help those who will be using computers every day on the job.

---
[i] Neal Swanson, *Information Management*, Glencoe/McGraw-Hill, Westerville, Ohio, 1992, p. 372.
[ii] Christine L. Seymour, "The Ins and Outs of Designing Your Computer System," *Information Processing Trends*, January 1991, p. 23.
[iii] Lee Bailey, *Computer Systems Management*, The University of New Mexico Press, Albuquerque, New Mexico, 1992, p. 413.

TRAINING OPERATORS

Many firms neglect this important phase of designing a computer system. It is not enough to offer a one-week training course in an applications package and then expect proficiency from a worker.[3] Training must occur over time to help those who will be using computers every day on the job.

1. Neal Swanson, *Information Management*, Glencoe/McGraw-Hill, Westerville, Ohio, 1992, p. 372.

2. Christine L. Seymour, "The Ins and Outs of Designing Your Computer System," *Information Processing Trends*, January 1991, p. 23.

3. Lee Bailey, *Computer Systems Management*, The University of New Mexico Press, Albuquerque, New Mexico, 1992, p. 413.

2

a real estate agent from North Georgia Realty, provided a copy of selected reports that are available only to real estate agents (Miller, 1995, p. 216). Statistics for the Chestnut Log school district for those homes selling during the past year are shown in Table 2.

TABLE 2. CHESTNUT LOG HOME SALES
January Through December

Selling Price	Number of Homes	Days Listed	Average Square Feet
Less than $90,000	55	145	1,571
$90,000-$109,000	29	81	1,917
$110,000-$129,999	7	105	2,094
$130,000-or more	14	185	2,391

The data reflected in Table 2 are based on used homes. According to one source, the typical residential community offers fewer new homes than resales, new homes sell faster, and they average about 20 percent larger than resales (Ashley, 1994, p. 143).

YOUNG FAMILY

Individuals in the young family submarket are making their first purchase of a new home. This submarket represents households from a rental or used-home arrangement. In the market, on the basis of current mortgage rates, these buyers cannot afford more than $107,000 for a home. And, since family size is still small (less than four), homes of approximately 2,000 square feet are considered to be an adequate size.

13

References

Connor, E. (1995, June). Exploring body language cues. Management Today, 14, 250-261, 273.

LePoole, A. (1989). Your tour of duty overseas (2nd ed.). Oklahoma City: American Press.

LePoole, A. (1991). What American business can (and must) learn from the Japanese. New York: Management Press.

Newby, C. J. (1995). Global implications for American business: The numbers don't lie. Marketing Research Quarterly, 50, 190-215.

Roncaro, P. L., & Lance, G. D. (1992, June 2). Losing something in the translation. Winston-Salem Herald, pp. 4A, 12A.

Tell it like it is: Making yourself understood in the new Russia. (1994, October 19). International Times, p. 38.

↓1" top margin

Jenson 1

Sherlon Jenson

Professor Zhao

BusCom 300

8 October 19—

Communication Skills Needed in International Business

International business plays an increasingly important role in the U.S. economy, and U.S. companies recognize that to be competitive nationally, they must be competitive internationally. Reflecting this trend, direct investment by U.S. private enterprises in foreign countries increased from $409 billion in 1990 to $528 billion in 1994, an increase of 29 percent in four years (Connor 253). Today, more than 3,000 U.S. corporations have over 25,000 subsidiaries and affiliates in 125 foreign countries, and more than 25,000 American firms are engaged in international marketing (Newby 193, 205).

International business is highly dependent on communication. According to Arnold LePoole, chief executive officer of Armstrand Industries, an international supplier of automotive parts:

If a company cannot communicate with its foreign subsidiaries, customers, suppliers, and governments, it cannot achieve success. The sad fact is that most American managers are ill-equipped to communicate with their international counterparts. (143-144)

Because competent business communications skills are one of the most important components for success in international business affairs, a survey instrument was designed to explore the importance of, level of competence in, and methods of

Jensen 13

↓3 DS

Works Cited

Connor, Earl. "Exploring Body Language Cues." Management Today, June 1994: 250-261, 273.

LePoole, Arnold. What American Business Can (and Must) Learn From the Japanese. New York: Management Press, 1990.

---. Your Tour of Duty Overseas. 2nd ed. Oklahoma City: American Press, 1988.

Newby, Corrine J. "Global Implications for American Business: The Numbers Don't Lie." Marketing Research Quarterly 50 (1994): 190-215.

Roncaro, Paul L., and Glenn D. Lance. "Losing Something in the Translation." Winston-Salem Herald 2 June 1992: 4A+.

"Tell It Like It Is: Making Yourself Understood in the New Russia." International Times 19 October 1993: 38.

↓6x

MILES HARDWARE EXECUTIVE COMMITTEE ↓2x

Meeting Agenda ↓2x

June 7, 19—, 3 p.m. ↓2x

1. Call to order
2. Approval of minutes of May 5 meeting
3. Progress report on building addition and parking lot restrictions (Norman Hedges and Anthony Pascarelli)
4. May 15 draft of Five-Year Plan
5. Review of National Hardware Association annual convention
6. Employee grievance filed by Ellen Burrows (John Landstrom)
7. New expense-report forms (Anne Richards)
8. Announcements
9. Adjournment

↓6x

RESOURCE COMMITTEE ↓2x

Minutes of the Meeting ↓2x

March 13, 19— ↓2x

ATTENDANCE The Resource Committee met on March 13, 19—, at the Airport Sheraton in Portland, Oregon, in conjunction with the western regional meeting. Members present were Michael Davis, Cynthia Giovanni, Don Madsen, and Edna Pointer. Michael Davis, chairperson, called the meeting to order at 2:30 p.m. ↓2x

OLD BUSINESS The members of the committee reviewed the sales brochure on electronic copyboards. They agreed to purchase an electronic copyboard for the conference room. Cynthia Giovanni will secure quotations from at least two vendors. ↓2x

NEW BUSINESS The committee reviewed a request from the Purchasing Department for three new computers. After extensive discussion regarding the appropriate use of the computers in the Purchasing Department and software to be purchased, the committee approved the request. ↓2x

ADJOURNMENT The meeting was adjourned at 4:45 p.m. The next meeting has been scheduled for May 4 in the headquarters conference room. Members are asked to bring with them copies of the latest resource planning document. ↓2x

Respectfully submitted, ↓4x

D. S. Madsen, Secretary

↓6x

PORTLAND SALES MEETING ↓2x

Itinerary for Arlene Gilsdorf ↓2x

March 12-15, 19— ↓2x

Thursday, March 12 ↓2x

Detroit/Minneapolis .... Northwest 83
    Depart 5:10 p.m.; arrive 5:55 p.m.
    Seat 8D; nonstop ↓2x

Minneapolis/Portland .... Northwest 2363
    Depart 6:30 p.m.; arrive 8:06 p.m.
    Seat 15C; nonstop; dinner ↓2x

Sunday, March 15

Portland/Minneapolis .... Northwest 360
    Depart 7:30 a.m.; arrive 12:26 p.m.
    Seat 15H; one stop; breakfast

Minneapolis/Detroit .... Northwest 748
    Depart 1 p.m.; arrive 3:32 p.m.
    Seat 10D; nonstop; snack ↓2x

NOTES ↓2x

1. Jack Weatherford, assistant western regional manager, will meet your flight on Thursday and drive you to the airport on Sunday.
2. All seat assignments are aisle seats; smoking is not allowed on any of the flights.
3. Important phone numbers:
    Jack Weatherford .... 503-555-8029, Ext. 87
    Airport Sheraton 503-555-4032

↓3 DS

POWER OF ATTORNEY

KNOW ALL MEN BY THESE PRESENTS that I, ATTORNEY LEE FERNANDEZ, of the City of Tulia, County of Swisher, State of Texas, do hereby appoint my son, Robert Fernandez, of this City, County, and State as my attorney-in-fact to act in my name, place, and stead as my agent in the management of my real estate transactions, chattel and goods transactions, banking transactions, and business operating transactions.

I give and grant unto my said attorney full power and authority to do and perform every act and thing requisite and necessary to be done in the said management as fully, to all intents and purposes, as I might or could do if personally present, with full power of revocation, hereby ratifying all that my said attorney shall lawfully do.

IN WITNESS WHEREOF, I have hereunto set my hand and seal this thirteenth day of April, 1995. ↓2 DS

centerpoint→ _____ (L.S.) ↓1 DS

SIGNED and affirmed in the presence of: ↓2 DS

_____ ↓2 DS

Page 1of 1

Resume

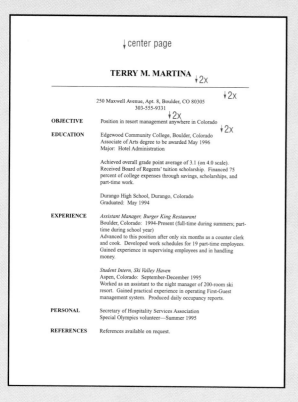

↓ center page

TERRY M. MARTINA ↓2x

↓2x

250 Maxwell Avenue, Apt. 8, Boulder, CO 80305
303-555-9331

↓2x

OBJECTIVE   Position in resort management anywhere in Colorado

↓2x

EDUCATION   Edgewood Community College, Boulder, Colorado
Associate of Arts degree to be awarded May 1996
Major: Hotel Administration

Achieved overall grade point average of 3.1 (on 4.0 scale).
Received Board of Regents' tuition scholarship. Financed 75
percent of college expenses through savings, scholarships, and
part-time work.

Durango High School, Durango, Colorado
Graduated: May 1994

EXPERIENCE   *Assistant Manager, Burger King Restaurant*
Boulder, Colorado: 1994-Present (full-time during summers; part-
time during school year)
Advanced to this position after only six months as a counter clerk
and cook. Developed work schedules for 19 part-time employees.
Gained experience in supervising employees and in handling
money.

Student Intern, Ski Valley Haven
Aspen, Colorado: September-December 1995
Worked as an assistant to the night manager of 200-room ski
resort. Gained practical experience in operating First-Guest
management system. Produced daily occupancy reports.

PERSONAL   Secretary of Hospitality Services Association
Special Olympics volunteer—Summer 1995

REFERENCES   References available on request.

Letter of application

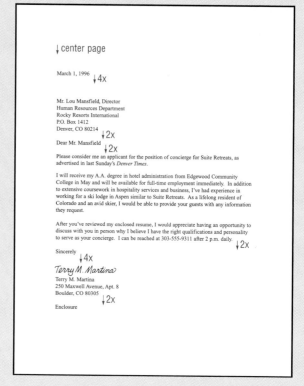

↓ center page

March 1, 1996 ↓4x

Mr. Lou Mansfield, Director
Human Resources Department
Rocky Resorts International
P.O. Box 1412
Denver, CO 80214 ↓2x

Dear Mr. Mansfield ↓2x

Please consider me an applicant for the position of concierge for Suite Retreats, as
advertised in last Sunday's *Denver Times*.

I will receive my A.A. degree in hotel administration from Edgewood Community
College in May and will be available for full-time employment immediately. In addition
to extensive coursework in hospitality services and business, I've had experience in
working for a ski lodge in Aspen similar to Suite Retreats. As a lifelong resident of
Colorado and an avid skier, I would be able to provide your guests with any information
they request.

After you've reviewed my enclosed resume, I would appreciate having an opportunity to
discuss with you in person why I believe I have the right qualifications and personality
to serve as your concierge. I can be reached at 303-555-9311 after 2 p.m. daily. ↓2x

Sincerely ↓4x

Terry M. Martina
Terry M. Martina
250 Maxwell Avenue, Apt. 8
Boulder, CO 80305 ↓2x

Enclosure ↓2x

PLACING INFORMATION ON PRINTED LINES

Because of the difficulty of aligning copy on a printed line with a computer and printer, lined forms such
as job-application forms are most efficiently completed on a typewriter.

When typing on a lined form, use the typewriter's
variable line spacer to adjust the paper so that the line
is in the position that a row of underlines would
occupy. (On many machines, this is accomplished by
pressing in the left platen knob.)

Do not leave any lines for requested information
blank; use *N/A* ("not applicable") if necessary.
Because of space limitations, it may be necessary to
abbreviate some words.

Because first impressions are important, ensure that
all your employment documents are in correct format,
are neat in appearance, and are free from errors.

Job-application form

(first page)

ROCKY RESORTS INTERNATIONAL
P.O. Box 1412   Denver, CO 80218

Employment Application

POSITION APPLIED FOR __Concierge__   DATE OF APPLICATION __3/18/97__

TYPE OF EMPLOYMENT DESIRED [X] Full-time [ ] Part-time [ ] Temporary [ ] Co-op/Internship

NAME __Martina__   __Terry__   __M__
      LAST   FIRST   MI

ADDRESS __250 Maxwell Avenue, Apt. B__ __Boulder__ __CO__ __80305__
          STREET   CITY   STATE   ZIP

TELEPHONE __303-555-9331__   SOCIAL SECURITY NO __247-72-8431__

If you are under 18, can you furnish a work permit? ____N/A____ [ ] Yes ... [ ] No

Have you ever worked here before? [X] Yes ... [ ] No

Are you legally eligible for employment in this country? [X] Yes ... [ ] No

Have you been convicted of a felony within the past seven years? [ ] Yes ... [X] No

If yes, please explain _____ N/A

EDUCATION (most recent first)

Institution	City/State	Degree/Major	Dates
Edgewood Community College, Boulder, CO		A.A.—Hotel Admin.	1995-97
Durango High School, Durango, CO		Diploma	1992-95

WORK EXPERIENCE (most recent first)

Organization	City/State	Position	Dates (inclusive)
Burger King Restaurant	Boulder, CO	Asst. Mgr.	1994-present
Ski Valley Haven	Aspen, CO	Intern	Sep-Dec 1994

AN EQUAL OPPORTUNITY EMPLOYER

Open table

(with centered column headings)

↓ center page

COMPUTER SUPPLIES UNLIMITED
Guide to Support Services*

↓1x

Support Service	Telephone	Hours
Product Literature	800-555-3867	6 a.m. to 5 p.m.
Replacement Parts	303-555-3388	24 hours a day
Technical Documentation	408-555-3309	24 hours a day
Troubleshooting	800-555-8277	6 a.m. to 5 p.m.
Printer Drivers	800-555-2377	6 a.m. to 5 p.m.
Software Notes	800-555-3496	24 hours a day
Hardware Information	303-555-4289	6 a.m. to 5 p.m.
Technical Support	800-555-1205	24 hours a day

Ruled table

(with blocked column headings)

↓ center page

COMPUTER SUPPLIES UNLIMITED
Guide to Support Services

↓1x

Support Service	Telephone	Hours
Product Literature	800-555-3867	6 a.m. to 5 p.m.
Replacement Parts	303-555-3388	24 hours a day
Technical Documentation	408-555-3309	24 hours a day
Troubleshooting	800-555-8277	6 a.m. to 5 p.m.
Printer Drivers	800-555-2377	6 a.m. to 5 p.m.
Software Notes	800-555-3496	24 hours a day
Hardware Information	303-555-4289	6 a.m. to 5 p.m.
Technical Support	800-555-1205	24 hours a day

Boxed table

(with blocked column headings)

↓ center page

COMPUTER SUPPLIES UNLIMITED
Guide to Support Services*

↓1x

Support Service	Telephone	Hours
Product Literature	800-555-3867	6 a.m. to 5 p.m.
Replacement Parts	303-555-3388	24 hours a day
Technical Documentation	408-555-3309	24 hours a day
Troubleshooting	800-555-8277	6 a.m. to 5 p.m.
Printer Drivers	800-555-2377	6 a.m. to 5 p.m.
Software Notes	800-555-3496	24 hours a day
Technical Support	800-555-1205	24 hours a day
Hardware Information	303-555-4289	6 a.m. to 5 p.m.
*All support services are available 7 days a week.		

Boxed table

(with centered column headings)

↓ center page

QUALITY INN SUITES

↓1x

Location	Rack Rate	Discount Rate
Los Angeles, California	$159.00	$89.50
Orlando, Florida	$125.00	$95.50
Chicago, Illinois	$149.00	$79.50
New York, New York	$239.00	$175.00
Minneapolis, Minnesota	$98.50	$59.50
Las Vegas, Nevada	$125.50	$85.00
Seattle, Washington	$79.00	$59.00
Dallas, Texas	$250.00	$185.00

Many business forms can be created and filled in by using templates that are provided within commercial word processing software. Template forms can be used "as is" or they can be edited. Templates can also be used to create customized forms for any business.

When a template is opened, the form is displayed on screen. The user can then fill in the necessary information, including personalized company information. Data is entered into cells or fields and you can move quickly from field to field with a single keystroke—usually by pressing Tab or Enter.

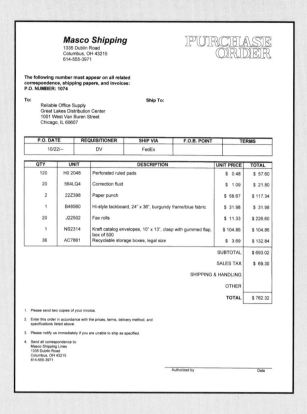

PROOFREADERS' MARKS

Proofreaders' Marks		Draft	Final Copy	Proofreaders' Marks		Draft	Final Copy
⌒	Omit space	data base	database	SS	Single-space	first line / second line	first line second line
∨ or ∧	Insert	if he's going not	if he's not going,	ds	Double-space	first line second line	first line / second line
≡	Capitalize	Maple street	Maple Street	⌐	Move right	Please send	Please send
⌀	Delete	a final draft	a draft	⌐	Move left	May I	May I
#	Insert space	allready to	all ready to	∿	Bold	Column Heading	**Column Heading**
when	Change word	and if you when	and when you	ital	Italic	Time magazine	*Time* magazine
/	Use lowercase letter	our President	our president	u/l	Underline	Time magazine	Time magazine readers
¶	Paragraph	¶ Most of the	Most of the	♂	Move as shown	readers will see	will see
•••	Don't delete	a true story	a true story				
○	Spell out	the only 1	the only one				
∽	Transpose	they all see	they see all				

AMPERSAND. One space before and after.

CLOSING QUOTATION MARK. *(a)* Typed *after* a period or comma and *before* a colon or semicolon. *(b)* Typed *after* a question mark or exclamation point if the quoted material is a question or an exclamation; otherwise, it is typed *before* the question mark or exclamation point.

COLON. Two spaces after.

COMMA. One space after.

EXCLAMATION POINT. Two spaces after.

PERIOD. *(a)* Two spaces after a period at the end of a sentence; *(b)* one space after the period following someone's initials or the abbreviation of a single word (for example, *Mrs. Jones*); *(c)* no space after each internal period in an abbreviation (for example, *a.m.*).

QUESTION MARK. Two spaces after.

SEMICOLON. One space after.

TABLE COLUMNS. Although six spaces are generally left between table columns, spacing varies when you use the Table feature of your word processor.

ITALICS/UNDERLINE. *(a)* Type a magazine or book title in italics or underline it, including internal spaces and punctuation. *(b)* To stress individual words, italicize or underline them separately; do not italicize or underline the punctuation or the spaces between the words.

ZIP CODE. One space before.

LANGUAGE ARTS FOR BUSINESS

PUNCTUATION

COMMAS

1. **, ind**   Use a comma between independent clauses joined by a conjunction. (An independent clause is one that can stand alone as a complete sentence.)

     We requested Brown Industries to change the date, and they did so within five days.

2. **, intro**   Use a comma after an introductory expression (unless it is a short prepositional phrase).

     Before we can make a decision, we must have all the facts.
     In 1992 our nation elected a president.

3. **, date**   Use a comma before and after the year in a complete date.

     We will arrive at the plant on June 2, 1995, for the conference.

4. **, place**   Use a comma before and after a state or country that follows a city (but not before a ZIP Code).

     Joan moved to Vancouver, British Columbia, in September.
     Send the package to Douglasville, GA 30135, by express mail.

5. **, ser**   Use a comma between each item in a series of three or more.

     We need to order paper, toner, and font cartridges.

6. **, tran**   Use a comma before and after a transitional expression (such as *therefore* and *however*).

     It is critical, therefore, that we finish the project on time.

7. **, quot**   Use a comma before and after a direct quotation.

     When we left, James said, "Let us return to the same location next year."

8. **, non**   Use a comma before and after a nonessential expression. (A nonessential expression is a word or group of words that may be omitted without changing the basic meaning of the sentence.)

     Let me say, to begin with, that the report has already been finalized.

9. **, adj**   Use a comma between two adjacent adjectives that modify the same noun.

     We need an intelligent, enthusiastic individual for this job.

SEMICOLONS

1.   ; noconj   Use a semicolon to join two closely related independent clauses that are not connected by a conjunction (such as *and*, *but*, or *nor*).

Management favored the vote; stockholders did not.

2.   ; ser   Use a semicolon to separate three or more items in a series if any of the items already contain commas.

Region 1 sent its reports on March, April, and May; and Region 2 sent its reports on September, October, and November.

HYPHENS

1.   - adj   Hyphenate compound adjectives that come before a noun (unless the first word is an adverb ending in *-ly*).

We reviewed an up-to-date report on Wednesday.
We attended a highly rated session on multimedia software.

2.   - num   Hyphenate compound numbers (between twenty-one and ninety-nine) and fractions that are expressed as words.

We observed twenty-nine infractions during the investigation.
Bancroft Industries reduced their sales force by one-third.

3.   - div   Turning on the hyphenation feature on your word processor takes care of most word division decisions for you. However, in some cases, you will need to make the correct choices. As a general rule, hyphenate words that are divided at the ends of lines. Do not divide one-syllable words, contractions, or abbreviations; divide other words only between syllables.

To appreciate the full significance of our actions, you must review the entire document that was sent to you.

APOSTROPHES

1.   ' sing   Use *'s* to form the possessive of singular nouns.

The hurricane caused major damage to Georgia's coastline.

2.   ' plur   Use only an apostrophe to form the possessive of plural nouns that end in *s*.

The investors' goals were outlined in the annual report.

3.   ' pro   Use *'s* to form the possessive of indefinite pronouns (such as *someone's* or *anybody's*); do not use an apostrophe with personal pronouns (such as *hers*, *his*, *its*, *ours*, *theirs*, and *yours*).

She was instructed to select anybody's paper for a sample.
Each computer comes carefully packed in its own container.

COLONS

1.   : expl   Use a colon to introduce explanatory material that follows an independent clause. (An independent clause is one that can stand alone as a complete sentence.)

The computer satisfies three criteria: speed, cost, and power.

DASHES

1. **—emph**   Use a dash instead of a comma, semicolon, colon, or parenthesis when you want to convey a more forceful separation of words within a sentence. (If your software has a special dash symbol, use it. Otherwise, form a dash by typing two hyphens, with no space before, between, or after.)

At this year's meeting, the speakers—and topics—were superb.

PERIODS

1. **. req**   Use a period to end a sentence that is a polite request. (Consider a sentence a polite request if you expect the reader to respond by doing as you ask rather than by giving a yes-or-no answer.)

Will you please call me if I can be of further assistance.

QUOTATION MARKS

1. **' title**   Use quotation marks around the titles of newspaper articles, magazine articles, chapters in a book, reports, conferences, and similar items.

The best article I found in my research was entitled "Multimedia for Everyone."

2. **" quote**   Use quotation marks around a direct quotation.

Harrison responded by saying, "This decision will not affect our merger."

ITALICS (OR UNDERLINE)

1. **_ title**   Italicize (or underline) the titles of books, magazines, newspapers, and other complete published works.

I read *The Pelican Brief* last month.

GRAMMAR

AGREEMENT

1. **Agr sing**   Use singular verbs and pronouns with singular subjects and plural verbs and pronouns with plural subjects.

    agr plur   I was pleased with the performance of our team.
Reno and Phoenix were selected as the sites for our next two meetings.

2. **Agr pro**   Some pronouns (*anybody, each, either, everybody, everyone, much, neither, no one, nobody,* and *one*) are always singular and take a singular verb. Other pronouns (*all, any, more, most, none,* and *some*) may be singular or plural, depending on the noun to which they refer.

Each employee is responsible for summarizing the day's activities.
Most of the workers are going to get a substantial pay raise.

3. **Agr inter**   Disregard any intervening words that come between the subject and verb when establishing agreement.

The box containing the books and pencils has not been found.

4. **Agr near**   If two subjects are joined by *or, either/or, neither/nor,* or *not only/but also,* the verb should agree with the subject nearer to the verb.

Neither the players nor the coach is in favor of the decision.

5. **Agr num**   The subject <u>a</u> *number* takes a plural verb; <u>the</u> *number* takes a singular verb.

<u>A</u> number of us are taking the train to the game.
<u>The</u> number of errors has increased in the last two attempts.

6.	**Agr comp**	Subjects joined by *and* take a plural verb unless the compound subject is preceded by *each*, *every*, or *many a* (*an*).

Every man, woman, and child is included in our survey.

7.	**Agr subj**	Verbs that refer to conditions that are impossible or improbable (that is, verbs in the *subjunctive mood*) require the plural form.

If the total eclipse were to occur tomorrow, it would be the second one this year.

PRONOUNS

1.	**Pro nom**	Use nominative pronouns (such as *I, he, she, we*, and *they*) as subjects of a sentence or clause.

They traveled to Minnesota last week but will not return until next month.

2.	**Pro obj**	Use objective pronouns (such as *me, him, her, us*, and *them*) as objects in a sentence or clause.

The package has been sent to her.

ADJECTIVES AND ADVERBS

1.	**Adj/Adv**	Use comparative adjectives and adverbs (*-er*, *more*, and *less*) when referring to two nouns; use superlative adjectives and adverbs (*-est*, *most*, and *least*) when referring to more than two.

Of the two movies you have selected, the shorter one is the more interesting.
The highest of the three mountains is Mount Everest.

WORD USAGE

1.	**Word**	Do not confuse the following pairs of words:

Accept means "to agree to"; *except* means "to leave out."

We accept your offer for developing the new product.
Everyone except Sam and Lisa attended the meeting.

Affect is most often used as a verb meaning "to influence"; *effect* is most often used as a noun meaning "result."

Mr. Smith's decision will not affect our programming plans.
It will be weeks before we can assess the effect of this action.

Farther refers to distance; *further* refers to extent or degree.

Did we travel farther today than yesterday?
We need to discuss our plans further.

Personal means "private"; *personnel* means "employees."

The letters were very personal and should not have been read.
We hope that all personnel will comply with the new regulations.

Principal means "primary"; *principle* means "rule."

The principal means of research were interviewing and surveying.
They must not violate the principles under which our company was established.

MECHANICS

CAPITALIZATION

1. ≡ **sent**   Capitalize the first word of a sentence.

Please prepare a summary of your activities for our next meeting.

2. ≡ **prop**   Capitalize proper nouns and adjectives derived from proper nouns. (A proper noun is the official name of a particular person, place, or thing.)

Judy Hendrix drove to Albuquerque in her new automobile, a Pontiac.

3. ≡ **time**   Capitalize the names of the days of the week, months, holidays, and religious days (but do not capitalize the names of the seasons).

On Thursday, November 25, we will celebrate Thanksgiving, the most popular fall holiday.

4. ≡ **noun #**   Capitalize nouns followed by a number or letter (except for the nouns *line, note, page, paragraph,* and *size*).

Please read Chapter 5, but not page 94.

5. ≡ **comp**   Capitalize compass points (such as *north, south,* or *northeast*) only when they designate definite regions.

The Crenshaws will vacation in the Northeast this summer.
We will have to drive north to reach the closest Canadian border.

6. ≡ **org**   Capitalize common organizational terms (such as *advertising department* and *finance committee*) when they are the actual names of the units in the writer's own organization and when they are preceded by the word *the*.

The quarterly report from the Advertising Department will be presented today.

7. ≡ **course**   Capitalize the names of specific course titles but not the names of subjects or areas of study.

I have enrolled in Accounting 201 and will also take a marketing course.

NUMBER EXPRESSION

1. **# gen**   In general, spell out numbers 1 through 10, and use figures for numbers above 10.

We have rented two movies for tonight.
The decision was reached after 27 precincts had sent in their results.

2. **# fig**   Use figures for:

Dates (use *st, d,* or *th* only if the day precedes the month).

We will drive to the camp on the 23d of May.
The tax report is due on April 15.

All numbers if two or more related numbers both above and below ten are used in the same sentence.

Mr. Carter sent in 7 receipts; Ms. Cantrell sent in 22 receipts.

Measurements (time, money, distance, weight, and percent).

At 10 a.m. we delivered the $500 coin bank in a 17-pound container.

Mixed numbers.

Our sales are up 9½ percent over last year.

3. # word

Spell out:

Numbers used as the first word in a sentence.

Seventy people attended the conference in San Diego last week.

The smaller of two adjacent numbers.

We have ordered two 5-pound packages for the meeting.

The words *million* and *billion* in even amounts (do not use decimals with even amounts).

The lottery is worth $28 million this month.

Fractions.

About one-half of the audience responded to the questionnaire.

ABBREVIATIONS

1. Abb no

In nontechnical writing, do not abbreviate common nouns (such as *dept.* or *pkg.*), compass points, units of measure, or the names of months, days of the week, cities, or states (except in addresses).

The Sales Department will meet on Tuesday, March 7, in Tempe, Arizona.

2. Abb meas

In technical writing, on forms, and in tables, abbreviate units of measure when they occur frequently; do not use periods (e.g., deg (degree), ft (foot/feet), hrs (hours), mi (mile), min (minute), mos (months), oz (ounce), and yrs (years).

14 oz   5 ft 10 in   50 mph   2 yrs 10 mo

3. Abb lc

In lowercase abbreviations made up of single initials, use a period after each initial but no internal spaces.

We will be including several states (e.g., Maine, New Hampshire, Vermont, Massachusetts, and Connecticut).

4. Abb ≡

In all-capital abbreviations made up of single initials, do not use periods or internal spaces. (Exception: Keep the periods in most academic degrees and in abbreviations of geographic names other than two-letter state abbreviations.)

You need to call the EEO office for clarification on that issue.
He earned a Ph.D. degree in business administration.

PART ONE
The Alphabet, Number, and Symbol Keys

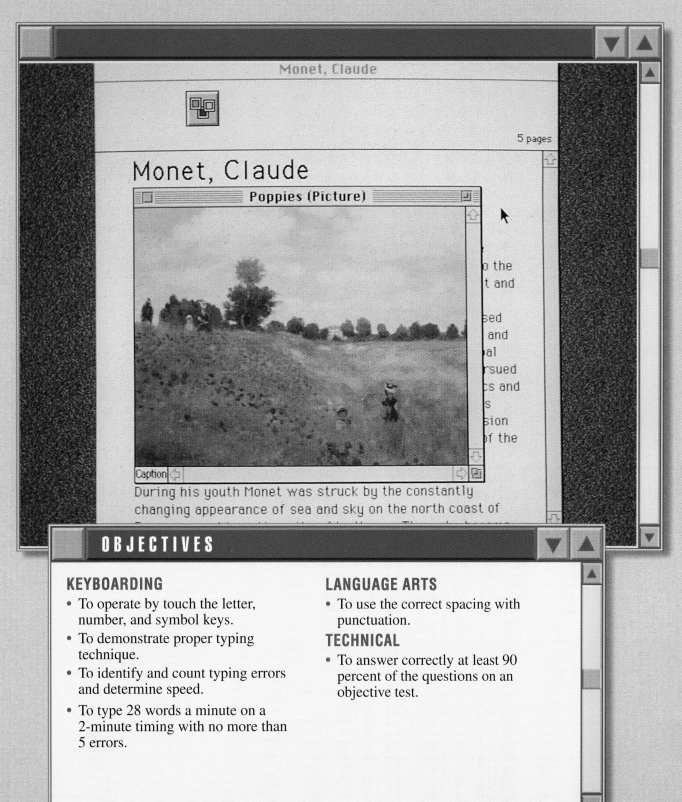

Monet, Claude

5 pages

Monet, Claude

Poppies (Picture)

Caption
During his youth Monet was struck by the constantly changing appearance of sea and sky on the north coast of

OBJECTIVES

KEYBOARDING
- To operate by touch the letter, number, and symbol keys.
- To demonstrate proper typing technique.
- To identify and count typing errors and determine speed.
- To type 28 words a minute on a 2-minute timing with no more than 5 errors.

LANGUAGE ARTS
- To use the correct spacing with punctuation.

TECHNICAL
- To answer correctly at least 90 percent of the questions on an objective test.

BEFORE YOU BEGIN

Using Microsoft Windows

If you are using *Gregg College Keyboarding & Document Processing, 8th Edition for Windows*, you must know how to use a mouse and you must know some basic information about Microsoft Windows.

Before you begin Lesson 1, turn to the Introduction section in your word processing manual and read the information presented there. Then, use Windows Help to learn how to navigate within a program and to learn the skills you need to use Windows.

Moving around, or navigating, within a program with a mouse involves pointing, clicking, double-clicking, and dragging.

Through Windows Help, you will learn the names and functions of the different parts of a window. You will want to pay close attention to the menu bar and command names, as well as how to select options in a dialog box.

Starting Your Program

Once you have completed the Introduction, you are ready to begin Lesson 1. If you are using the *Gregg College Keyboarding & Document Processing for Windows* software (sometimes referred to as GDP) that is correlated with this textbook, you must first start Windows.

To start the *Gregg College Keyboarding & Document Processing for Windows* software, locate the Glencoe Keyboarding group icon. Open the group window. If you will be saving your data to a floppy disk, insert your data disk into the correct drive before you continue.

In the Glencoe Keyboarding group window, if there is a GDP Classes icon, use that icon to start the program. Choose the correct class; then choose your name from the class list. If your name does not appear on the list, click *New* to add your name to the list. Then follow the instructions to log in and begin Lesson 1.

If there is no GDP Classes icon, select the icon that corresponds to your course name and the location of your data. For example, if your course is called *Lessons 1-60* and you will be saving your data to a disk in drive A, use the GDP Lessons 1-60 (Drive A) icon. If you will be saving your data to a disk in drive B, use the GDP Lessons 1-60 (Drive B) icon. If you will be saving your data to a hard drive or network drive, you may have an icon specified for your use only. (If you are unsure of which icon to use, ask your instructor.) Use the correct program icon, and follow the on-screen directions to log in and begin Lesson 1.

Lesson 1   Home Keys

GOALS: To control the home keys (A S D F J K L ;), the space bar, and the enter key.

 NEW KEYS

A. A semicolon (;) is commonly called the sem key.

A. THE HOME KEYS

The **A S D F J K L ;** keys are known as the home keys.

1. Place the fingers of your left hand on the home keys as follows: first finger on **F**; second finger on **D**; third finger on **S**; fourth finger on **A**.
2. Place the fingers of your right hand on the home keys as follows: first finger on **J**; second finger on **K**; third finger on **L**; and fourth finger on **;**.
3. Curve your fingers.
4. Using the correct fingers, type each letter as you say it to yourself: a s d f j k l ;.
5. Remove your fingers from the keyboard and replace them on the home keys.
6. Press each home key again as you say each letter: a s d f j k l ;.

B. THE [SPACE BAR]

The space bar, located beneath the letter keys, is used to space between words and after marks of punctuation.

1. With fingers held motionless on the home keys, poise your right thumb about a half inch above the space bar.
2. Type the letters a s d f, then press the space bar once. Bounce your thumb off.
3. Type the letters j k l ;, then press the space bar once.
4. Type the letters a s d f, press the space bar once, then type the letters j k l ;.

C. THE [ENTER] KEY

The enter key moves the insertion point to the beginning of a new line. Reach to the enter key with the fourth finger of your right hand. Keep your **J** finger at home. Lightly press the enter key.

Practice using the enter key until you can do so with confidence and without looking at your hands.

C. Type each line once, pressing the space bar where you see a space and pressing the enter key at the end of a line.

```
asdf jkl; asdf jkl;↵
asdf jkl; asdf jkl;↵
```

LEFT HAND

First Finger	F
Second Finger	D
Third Finger	S
Fourth Finger	A

RIGHT HAND

J	First finger
K	Second Finger
L	Third Finger
;	Fourth Finger
Space Bar	Thumb

D. Press the space bar with your right thumb. Type each line 2 times.
Use first fingers on F and J.

D. THE F AND J KEYS

1 fff fff jjj jjj fff jjj ff jj ff jj f j
2 fff fff jjj jjj fff jjj ff jj ff jj f j

E. The A and Sem fingers remain in home position. Type each line 2 times.
Use second fingers on D and K.

E. THE D AND K KEYS

3 ddd ddd kkk kkk ddd kkk dd kk dd kk d k
4 ddd ddd kkk kkk ddd kkk dd kk dd kk d k

F. The A and Sem fingers remain on the home keys. Type each line 2 times.
Use third fingers on S and L.

F. THE S AND L KEYS

5 sss sss lll lll sss lll ss ll ss ll s l
6 sss sss lll lll sss lll ss ll ss ll s l

G. The F and J fingers remain on the home keys. Type each line 2 times.
Use fourth fingers on A and Sem.

G. THE A AND ; KEYS

7 aaa aaa ;;; ;;; aaa ;;; aa ;; aa ;; a ;
8 aaa aaa ;;; ;;; aaa ;;; aa ;; aa ;; a ;

SKILLBUILDING

H. Type lines 9–15 twice. Press Enter twice to leave a blank line after each pair. Note the word patterns.
Space once after a semicolon.

H. WORD BUILDING

9   aaa ddd ddd add aaa lll lll all add all
10 aaa sss kkk ask ddd aaa ddd dad ask dad
11 lll aaa ddd lad fff aaa ddd fad lad fad
12 aaa ddd ;;; ad; aaa sss ;;; ad; as; ad;
13 f fa fad fads; a as ask asks; d da dad;
14 l la las lass; f fa fal fall; s sa sad;
15 a ad add adds; l la lad lads; a ad ads;

I. Type lines 16–17 twice, leaving a blank line after each pair. Note the phrase patterns.

I. PHRASES

16 dad ask; ask a lad; dad ask a lad; as a
17 a fall; a lass; ask a lass; a lad asks;

J. Take two 1-minute timings. Try to complete the line each time.

J. 1-MINUTE TIMING

18 ask a sad lad; a fall fad; add a salad;

Lesson 2   New Keys

GOAL: To control the H, E, O, and R keys.

Fingers are named for home keys. (Example: the second finger of the left hand is the D finger.)

A. Type each line 2 times.

A. WARMUP

1 fff jjj ddd kkk sss lll aaa ;;; fff jjj
2 a salad; a lad; alas a fad; ask a lass;

NEW KEYS

B. Type each line 2 times. Space once after a semicolon.

Use the J finger.

B. THE H KEY

3 jjj jhj jhj hjh jjj jhj jhj hjh jjj jhj
4 has has hah hah had had aha aha ash ash
5 hash half sash lash dash hall shad shah
6 as dad had; a lass has half; add a dash

C. Type each line 2 times. Keep your eyes on the copy as you type.

Use the D finger.

C. THE E KEY

7 ddd ded ded ede ddd ded ded ede ddd ded
8 lea led see he; she eke fed sea lee fee
9 feed keel ease heal held seal lead fake
10 he fed a seal; she held a lease; a keel

D. Type each line 2 times. Keep fingers curved.

Use the L finger.

D. THE O KEY

11 lll lol lol olo lll lol lol olo lll lol
12 doe off foe hod oh; oak odd ode old sod
13 shoe look kook joke odes does solo oleo
14 he held a hook; a lass solos; old foes;

E. Type each line 2 times. Keep the A finger at home.

Use the F finger.

E. THE R KEY

```
15  fff frf frf rfr fff frf frf rfr fff frf
16  red ark ore err rah era rod oar her are
17  oars soar dear fare read role rare door
18  a dark red door; he read a rare reader;
```

SKILLBUILDING

F. Type each line 2 times. Do not pause at the vertical lines that mark off the word patterns.

F. WORD PATTERNS

```
19  dale kale sale hale|fold sold hold old;
20  feed deed heed seed|dash sash lash ash;
21  lake rake sake fake|dear sear rear ear;
```

G. Take two 1-minute timings. Try to complete both lines each time. Press Enter only at the end of line 23.

G. 1-MINUTE TIMING

```
22  she asked for a rare old deed; he had a
23  door ajar;
```

Lesson 3   New Keys

GOAL: To control the M, T, P, and C keys.

A. Type each line 2 times.

A. WARMUP

```
1  aa ;; ss ll dd kk ff jj hh ee oo rr aa;
2  he held a sale for her as she had asked
```

NEW KEYS

B. Type each line 2 times.

Use the J finger.

B. THE M KEY

```
3  jjj jmj jmj mjm jjj jmj jmj mjm jjj jmj
4  mad mom me; am jam; ram dam ham mar ma;
5  arms loam lame roam make fame room same
6  she made more room for some of her ham;
```

C. Type each line 2 times.
   Use the F finger.

C. THE T KEY

7 fff ftf ftf tft fff ftf ftf tft fff ftf
8 tar tam mat hot jot rat eat lot art sat
9 told take date late mart mate tool fate
10 he told her to set a later date to eat;

D. Type each line 2 times.
   Use the Sem finger.

D. THE P KEY

11 ;;; ;p; ;p; p;p ;;; ;p; ;p; p;p ;;; ;p;
12 pat pal sap rap pet par spa lap pad mop
13 pale palm stop drop pelt plea slap trap
14 please park the red jeep past the pool;

E. Type each line 2 times.
   Use the D finger.

E. THE C KEY

15 ddd dcd dcd cdc ddd dcd dcd cdc ddd dcd
16 cot cod sac act car coo arc ace cop cat
17 pack tack chat coat face aces deck cost
18 call her to race cool cars at the track

SKILLBUILDING

F. Sit in the correct position as you type these drills. Refer to the illustration on page vii in the Introduction. Type each line 2 times.

F. SHORT PHRASES

19 as so | she had | has met | let her | fast pace
20 to do | ask her | for the | had pop | look past
21 do as | lap top | her pad | let pat | halt them
22 as he | had for | red cap | she let | fast plot

G. Take two 1-minute timings. Try to complete both lines each time. Use word wrap. Press Enter only at the end of line 24.

G. 1-MINUTE TIMING

23 the old store at home had lots of cheap
24 stools for the sale;

Lesson 4 New Keys

GOALS: To control the right shift, V, period, and W keys; to count errors.

A. Type each line 2 times.

A. WARMUP

1 the farmer asked her to feed the mares;
2 the late callers came to mop the floor;

NEW KEYS

B. Type each line 2 times.
Use the Sem finger.

B. THE RIGHT SHIFT KEY

To capitalize letters on the left half of the keyboard:
1. With the J finger at home, press and hold down the right shift key with the

Sem finger.
2. Press the letter key.
3. Release the shift key and return fingers to home position.

3 ;;; ;A; ;A; ;;; ;S; ;S; ;;; ;D; ;D; ;;;
4 Art Alf Ada Sal Sam Dee Dot Flo Ted Tom
5 Amos Carl Chet Elsa Fred Sara Todd Elda
6 Carl Amos took Sara Carter to the races

C. Type each line 2 times.
Use the F finger.

C. THE V KEY

7 fff fvf fvf vfv fff fvf fvf vfv fff fvf
8 Val eve Eva vet Ava vat Eve ova Vel vee
9 have vase Vera ever vast Reva dove vest
10 Dave voted for Vassar; Val voted for me

D. Type each line 2 times. Space once after a period following an abbreviation; do not space after a period within an abbreviation; space twice after a period ending a sentence.
Use the L finger.

D. THE . KEY

11 111 1.1 1.1 .1. 111 1.1 1.1 .1. 111 1.1
12 dr. dr. ea. ea. sr. sr. Dr. Dr. Sr. Sr.
13 a.m. acct. A.D. p.m. Corp. amt. Dr. Co.
14 Elsa left. Dave left. Sara came home.

E. Type each line 2 times.
Use the S finger.

E. THE W KEY

15 sss sws sws wsw sss sws sws wsw sss sws
16 wow sow war owe was mow woe few wee row
17 wake ward wart wave wham whom walk what
18 Wade watched Walt Shaw walk for a week.

F. Compare the copy with lines 19–21 below.

F. COUNTING ERRORS

Count an error when:
1. Any stroke is incorrect.
2. Any punctuation after a word is incorrect or omitted. Count the word before the punctuation as incorrect.
3. The spacing after a word or after its punctuation is incorrect. Count the word as incorrect.
4. A letter or word is omitted.
5. A letter or word is repeated.
6. A direction about spacing, indenting, and so on, is violated.
7. Words are transposed.

Note: Only one error is counted for each word, no matter how many errors it may contain.

```
Ada lost her letter; Dee lost her her card.
 Ada lost her letter;  Dee lost her card.
Dave sold some of thr food to a market.
Dave some sold of the food to a market.
Alva asked Walt for three more matches
Alva asked Walt three more matches.
```

G. Type each line once. After typing all three lines, count your errors.

G. SENTENCES

```
19 Ada lost her letter; Dee lost her card.
20 Dave sold some of the food to a market.
21 Alva asked Walt for three more matches.
```

H. Take two 1-minute timings. Try to complete both lines each time.

H. 1-MINUTE TIMING

```
22 Val asked them to tell the major to see
23 Carla at the local farm.
```

Lesson 5   Determining Speed

GOALS: To reinforce new-key reaches; to learn to determine speed.

A. Type each line 2 times.

A. WARMUP

```
1 Dave called Drew to ask for a road map.
2 Elsa took three old jars to her mother.
```

B. WORD PATTERNS

B. Type each line 2 times.

3 feed seed deed heed|fold cold mold told
4 fame tame lame same|mate late date fate
5 lace face mace race|vast last cast fast

C. PHRASES

C. Type each line 2 times.

6 at the|he has|her hat|for the|come home
7 or the|he had|her top|ask the|late date
8 to the|he met|her mop|ask her|made more
9 of the|he was|her pop|ask too|fast pace

D. DETERMINING SPEED

D. The software you are using with this text will compute your speed automatically.

Typing speed is measured in words a minute (wam). To compute wam, count every 5 strokes, including spaces, as 1 "word." Horizontal word scales below an activity divide lines into 5-stroke words (see Activity E). Vertical word scales beside an activity show the number of words in each line cumulatively totaled (see Activity F). For example, if you complete a line, you have typed 8 words. If you complete 2 lines, you have typed 16 words. Use the bottom word scale to determine the word count of a partial line. Add that number to the cumulative total for the last complete line. In the illustration, speed is 28 wam (24 + 4).

Compare with lines 13–15.

Rachael asked Sal to take her to school
for three weeks. She had to meet Freda
or Walter at the school to start a map.
Rachael asked Sal to
| 1 | 2 | 3 | 4 | 5 | 6 | 7 | 8

E. SENTENCES

E. Take a 1-minute timing on each line. Determine your speed and errors.

10 Carl loved to talk to the tall teacher.
11 She dashed to take the jet to her home.
12 Carl asked her to deed the farm to Ted.

| 1 | 2 | 3 | 4 | 5 | 6 | 7 | 8   = Number of 5-stroke words

F. PARAGRAPH

F. Take two 1-minute timings on the paragraph. Press Enter only at the end of the paragraph. Determine your speed and errors.

CUMULATIVE WORDS

13 Rachael asked Sal to take her to school   8
14 for three weeks. She had to meet Freda   16
15 or Walter at the school to start a map.   24

| 1 | 2 | 3 | 4 | 5 | 6 | 7 | 8

G. 1-MINUTE TIMING

G. Take two 1-minute timings. Determine your speed and errors.

16 Dot Crews asked Al Raper to meet her at   8
17 three to look for the jacket.   14

| 1 | 2 | 3 | 4 | 5 | 6 | 7 | 8

Lesson 6　　New Keys

GOALS: To control the I, left shift, hyphen, and G keys; to type 15 wam/1'/3e. "15 wam/1'/3e" means to type at the rate of 15 words a minute for 1 minute with no more than 3 errors.

A. Type each line 2 times.

A. WARMUP

1　The major sold three wool hats at cost.
2　Dale took her cats to the vet at three.

 NEW KEYS

B. Type each line 2 times.

　　Use the K finger.

B. THE 🄸 KEY

3　kkk kik kik iki kkk kik kik iki kkk kik
4　aid did fir him kid lid mid pit sip tip
5　chip dice itch film hide iris kite milk
6　This time he left his tie at the store.

C. Type each line 2 times.

　　Use the A finger.

C. THE LEFT ⎗SHIFT⎘ KEY

To capitalize letters on the right half of the keyboard:

1. With the F finger at home, press and hold down the left shift key with the A finger.

2. Press the letter key.

3. Release the shift key and return fingers to home position.

7　aaa Jaa Jaa aaa Kaa Kaa aaa Laa Laa aaa
8　Joe Kip Lee Hal Mat Pat Jim Kim Les Pam
9　Jake Karl Lake Hope Mark Jack Kate Hale
10　Les Lee rode with Pat Mace to the park.

D. Type each line 2 times. Do not space before or after a hyphen; keep the J finger in home position.

　　Use the Sem finger.

D. THE ⊡ KEY

11　;;; ;p; ;-; ;-; -;- ;;; ;-; -;- ;;; ;-;
12　two-thirds two-fifths trade-off tip-off
13　look-alike jack-of-all-trades free-fall
14　I heard that Ms. Lee-Som is well-to-do.

E. Type each line 2 times. Keep wrists low, but not resting on the keyboard.

Use the F finger.

E. THE G KEY

15 fff fgf fgf gfg fff fgf fgf gfg fff fgf
16 age cog dig fig hog jog lag peg rag sag
17 gold rage sage grow page cage gate wage
18 Gail G. Grove greeted the great golfer.

SKILLBUILDING

F. Type each line 2 times.

F. TECHNIQUE PRACTICE: SPACE BAR

19 Vi will meet. Ed is here. Al is here.
20 See them. Do it. Make them. Hold it.
21 See Les. See Kate. See Dad. See Mom.
22 Take the car. Make the cake. Hide it.

G. Type each line 2 times.

G. TECHNIQUE PRACTICE: HYPHEN KEY

23 Two-thirds were well-to-do look-alikes.
24 Jo Hames-Smith is a jack-of-all-trades.
25 Phil saw the trade-offs at the tip-off.
26 Two-fifths are packed for Jo Mill-Ross.

H. Take two 1-minute timings. Determine your speed and errors.

Goal: 15 wam/1'/3e

H. 1-MINUTE TIMING

WORDS

27 Al Hall left the firm two weeks ago. I   8
28 will see Al at the park at three.   15

| 1 | 2 | 3 | 4 | 5 | 6 | 7 | 8

Lesson 7   New Keys

GOALS: To control the U, B, colon, and X keys; to type 16 wam/1'/3e.

A. Type each line 2 times.

A. WARMUP

1 Evette jogged eight miles with Christi.
2 Philip gave Shari the award for spirit.

B. Type each line 2 times. Keep your other fingers at home as you reach to U.

Use the J finger.

B. THE U KEY

```
3  jjj juj juj uju jjj juj juj uju jjj juj
4  cue due hue put rut cut dug hut pup rum
5  cult duet fuel hulk just lump mule pull
6  Hugh urged us to put out the hot fires.
```

C. Type each line 2 times.

Use the F finger.

C. THE B KEY

```
7  fff fbf fbf bfb fff fbf fbf bfb fff fbf
8  bag cab bad lab bat rib bar tab beg web
9  bake back bead beef bath bail beam both
10 Bart backed Bill for a big blue bumper.
```

D. The colon is the shift of the semicolon key. Type each line 2 times. Space once after a period following an abbreviation; twice after a colon.

Use the Sem finger.

D. THE : KEY

```
11 ;;; ;:; ;:; :;: ;;; ;:; ;:; :;: ;;; ;:;
12 Dr. Poe:   Ms. Shu:   Mr. Roe:   Mrs. Tam:
13 Dear Ed:   Dear Flo:   Dear Al:   Dear Di:
14 Date:  To:  From:  Subject:  as listed:
```

E. Type each line 2 times.

Use the S finger.

E. THE X KEY

```
15 sss sxs sxs xsx sss sxs sxs xsx sss sxs
16 box fox hex lax lux mix six tax vex wax
17 apex axle exam flax flex flux taxi text
18 Max asked six pals to fix a sixth taxi.
```

F. Type each line 2 times.

F. TECHNIQUE PRACTICE: COLON KEY

```
19 as follows:  these dates:  for example:
20 Dear Sir:  Dear Madam:  Dear Ms. Smith:
21 Dear Di:  Dear Bo:  Dear Pa:  Dear Mom:
22 for these parts:  as listed:  as usual:
```

G. WORD PRACTICE

G. Type each line 2 times.

Top row

23 We were told to take our truck to Hugo.
24 There were two tired people at the hut.
25 Please write to their home to tell Tom.

Home row

26 Jake asked his dad for small red flags.
27 Sara added a dash of salt to the salad.
28 Dale said she had a fall sale at Drake.

Bottom row

29 He came to the mall at five to meet me.
30 Victoria came to vote with ample vigor.
31 Mable Baxter visited via the Marta bus.

H. 1-MINUTE TIMING

H. Take two 1-minute timings. Determine your speed and errors.

Goal: 16 wam/1'/3e

WORDS

32 Dear Jack: Fred would like to take Pam   8
33 Hall to the home game at five tomorrow.   16

| 1 | 2 | 3 | 4 | 5 | 6 | 7 | 8 |

Lesson 8   New Keys

GOALS: To control the Y, comma, Q, and / keys; to type 17 wam/1'/3e.

A. WARMUP

A. Type each line 2 times.

1 Jack asked Philip if Charlie came home.
2 Kim had a short meal with Victor Baker.

 NEW KEYS

B. THE Y KEY

B. Type each line 2 times.

Use the J finger.

3 jjj jyj jyj yjy jjj jyj jyj yjy jjj jyj
4 boy cry day eye fly guy hay joy key may
5 yard year yelp yoke yolk your yule play
6 Peggy told me that she may try to stay.

C. Type each line 2 times.

  Use the K finger.

C. THE , KEY

7 kkk k,k k,k ,k kkk k,k k,k ,k kkk k,k
8 as, at, do, if, is, it, of, oh, or, so,
9 if so, if it is, what if, what of, too,
10 Dale, Barbra, Sadie, or Edith left too.

D. Type each line 2 times.

  Use the A finger.

D. THE Q KEY

11 aaa aqa aqa qaq aaa aqa aqa qaq aaa aqa
12 quip quit quack quail quake quart quash
13 quest quick quilts quotes quaver queasy
14 Four quiet squires quilted aqua quilts.

E. Type each line 2 times. Do not space before or after a slash.

  Use the Sem finger.

E. THE / KEY

15 ;;; ;/; ;/; /;/ ;;; ;/; ;/; /;/ ;;; ;/;
16 his/her him/her he/she either/or ad/add
17 do/due/dew hale/hail fir/fur heard/herd
18 Ask him/her if he/she chose true/false.

SKILLBUILDING

F. Type each line 2 times.

F. PHRASES

19 if it is she will do will he come he is
20 he said so who left them will she drive
21 after all he voted just wait to ask her
22 some said it for that firm did she seem

G. Type each line 2 times.

G. TECHNIQUE PRACTICE: SHIFT KEY

23 Ada, Idaho; Kodiak, Alaska; Lima, Ohio;
24 Lula, Georgia; Sully, Iowa; Alta, Utah;
25 Mr. Ray Tims; Mr. Ed Chu; Mr. Cal York;
26 Ms. Vi Close; Ms. Di Ray; Ms. Sue Ames;

H. Take two 1-minute timings. Determine your speed and errors.

Goal: 17 wam/1'/3e

H. 1-MINUTE TIMING

27 George predicted that Lu will have five · 8
28 boxed meals. Dave Quayle was to pack a · 16
29 mug. · 17

| 1 | 2 | 3 | 4 | 5 | 6 | 7 | 8

Lesson 9 · New Keys

GOALS: To control the N, Z, and ? keys; to type 18 wam/1'/3e.

A. Type each line 2 times.

A. WARMUP

1 I quit the sales job at Huber, Georgia.
2 Alice packed two boxes of silver disks.

 NEW KEYS

B. Type each line 2 times.

Use the J finger.

B. THE N KEY

3 jjj jnj jnj njn jjj jnj jnj njn jjj jnj
4 and ban can den end fan nag one pan ran
5 aunt band chin dent find gain hang lawn
6 Al and Dan can enter the main entrance.

C. Type each line 2 times. Keep the F finger at home as you reach to the Z.

Use the A finger.

C. THE Z KEY

7 aaa aza aza zaz aaa aza aza zaz aaa aza
8 zap zig buzz gaze haze jazz mazes oozes
9 zip zoo zinc zing zone zoom blaze craze
10 The size of the prized pizza amazed us.

D. The question mark is the shift of the slash. Space twice after a question mark at the end of a sentence. Type each line 2 times.

Use the Sem finger.

D. THE ? KEY

11 ; ; ;   ; / ?   ; / ?   ? ; ?   ; ; ;   ; / ?   ; / ?   ? ; ?   ; ; ;   ; ? ;
12 Can Joe go?   If not Jan, who?   Can Ken?
13 Who will see?   Can it be?   Is that you?
14 Why not bat?   Can they go?   Did he ask?

SKILLBUILDING

E. Type each line 2 times.

E. TECHNIQUE PRACTICE: QUESTION MARK

15 Who?   Why?   How?   When?   Where?   Whose?
16 Is it?   Why not?   What for?   Which one?
17 Did Mary go?   Is Clint ready?   Why not?
18 Who competed?   Donna?   Jim?   Kay?   Dan?

F. Type each line 2 times.

F. PHRASES

19 and the for the she is able can they go
20 ask him for him they still did they fly
21 of them with us can he send ought to be
22 has been able they need it he will call

G. Type lines 23-28 two times.

G. TECHNIQUE PRACTICE: HYPHEN

Hyphens are used:

1. To show that a word is divided (lines 23 and 27).

2. To make a dash (two hyphens with no space before or after, see lines 24 and 27).

3. To join words in a compound (lines 25, 26, and 28).

23 Can Larry go to the next tennis tourna-
24 ment?   I am positive he--like you--will
25 find it a first-class sports event.   If
26 he can go, I will get first-rate seats.
27 Larry--like Ellen--likes tennis tourna-
28 ments that are first-rate, first-class.

H. Space once after a semicolon and comma, twice after a period and question mark at the end of a sentence, and twice after a colon. Type each line 2 times.

H. PUNCTUATION PRACTICE

29 Kay writes; John sings.   Are they good?
30 Send these items: pens, pencils, lead.
31 He left; she stayed.   Will they attend?
32 We made these stops: Rome, Bern, Kiev.

I. Take two 1-minute timings. Determine your speed and errors.

Goal: 18 wam/1'/3e

I. 1-MINUTE TIMING

33 Zelik judged six typing contests that a   8
34 local firm held in Piqua. Vic Bass was   16
35 a winner.   18

| 1 | 2 | 3 | 4 | 5 | 6 | 7 | 8

Lesson 10   New Key

GOALS: To learn the tab key; to type 19 wam/1'/3e.

A. Type each line 2 times.

A. WARMUP

1 Gwen Dunne expects too much from a job.
2 Keith had a very quiet, lazy afternoon.

NEW KEY

B. The word counts in this book credit you with 1 stroke for each paragraph indention in a timing. Press the tab key after the timing starts.
Use the A finger.

B. THE [TAB] KEY

The tab key is used to indent paragraphs. Reach to the tab key with the A finger. Keep your other fingers on home keys as you quickly press the tab key.

Pressing the tab key moves the insertion point 0.5 inch (the default setting) to the right.

SKILLBUILDING

C. Take a 1-minute timing on each paragraph. Determine your speed and errors.

C. SHORT PARAGRAPHS

3   You can use your typing skills to   7
4 do quite a few jobs. Many jobs might   15
5 need to be printed.   19

6   You will be amazed as to how easy   7
7 and exact your typing can be when you   15
8 draft all your work.   19

| 1 | 2 | 3 | 4 | 5 | 6 | 7 | 8

D. Type each line 2 times.

D. WORD PATTERNS

9 banister minister adapter filter master
10 disable disband discern discord discuss
11 embargo emerge embody empty employ emit
12 enforce endure energy engage engine end
13 precept precise predict preside premier
14 subtract subject subsist sublime subdue
15 teamster tearful teaches teak team tear
16 theater theirs theory thefts therm them
17 treason crimson season prison bison son
18 tribune tribute tripod trial tribe trim

E. Type each line 2 times. Keep fingers curved and wrists low but not resting on the keyboard as you practice these lines.

E. ALPHABET REVIEW

19 Alda asked Alma Adams to fly to Alaska.
20 Both Barbara and Bill liked basketball.
21 Carl can accept a classic car in Cairo.
22 David dined in a dark diner in Detroit.
23 Elmo said Eddie edited the entire text.
24 Five friars focused on the four fables.
25 Guy gave a bag of green grapes to Gina.
26 Haughty Hugh hoped Hal had helped Seth.
27 Irene liked to pickle pickles in brine.
28 Jon Jones joined a junior jogging team.
29 Kenny kept a kayak for a trek to Koyuk.
30 Lowell played a well-planned ball game.
31 Monica made more money on many markups.
32 Ned knew ten men in a main dining room.
33 Opal Orem opened four boxes of oranges.
34 Pat paid to park the plane at the pump.
35 Quincy quickly quit his quarterly quiz.
36 Robin read rare books in their library.
37 Sam signed, sealed, and sent the lease.
38 Todd caught trout in the little stream.
39 Uncle Rubin urged Julie to go to Utica.
40 Viva Vista vetoed the five voice votes.
41 Walt waited while Wilma went to Weston.
42 Xu mixed extra extract exactly as told.
43 Yes, your young sister played a cymbal.
44 Zesty zebras zigzagged in the Ohio zoo.

F. Take two 1-minute timings. Determine your speed and errors.

Goal: 19 wam/1'/3e

F. 1-MINUTE TIMING

45   Zoe expected a quiet morning to do   7
46 all of her work. Joy Day was to bring   15
47 five of the tablets.   19

| 1 | 2 | 3 | 4 | 5 | 6 | 7 | 8

Lesson 11   Number Keys

GOALS: To control the 5, 7, 3, and 9 keys; to type 19 wam/2'/5e.

A. Type the paragraph 2 times.

A. WARMUP

```
1      The law firm of Quayle, Buster, Given, and     9
2  Rizzo processed all the cases last June and July;  19
3  however, we will seek a new law firm next summer.  29
   |  1  |  2  |  3  |  4  |  5  |  6  |  7  |  8  |  9  |  10
```

 NEW KEYS

B. Type each line 2 times.

   Use the F finger.

B. THE ⑤ KEY

```
4  fr5f fr5f f55f f55f f5f5 f5f5 5 55 555 5,555 5:55
5  55 fury 55 foes 55 fibs 55 fads 55 furs 55 favors
6  The 55 students read the 555 pages in 55 minutes.
7  He found Item 5 that weighed 55 pounds, 5 ounces.
```

C. Type each line 2 times.

   Use the J finger.

C. THE ⑦ KEY

```
8  ju7j ju7j j77j j77j j7j7 j7j7 7 77 777 7,777 7:77
9  77 jigs 77 jobs 77 jugs 77 jets 77 jars 77 jewels
10 The 77 men bought Items 77 and 777 for their job.
11 Joe had 57 books and 77 tablets for a 7:57 class.
```

D. Type each line 2 times.

   Use the D finger.

D. THE ③ KEY

```
12 de3d de3d d33d d33d d3d3 d3d3 3 33 333 3,333 3:33
13 33 dots 33 died 33 dine 33 days 33 dogs 33 drains
14 The 33 vans moved 73 cases in less than 33 hours.
15 Add 55 to 753; subtract 73 to get a total of 735.
```

E. Type each line 2 times.

   Use the L finger.

E. THE ⑨ KEY

```
16 lo91 lo91 1991 1991 1919 1919 9 99 999 9,999 9:99
17 99 lads 99 lights 99 labs 99 legs 99 lips 99 logs
18 Their 99 cans of No. 99 were sold to 99 managers.
19 He had 39 pens, 59 pads, 97 pencils, and 9 clips.
```

F. Type each line 2 times.

F. NUMBER PRACTICE: 5, 7, 3, AND 9

20 The 57 tickets were for the April 3 show at 9:59.
21 Mary was to read pages 33, 57, 95, and 97 to him.
22 Kate planted 53 tulips, 39 mums, and 97 petunias.
23 Only 397 of the 573 coeds could register at 5:39.

G. Type each line 2 times. Keep other fingers at home as you reach to the shift keys.

G. TECHNIQUE PRACTICE: SHIFT KEY

24 Vera Rosa Tao Fay Jae Tab Pat Yuk Sue Ann Sal Joe
25 Andre Fidel Pedro Chong Alice Mike Juan Fern Dick
26 Carlos Caesar Karen Ojars Julie Marta Scott Maria
27 Marge Jerry Joan Mary Bill Ken Bob Ray Ted Mel Al

H. PROGRESSIVE PRACTICE: ALPHABET

Turn to the Progressive Practice: Alphabet routine beginning on page SB-7. Take a 1-minute timing on the Entry Timing paragraph. Then follow the directions at the top of page SB-7 for completing the activity.

I. Take two 2-minute timings. Determine your speed and errors.

Goal: 19 wam/2′/5e

I. 2-MINUTE TIMING

28   Jazz paid for six seats and quit because he   9
29 could not get the views he wanted near the middle   19
30 of the field. In August he is thinking of going   29
31 to the ticket office early to purchase tickets.   38

| 1 | 2 | 3 | 4 | 5 | 6 | 7 | 8 | 9 | 10

Lesson 12 Review

GOAL: To type 20 wam/2′/5e.

A. Type the paragraph 2 times.

A. WARMUP

1   Rex played a very quiet game of bridge with   9
2 Zeke. In March they played in competition with   19
3 39 players; in January they played with 57 more.   28

| 1 | 2 | 3 | 4 | 5 | 6 | 7 | 8 | 9 | 10

B. 12-SECOND SPEED SPRINTS

B. Take three 12-second timings on each line. The scale below the last line shows your wam speed for a 12-second timing.

4 A good neighbor paid for these ancient ornaments.
5 Today I sit by the big lake and count huge rocks.
6 The four chapels sit by the end of the old field.
7 The signal means help is on its way to the child.

| | | |5 | | |10 | | |15 | | |20 | | |25 | | |30 | | |35 | | |40 | | |45 | | |50

C. SUSTAINED PRACTICE: SYLLABIC INTENSITY

C. Take a 1-minute timing on the first paragraph to establish your base speed. Then take four 1-minute timings on the remaining paragraphs. As soon as you equal or exceed your base speed on one paragraph, advance to the next, more difficult paragraph.

8   People continue to rent autos for personal   9
9 use and for their work, and car rental businesses   19
10 just keep growing. You may want to try one soon.   29

11   It is likely that a great deal of insurance   9
12 protection is part of the standard rental cost to   19
13 you. You may, however, make many other choices.   29

14   Perhaps this is not necessary, as you might   9
15 already have the kind of protection you want in a   19
16 policy that you currently have on the automobile.   29

17   Paying separate mileage charges could evolve   9
18 into a very large bill. This will undoubtedly be   19
19 true if your trip involves distant destinations.   29

| | 1 | 2 | 3 | 4 | 5 | 6 | 7 | 8 | 9 | 10

D. ALPHABET PRACTICE

D. Type each line 2 times.

20 Packing jam for the dozen boxes was quite lively.
21 Fay quickly jumped over the two dozen huge boxes.
22 We vexed Jack by quietly helping a dozen farmers.
23 The quick lynx from the zoo just waved a big paw.
24 Lazy brown dogs do not jump over the quick foxes.

E. NUMBER PRACTICE

E. Type each line 2 times.

25 Mary was to read pages 37, 59, 75, and 93 to Zoe.
26 He invited 53 boys and 59 girls to the 7:35 show.
27 The 9:37 bus did not come to our stop until 9:55.
28 Purchase Order 53 listed Items 35, 77, 93, and 9.
29 Flight 375 will be departing Gate 37 at 9:59 p.m.

F. TECHNIQUE PRACTICE: ENTER KEY

F. Type each sentence on a separate line. Type 2 times.

30 Can he go? If so, what? I am lost. Joe is ill.
31 Did he type the memo? Tina is going. Jane lost.
32 Max will drive. Xenia is in Ohio. He is taller.
33 Nate is fine; Ty is not. Who won? Where is Nan?
34 No, he cannot go. Is he here? Where is Roberta?

G. Type each line 2 times. Space without pausing.

G. TECHNIQUE PRACTICE: SPACE BAR

35 a b c d e f g h i j k l m n o p q r s t u v w x y
36 an as be by go in is it me no of or to we but for
37 Do you go to Ada or Ida for work every day or so?
38 I am sure he can go with you if he has some time.
39 He is to be at the car by the time you get there.

H. Take two 2-minute timings. Determine your speed and errors.

Goal: 20 wam/2'/5e

H. 2-MINUTE TIMING

40   Jack and Alex ordered six pizzas at a price   9
41 that was quite a bit lower than for the one they   19
42 ordered yesterday. They will order from the same   29
43 place tomorrow for the party they are planning to   39
44 have.   40

| 1 | 2 | 3 | 4 | 5 | 6 | 7 | 8 | 9 | 10

Lesson 13   Number Keys

GOALS: To control the 8, 2, and 0 keys; to type 21 wam/2'/5e.

A. Type the paragraph 2 times.

A. WARMUP

1   Mary, Jenny, and Quinn packed 79 prizes in   9
2 53 large boxes for the party. They will take all   19
3 of the boxes to 3579 North Capitol Avenue today.   28

| 1 | 2 | 3 | 4 | 5 | 6 | 7 | 8 | 9 | 10

 NEW KEYS

B. Type each line 2 times.

Use the K finger.

B. THE 8 KEY

4 ki8k ki8k k88k k88k k8k8 k8k8 8 88 888 8,888 8:88
5 88 inks 88 inns 88 keys 88 kits 88 kids 88 knives
6 Bus 38 left at 3:38 and arrived here at 8:37 p.m.
7 Kenny called Joe at 8:38 at 883-7878 or 585-3878.

C. Type each line 2 times.

Use the S finger.

C. THE 2 KEY

8 sw2s sw2s s22s s22s s2s2 s2s2 2 22 222 2,222 2:22
9 22 seas 22 sets 22 sons 22 subs 22 suns 22 sports
10 The 22 seats sold at 2:22 to 22 coeds in Room 22.
11 He added Items 22, 23, 25, 27, and 28 on Order 2.

D. Type each line 2 times.

Use the Sem finger.

D. THE 0 KEY

12 ;p0; ;p0; ;00; ;00; ;0;0 ;0;0 0 00 000 0,000 0:00
13 20 pads 30 pegs 50 pens 70 pins 80 pits 900 parks
14 You will get 230 when you add 30, 50, 70, and 80.
15 The 80 men met at 3:05 with 20 agents in Room 90.

SKILLBUILDING

E. Type each line 2 times.

E. NUMBER PRACTICE

16 Jill bought 55 tickets for the 5:50 or 7:50 show.
17 Maxine called from 777-7370 or 777-7570 for Mary.
18 Sally had 23 cats, 23 dogs, and 22 birds at home.
19 Items 35, 37, 38, and 39 were sent on October 30.
20 Did Flight 2992 leave from Gate 39 at 9:39 today?
21 Sue went from 852 28th Street to 858 28th Street.
22 He sold 20 tires, 30 air filters, and 200 wipers.

F. Indent and type each sentence on a separate line. Type 2 times.

F. TECHNIQUE PRACTICE: TAB KEY

23 Casey left. Where is John? Susan asked for Tom.
24 I drive. Where do you drive? When do you drive?
25 Pat sold cars. Don sold vans. Pete sold trucks.
26 Nick has nails. Chris has bolts. Dave has wood.

G. PACED PRACTICE

Turn to the Paced Practice routine beginning on page SB-14. Take a 1-minute timing on the Entry Timing paragraph. Then follow the directions at the top of page SB-14 for completing the activity.

H. DIAGNOSTIC PRACTICE: ALPHABET

Turn to the Diagnostic Practice: Alphabet routine beginning on page SB-2. Type one of the Pretest/Posttest paragraphs and identify any errors made. Then type the corresponding drill lines 2 times for each letter on which you made 2 or more errors and 1 time for each letter on which you made only 1 error. Finally, repeat the same Pretest paragraph and compare your performance.

I. Take two 2-minute timings. Determine your speed and errors.

Goal: 21 wam/2'/5e

I. 2-MINUTE TIMING

```
27      Jim told Bev that they must keep the liquid      9
28  oxygen frozen so that it could be used by the new    19
29  plant foreman tomorrow.  The oxygen will then be     29
30  moved quickly to its new location by transport or    39
31  rail next evening.                                   42
    |  1  |  2  |  3  |  4  |  5  |  6  |  7  |· 8  |  9  |  10
```

Lesson 14   Number Keys

GOALS: To control the 4, 6, and 1 keys; to type 22 wam/2'/5e.

A. Type the paragraph 2 times.

A. WARMUP

```
1       We quickly made 30 jars of jam and won a big     9
2   prize for our efforts on March 29.  Six of the       19
3   jars were taken to 578 Culver Drive on April 28.     28
    |  1  |  2  |  3  |  4  |  5  |  6  |  7  |  8  |  9  |  10
```

NEW KEYS

B. Type each line 2 times.

Use the F finger.

B. THE 4 KEY

```
4   fr4f fr4f f44f f44f f4f4 f4f4 4 44 444 4,444 4:44
5   44 fans 44 feet 44 figs 44 fins 44 fish 44 flakes
6   The 44 boys had 44 tickets for the games at 4:44.
7   Matthew read 4 books, 54 articles, and 434 lines.
```

C. Type each line 2 times.

Use the J finger.

C. THE 6 KEY

8 jy6j jy6j j66j j66j j6j6 j6j6 6 66 666 6,666 6:66
9 66 jabs 66 jams 66 jobs 66 join 66 jots 66 jewels
10 Tom Lux left at 6:26 on Train 66 to go 600 miles.
11 There were 56,640 people in Bath; 26,269 in Hale.

D. Type each line 2 times.

Use the A finger.

D. THE 1 KEY

12 aqla aqla alla alla alal alal 1 11 111 1,111 1:11
13 11 aces 11 adds 11 aims 11 arts 11 axes 11 arenas
14 Sam left here at 1:11; Sue at 6:11; Don at 11:11.
15 Eric moved from 1661 Main Street to 1116 in 1995.

SKILLBUILDING

E. Type each line 2 times. Focus on accuracy rather than speed as you practice the number drills.

E. NUMBER PRACTICE

16 Adding 10 and 20 and 30 and 40 and 70 totals 170.
17 On July 25, 1996, 130 girls ran in a 4-mile race.
18 Al selected Nos. 16, 17, 18, 19, and 20 to study.
19 The test took Sam 10 hours, 8 minutes, 3 seconds.
20 Alice took 14 men and 23 women to the 128 events.

21 Did the 33 men drive 567 miles on Route 23 or 27?
22 On 10/29/96, she typed lines 16-47 in 35 minutes.
23 In 1995 there were 2,934 people in the 239 camps.
24 The 18 shows were sold out by 8:37 on October 18.
25 On April 29-30 we will be open from 7:45 to 9:30.

F. PROGRESSIVE PRACTICE: NUMBERS

Turn to the Progressive Practice: Numbers routine beginning on page SB-11. Take a 1-minute timing on the Entry Timing paragraph. Then follow the directions at the top of page SB-11 for completing the activity.

G. Take two 1-minute timings. Determine your speed and errors.

G. HANDWRITTEN PARAGRAPH

26   *Good writing skills are critical for success*   9
27   *in business. Numerous studies have shown*   19
28   *that these skills are essential for job advancement.*   28

H. Take two 2-minute timings. Determine your speed and errors.

Goal: 22 wam/2'/5e

H. 2-MINUTE TIMING

```
29        James scheduled a science quiz next week for        9
30  George, but he did not let him know what time the        19
31  exam was to be taken.  It is very important that          29
32  George scores well in this exam to be admitted to         39
33  the Mount Garland Academy.                                44
    |  1  |  2  |  3  |  4  |  5  |  6  |  7  |  8  |  9  |  10
```

Lesson 15   Review

GOAL: To type 23 wam/2'/5e.

A. Type the paragraph 2 times.

A. WARMUP

```
1         Jeffrey Mendoza quickly plowed six fields so       9
2   that he could plant 19 rows of beets, 28 rows of         19
3   corn, 37 rows of grapes, and 45 rows of olives.          28
    |  1  |  2  |  3  |  4  |  5  |  6  |  7  |  8  |  9  |  10
```

SKILLBUILDING

B. Take three 12-second timings on each line. The scale below the last line shows your wam speed for a 12-second timing.

B. 12-SECOND SPEED SPRINTS

```
4   The lane to the lake might make the auto go away.
5   They go to the lake by bus when they work for me.
6   He just won and lost, won and lost, won and lost.
7   The man and the girl rush down the paths to town.
    | | | 5 | | | 10 | | | 15 | | | 20 | | | 25 | | | 30 | | | 35 | | | 40 | | | 45 | | | 50
```

C. Tab once between columns. Type 2 times.

C. TECHNIQUE PRACTICE: TAB KEY

8 aisle	break	crank	draft	earth
9 frame	guide	hitch	input	juice
10 knack	learn	mason	night	ocean
11 print	quest	rinse	slide	title
12 usual	vapor	where	extra	zesty

D. Type each line 2 times. Try not to slow down for the capital letters.

D. TECHNIQUE PRACTICE: SHIFT KEY

13 Sue, Pat, Ann, and Gail left for Rome on June 10.
14 The St. Louis Cardinals and New York Mets played.
15 Dave Herr took Flight 481 for Memphis and Toledo.
16 An address for Karen Cook is 5 Bar Street, Provo.
17 Harry Truman was born in Missouri on May 8, 1884.

E. Type each line 2 times.

E. PUNCTUATION PRACTICE

18 Jan Brooks-Smith was a go-between for the author.
19 The off-the-record comment led to a free-for-all.
20 Louis was a jack-of-all-trades as a clerk-typist.
21 Ask Barbara--who is in Central Data--to find out.
22 Joanne is too old-fashioned to be that outspoken.

Pretest
Take a 1-minute timing. Determine your speed and errors.

F. PRETEST: VERTICAL REACHES

23   A few of our business managers attribute the   9
24 success of the bank to a judicious and scientific   19
25 reserve program. The bank cannot drop its guard.   29
   | 1 | 2 | 3 | 4 | 5 | 6 | 7 | 8 | 9 | 10

Practice
Speed Emphasis: If you made 2 or fewer errors on the Pretest, type each *individual* line 2 times.
Accuracy Emphasis: If you made 3 or more errors, type each *group* of lines (as though it were a paragraph) 2 times.

G. PRACTICE: UP REACHES

26 at atlas plate water later batch fatal match late
27 dr draft drift drums drawn drain drama dress drab
28 ju jumpy juror junky jumbo julep judge juice just

H. PRACTICE: DOWN REACHES

29 ca cable cabin cadet camel cameo candy carve cash
30 nk trunk drink prank rinks brink drank crank sink
31 ba batch badge bagel baked banjo barge basis bank

Posttest
Repeat the Pretest timing and compare performance.

I. POSTTEST: VERTICAL REACHES

J. PROGRESSIVE PRACTICE: ALPHABET

Turn to the Progressive Practice: Alphabet routine beginning on page SB-7. Take six 30-second timings, starting at the point where you left off the last time.

K. Take two 2-minute timings. Determine your speed and errors.

Goal: 23 wam/2'/5e

K. 2-MINUTE TIMING

32   Jeff Malvey was quite busy fixing all of the   9
33 frozen pipes so that his water supply would not   19
34 be stopped. Last winter he kept the pipes from   28
35 freezing by wrapping them with an electric cord   38
36 that did not allow in any of the cold air.   46
   | 1 | 2 | 3 | 4 | 5 | 6 | 7 | 8 | 9 | 10

Lesson 16 — Symbol Keys

GOALS: To control the $, (,), and ! keys; to type 24 wam/2'/5e.

A. Type 2 times.

A. WARMUP

```
1        Gill was quite vexed by that musician who      9
2   played 5 jazz songs and 13 country songs at the   18
3   fair.  He wanted 8 rock songs and 4 blues songs.  28
    | 1 | 2 | 3 | 4 | 5 | 6 | 7 | 8 | 9 | 10
```

NEW KEYS

B. $ DOLLAR is the shift of 4. Do not space between the dollar sign and the number. Type each line 2 times.

Use the F finger.

B. THE $ KEY

```
4   frf fr4f f4f f4$f f$$f f$$f $44 $444 $4,444 $4.44
5   I quoted $48, $64, and $94 for the set of chairs.
6   Her insurance paid $150; our insurance paid $175.
7   Season concert seats were $25, $30, $55, and $75.
```

C. ( ) PAREN- THESES are the shifts of 9 and 0. Do not space between the parentheses and the text within them. Type each line 2 times.

Use the L finger on (.

Use the Sem finger on).

C. THE (AND) KEYS

```
8    lo9l lo9l lo(l lo(l l(((l ;p0; ;p0; ;p); ;p); ;));
9    Please ask (1) Al, (2) Pat, (3) Ted, and (4) Dee.
10   Sue has some (1) skis, (2) sleds, and (3) skates.
11   Mary is (1) prompt, (2) speedy, and (3) accurate.

12   Our workers (Lewis, Jerry, and Ty) were rewarded.
13   The owner (Ms. Parks) went on Friday (August 18).
14   The Roxie (a cafe) had fish (salmon) on the menu.
15   The clerk (Ms. Fay Green) will vote yes (not no).
```

D. ! EXCLAMATION is the shift of 1. Space twice after an exclamation point at the end of a sentence. Type each line 2 times.

Use the A finger.

D. THE ! KEY

```
16   aqa aqla aq!a a!!a a!!a Where!  Why!  How!  When!
17   Put it down!  Do not move!  No!  Yes!  Stop!  Go!
18   He did say that!  Jay cannot take a vacation now!
19   You cannot leave at this time!  Jane will not go!
```

E. TECHNIQUE PRACTICE: SPACE BAR

E. Type the paragraph 2 times.

20 We will all go to the race if I win the one
21 I am going to run today. Do you think I will be
22 able to run at the front of the pack and win it?

F. 12-SECOND SPEED SPRINTS

F. Take three 12-second timings on each line. The scale below the last line shows your wam speed for a 12-second timing.

23 Walking can perk you up if you are feeling tired.
24 Your heart and lungs can work harder as you walk.
25 It may be that a walk is often better than a nap.
26 If you walk each day, your health will be better.

| | | 5 | | | 10 | | | 15 | | | 20 | | | 25 | | | 30 | | | 35 | | | 40 | | | 45 | | | 50

G. PACED PRACTICE

Turn to the Paced Practice routine beginning on page SB-14. Take three 2-minute timings, starting at the point where you left off the last time.

H. 2-MINUTE TIMING

H. Take two 2-minute timings. Determine your speed and errors.

Goal: 24 wam/2′/5e

27 Katie quit her zoo job seven days after she   9
28 learned that she was expected to travel to four   19
29 different zoos in the first year of employment.   28
30 After quitting that job, she found an excellent   38
31 job that required her to travel less frequently.   48

| 1 | 2 | 3 | 4 | 5 | 6 | 7 | 8 | 9 | 10

Lesson 17   Review

GOAL: To type 25 wam/2′/5e.

A. WARMUP

A. Type 2 times.

1 Yes! We object to the dumping of 25 toxic   9
2 barrels at 4098 Nix Street. A larger number (36)   19
3 were dumped on the 7th, costing us over $10,000.   28

| 1 | 2 | 3 | 4 | 5 | 6 | 7 | 8 | 9 | 10

B. NUMBER PRACTICE

B. Type each line 2 times.

```
4  we 23 pi 08 you 697 row 492 tire 5843 power 09234
5  or 94 re 43 eye 363 top 590 quit 1785 witty 28556
6  up 70 ye 63 pit 085 per 034 root 4995 wrote 24953
7  it 85 ro 49 rip 480 two 529 tour 5974 quite 17853
8  yi 68 to 59 toy 596 rot 495 tier 5834 queue 17373
9  op 90 qo 19 wet 235 pet 035 rope 4903 quote 17953
```

C. WORD BEGINNINGS

C. Type each line 2 times.

```
10  tri trinkets tribune trifle trick trial trip trim
11  mil million mileage mildew mills milky miles mild
12  spo sponsor sponge sports spore spoon spool spoke
13  for forgiving forbear forward forbid forced force

14  div dividend division divine divide diving divers
15  vic vicinity vicious victory victims victor vices
16  aff affliction affiliates affirms affords affairs
17  tab tablecloth tabulates tableau tabloids tablets
```

D. WORD ENDINGS

D. Type each line 2 times.

```
18  ive repulsive explosive alive drive active strive
19  est nearest invest attest wisest nicest jest test
20  ply supply simply deeply damply apply imply reply
21  ver whenever forever whoever quiver waiver driver

22  tor inventor detector debtor orator doctor factor
23  lly industrially logically legally ideally really
24  ert convert dessert expert invert diverts asserts
25  ink shrink drink think blink clink pink sink rink
```

E. PROGRESSIVE PRACTICE: ALPHABET

Turn to the Progressive Practice: Alphabet routine beginning on page SB-7. Take six 30-second timings, starting at the point where you left off the last time.

F. HANDWRITTEN PARAGRAPH

F. Take two 1-minute timings. Determine your speed and errors.

```
26  In this book you have learned the reaches         9
27  for all alphabetic and number keys. You have      18
28  also learned a few of the symbol keys. In the     27
29  remaining lessons you will learn the remaining    36
30  symbol keys, and you will also build your         45
31  speed and accuracy when typing.                   51
```

G. DIAGNOSTIC PRACTICE: NUMBERS

Turn to the Diagnostic Practice: Numbers routine beginning on page SB-5. Type one of the Pretest/Posttest paragraphs and identify any errors made. Then type the corresponding drill lines 2 times for each number on which you made 2 or more errors and 1 time for each number on which you made only 1 error. Finally, repeat the same Pretest paragraph and compare your performance.

H. 2-MINUTE TIMING

H. Take two 2-minute timings. Determine your speed and errors.

Goal: 25 wam/2'/5e

```
32        From the tower John saw that the six big       8
33   planes would crash as they zoomed quickly over      18
34   treetops on their way to the demonstration that     27
35   was scheduled to begin early.  We hope there is      37
36   no accident and that those pilots reach their       46
37   destinations safely.                                50
     |  1  |  2  |  3  |  4  |  5  |  6  |  7  |  8  |  9  |  10
```

Lesson 18   Symbol Keys

GOALS: To control the *, #, and ' keys; to type 26 wam/2'/5e.

A. WARMUP

A. Type 2 times.

```
1        Bill Waxmann quickly moved all 35 packs of      9
2   gear for the Amazon trip (worth $987) 26 miles       18
3   into the jungle.  The move took 14 days in all.      28
     |  1  |  2  |  3  |  4  |  5  |  6  |  7  |  8  |  9  |  10
```

 NEW KEYS

B. THE KEY

B. * ASTERISK is the shift of 8. Type each line 2 times.
   Use the K finger.

```
4   kik ki8k k8*k k8*k k**k k**k This book* is great.
5   Use an * to show that a table source is included.
6   Asterisks keyed in a row (*******) make a border.
7   The article quoted Hanson,* Pyle,* and Peterson.*
```

C. # NUMBER (if before a figure) or POUNDS (if after a figure) is the shift of 3. Type each line 2 times.

Use the D finger.

C. THE # KEY

8 de3d de3#d d3#d d3#d d#d d#d #3 #33 #333 #3,333
9 Al wants 33# of #200 and 38# of #400 by Saturday.
10 My favorite seats are #2, #34, #56, #65, and #66.
11 Please order 45# of #245 and 13# of #24 tomorrow.

D. ' APOSTROPHE is to the right of the semicolon. Type each line 2 times.

Use the Sem finger.

D. THE ' KEY

12 ;'; ;'; ;'; ;'' Can't we go in Sue's or Al's car?
13 It's Bob's job to cover Ted's work when he's out.
14 What's in Joann's lunch box for Sandra's dessert?
15 He's left for Ty's banquet which is held at Al's.

SKILLBUILDING

E. PACED PRACTICE

Turn to the Paced Practice routine beginning on page SB-14. Take three 2-minute timings, starting at the point where you left off the last time.

F. DIAGNOSTIC PRACTICE: ALPHABET

Turn to the Diagnostic Practice: Alphabet routine beginning on page SB-2. Type one of the Pretest/Posttest paragraphs and identify any errors made. Then type the corresponding drill lines 2 times for each letter on which you made 2 or more errors and 1 time for each letter on which you made only 1 error. Finally, repeat the same Pretest paragraph and compare your performance.

G. Take two 1-minute timings. Determine your speed and errors.

G. HANDWRITTEN PARAGRAPH

16 *You have completed the first segment of* 8
17 *your class and have learned your alphabetic* 17
18 *keys, the number keys, and some of the* 25
19 *symbol keys. Next you will learn the* 32
20 *remaining symbol keys on the top row.* 40

H. Take two 2-minute timings. Determine your speed and errors.

Goal: 26 wam/2'/5e

H. 2-MINUTE TIMING

```
21        Max had to make one quick adjustment to his        9
22   television before the football game began.  The        19
23   picture during the last game was fuzzy and hard         28
24   to see.  If he cannot fix the picture, he may           37
25   have to purchase a new television set; and that         47
26   may not be possible today.                              52
     |  1  |  2  |  3  |  4  |  5  |  6  |  7  |  8  |  9  |  10
```

Lesson 19 Symbol Keys

GOALS: To control the &, %, ", and @ keys; to type 27 wam/2'/5e.

A. Type 2 times.

A. WARMUP

```
1        The teacher (Jane Quayler) gave us some work       9
2   to do as homework for 11-28-96.   Chapters 3 and        19
3   4 from our text* are to be read for a hard quiz.        28
    |  1  |  2  |  3  |  4  |  5  |  6  |  7  |  8  |  9  |  10
```

NEW KEYS

B. & AMPERSAND (sign for *and*) is the shift of 7. Space before and after the ampersand. Type each line 2 times.
Use the J finger.

B. THE & KEY

```
4   juj ju7j j7j j7&j j&&j j&&j Max & Dee & Sue & Ken
5   Brown & Sons shipped goods to Crum & Lee Company.
6   Johnson & Loo brought a case against May & Green.
7   Ball & Trump vs. Vens & See is being decided now.
```

C. % PERCENT is the shift of 5. Do not space between the number and the percent sign. Type each line 2 times.
Use the F finger.

C. THE % KEY

```
8    ft5f ft5%f f5%f f5%f f%%f f%%f 5% 55% 555% 5,555%
9    Robert quoted rates of 8%, 9%, 10%, 11%, and 12%.
10   Pat scored 82%, Jan 89%, and Ken 90% on the test.
11   Only 55% of the students passed 75% of the exams.
```

D. QUOTATION is the shift of the apostrophe. Do not space between the quotation marks and the text they enclose. Type each line 2 times.

Use the Sem finger.

D. THE " KEY

12 ;'; ";" ;"; ";" "That's a super job," said Mabel.
13 The theme of the meeting is "Improving Your Job."
14 John said, "Those were good." Sharon said, "No."
15 Allison said, "I'll take Janice and Ed to Flint."

E. AT is the shift of 2. Space before and after @ except when used in an e-mail address. Type each line 2 times.

Use the S finger.

E. THE @ KEY

16 sws sw2s s2@s s2@s s@@s s@@s Buy 15 @ $5 in June.
17 You can e-mail us at this address: proj@edu.com.
18 Order 12 items @ $14 and another 185 items @ $16.
19 Lee said, "I'll buy 8 shares @ $6 and 5 @ $7.55."

FORMATTING

F. PLACEMENT OF QUOTATION MARKS

Read these rules about the placement of quotation marks. Then type lines 20–23 twice.

1. The closing quotation mark is always typed *after* a period or comma but *before* a colon or semicolon.

2. The closing quotation mark is typed *after* a question mark or exclamation point if the quoted material is a question or an exclamation; otherwise, the quotation mark is typed *before* the question mark or exclamation point.

20 "Hello," I said. "My name is Al; I am new here."
21 Zack read the article "Can She Succeed Tomorrow?"
22 James said, "I'll mail the check"; but he didn't.
23 Did he say, "We lost"? She said, "I don't know."

SKILLBUILDING

G. Type each line 2 times.

G. ALPHABET AND SYMBOL PRACTICE

24 Gaze at views of my jonquil or red phlox in back.
25 Jan quickly moved the six dozen big pink flowers.
26 Joe quietly picked six razors from the woven bag.
27 Packing jam for the dozen boxes was quite lively.

28 Mail these "Rush": #38, #45, and #67 (software).
29 No! Joe's note did not carry a rate of under 9%.
30 Lee read "The Computer Today." It's here Monday.
31 This book* cost us $48.10; 12% higher than yours.

H. Take a 1-minute timing on the first paragraph to establish your base speed. Then take four 1-minute timings on the remaining paragraphs. As soon as you equal or exceed your base speed on one paragraph, advance to the next, more difficult paragraph.

H. SUSTAINED PRACTICE: NUMBERS AND SYMBOLS

```
32      We purchased several pieces of new computer        9
33  equipment for our new store in Boston.  We were       19
34  amazed at all the extra work we could get done.       28

35      For our department, we received 5 printers,        9
36  12 computers, and 3 fax machines.  We heard that      19
37  the equipment cost us several thousand dollars.       28

38      Next week 6 computers (Model ZS86), 4 old          9
39  copiers (drums are broken), and 9 shredders will      18
40  need to be replaced.  Total cost will be high.        28

41      Last year $150,890 was spent on equipment          9
42  for Iowa's offices.  Breaman & Sims predicted a       18
43  17% to 20% increase (*over '95); that's amazing.      28
    |  1  |  2  |  3  |  4  |  5  |  6  |  7  |  8  |  9  |  10
```

I. Take two 2-minute timings. Determine your speed and errors.

Goal: 27 wam/2'/5e

I. 2-MINUTE TIMING

```
44      Topaz and onyx were for sale at a reasonable       9
45  price last week.  When Mavis saw the rings with       19
46  these stones, she quickly bought them both for        28
47  her sons.  These jewels were difficult to find,       38
48  and Mavis was happy.  She was able to purchase        47
49  the rings before someone else did.                    54
    |  1  |  2  |  3  |  4  |  5  |  6  |  7  |  8  |  9  |  10
```

Lesson 20   Review

GOAL: To type 28 wam/2'/5e.

A. Type 2 times.

A. WARMUP

```
1       Vin went to see Exhibits #794 and #860.  He        9
2   had quickly judged these zany projects that cost      19
3   $321 (parts & labor)--a 5% markup from last year.     29
    |  1  |  2  |  3  |  4  |  5  |  6  |  7  |  8  |  9  |  10
```

B. PUNCTUATION PRACTICE

4 Go to Reno. Drive to Yuma. Call Mary. Get Sam.
5 We saw Nice, Paris, Bern, Rome, Munich, and Bonn.
6 Type a memo; read a report. Get pens; get paper.
7 Read the following pages: 1-8, 10-22, and 34-58.
8 No! Stop! Don't look! Watch out! Move! Jump!

9 Can you wait? Why not? Can he drive? Where to?
10 I have these reports: Sue's, Bill's, and Lisa's.
11 It's the best--and cheapest! Don't use it--ever.
12 "I can," he said, "right now." Val said, "Wait!"
13 Allen called Rome (GA), Rome (NY), and Rome (WI).

C. PRETEST: ALTERNATE- AND ONE-HAND WORDS

14   The chairman should handle the tax problem   9
15 downtown. If they are reversed, pressure tactics   19
16 might have changed the case as it was discussed.   28

   | 1 | 2 | 3 | 4 | 5 | 6 | 7 | 8 | 9 | 10

D. PRACTICE: ALTERNATE-HAND WORDS

17 the with girl right blame handle antique chairman
18 for wish town their panel formal problem downtown
19 pan busy they flair signs thrown signals problems

E. PRACTICE: ONE-HAND WORDS

20 lip fact yolk poplin yummy affect reverse pumpkin
21 you cast kill uphill jumpy grease wagered opinion
22 tea cage lump limply hilly served bravest minimum

F. POSTTEST: ALTERNATE- AND ONE-HAND WORDS

G. 12-SECOND SPEED SPRINTS

23 Paul likes to work for the bank while in college.
24 They will make a nice profit if the work is done.
25 The group of friends went to a movie at the mall.
26 The man sent the forms after she called for them.

| | | | 5 | | | 10 | ·| | 15 | | | 20 | | | 25 | | | 30 | | | 35 | | | 40 | | | 45 | | | 50

H. Take two 1-minute timings. Determine your speed and errors.

H. HANDWRITTEN PARAGRAPH

27 *In your career, you will use the* 7
28 *skills you are learning in this course.* 15
29 *However, you will soon discover that you* 23
30 *must also possess human relations skills.* 31

I. Take two 2-minute timings. Determine your speed and errors.

Goal: 28 wam/2'/5e

I. 2-MINUTE TIMING

31   Jake or Peggy Zale must quickly fix the fax 9
32 machine so that we can have access to regional 18
33 reports that we think might be sent within the 28
34 next few days. Without the fax, we will not be 37
35 able to complete all our monthly reports by the 47
36 deadline. Please let me know of any problems. 56

| 1 | 2 | 3 | 4 | 5 | 6 | 7 | 8 | 9 | 10 |

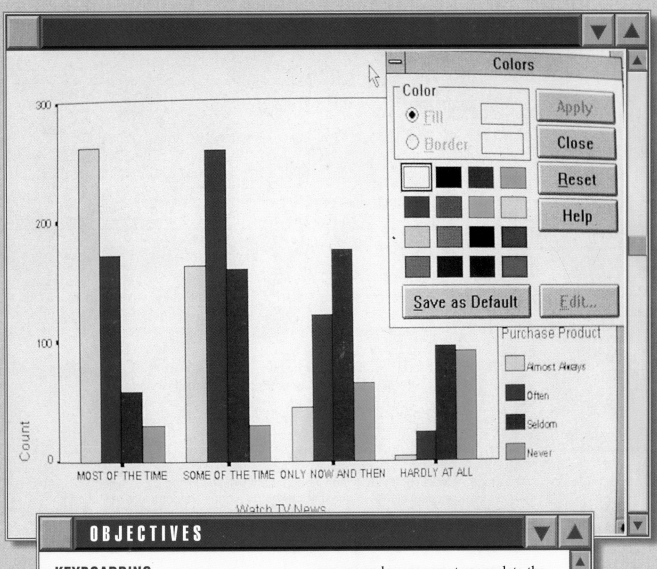

OBJECTIVES

KEYBOARDING
- To operate the keyboard by touch.
- To type 36 wam/3'/4e.

LANGUAGE ARTS
- To develop proofreading skills and correctly use proofreaders' marks.
- To correctly use capitals, commas, apostrophes, and numbers.
- To develop composing and spelling skills.

WORD PROCESSING
- To use the word processing commands necessary to complete the document processing activities.

DOCUMENT PROCESSING
- To format reports, block-style business letters, envelopes, memos, and tables.

TECHNICAL
- To answer correctly at least 90 precent of the questions on an objective test.

UNIT FIVE ▶ Word Processing and Reports

Lesson 21 Orientation to Word Processing—A

GOALS: To improve speed and accuracy; to refine language-arts skills in punctuation; to practice basic word processing commands.

A. WARMUP

```
1        Juan Valdez will lead 10 managers during this sales      11
2  period; his expert input has always been valuable.  Will      23
3  Quentin earn 8% commission ($534) after order #K76 arrives?    35
   | 1 | 2 | 3 | 4 | 5 | 6 | 7 | 8 | 9 | 10 | 11 | 12
```

SKILLBUILDING

B. PROGRESSIVE PRACTICE: NUMBERS

Turn to the Progressive Practice: Numbers routine beginning on page SB-11.
Take six 30-second timings, starting at the point where you left off the last time.

C. PACED PRACTICE

Turn to the Paced Practice routine beginning on page SB-14. Take three 2-minute timings, starting at the point where you left off the last time.

LANGUAGE ARTS

D. COMMAS

D. Study the rules at the right.

Rule: Use a comma between independent clauses joined by a conjunction. (An independent clause is one that can stand alone as a complete sentence.)

,ind

Ms. Morimoto is the new president, and she will begin her term immediately.
But: Ms. Morimoto is the new president and will begin her term immediately.

Rule: Use a comma after an introductory expression (unless it is a short prepositional phrase).

,intro

When you become a network manager, you will be able to find a good job.
But: You will be able to find a good job when you become a network manager.
But: At the meeting she was very quiet.

Edit the paragraph to insert any needed punctuation.

```
4        Many companies have work-study programs in effect and
5  employ a high percentage of students after graduation.
6  Because these students have worked hard and have set goals
7  for themselves many employers will be eager to hire them.
8  On Monday interviews will be scheduled.  If students are
9  interested they should call us immediately.  A resume will
10 be required from all applicants and a letter of application
11 must be written before the interview is scheduled.
```

E. WORD PROCESSING

Study Lesson 21 in your word processing manual. Complete all of the shaded steps while at your computer.

Lesson 22 — Orientation to Word Processing—B

GOALS: To type 28 wam/3′/5e; to practice basic word processing commands.

A. Type 2 times.

A. WARMUP

```
1        Zenobia bought 987 reams of 16# bond paper from V & J    11
2  Co.  Only 2/3 of this week's order is acceptable.  About      22
3  45 percent is excellent quality; the rest cannot be used.     34
   |  1  |  2  |  3  |  4  |  5  |  6  |  7  |  8  |  9  | 10 | 11 | 12
```

B. PROGRESSIVE PRACTICE: ALPHABET

Turn to the Progressive Practice: Alphabet routine beginning on page SB-7. Take six 30-second timings, starting at the point where you left off the last time.

C. Take three 12-second timings on each line. The scale below the last line shows your wam speed for a 12-second timing.

C. 12-SECOND SPEED SPRINTS

```
4  Mary will be glad to see when the girls will be able to go.
5  She will not come to their office for the first time today.
6  The blue car was not very fast when he tried to speed away.
7  The work must be done when she comes to work or he will go.
   | | | |5| | | |10| | |15| | |20| | |25| | |30| | |35| | |40| | |45| | |50| | |55| | |60
```

D. Take two 3-minute timings. Determine your speed and errors.

Goal: 28 wam/3′/5e

D. 3-MINUTE TIMING

```
8         Once you learn to use a variety of software programs,    11
9  you will feel confident and comfortable when you are using      23
10 a computer.  All you have to do is take the first step and      35
11 decide to strive for excellence.                                41
12        Initially, you might have several questions as you       52
13 gaze up at a screen filled with icons.  If you try using        63
14 just one or two commands each day, you will soon find that      75
15 learning to use software can be very exciting.                  84
   |  1  |  2  |  3  |  4  |  5  |  6  |  7  |  8  |  9  | 10 | 11 | 12
```

FORMATTING

go TO

E. WORD PROCESSING

Study Lesson 22 in your word processing manual. Complete all of the shaded steps while at your computer.

Lesson 23   Orientation to Word Processing—C

GOALS: To improve speed and accuracy; to refine language-arts skills in proofreading; to practice basic word processing commands.

A. Type 2 times.

A. WARMUP

```
1        We expect the following sizes to be mailed promptly      11
2   on January 8:  5, 7, and 9.  Send your payment quickly so     22
3   that the items will be sure to arrive before 2:34* (*p.m.)!   34
    |  1  |  2  |  3  |  4  |  5  |  6  |  7  |  8  |  9  |  10  |  11  |  12
```

SKILLBUILDING

B. Take a 1-minute timing on the first paragraph to establish your base speed. Then take four 1-minute timings on the remaining paragraphs. As soon as you equal or exceed your base speed on one paragraph, advance to the next, more difficult paragraph.

B. SUSTAINED PRACTICE: CAPITALS

```
4        The insurance industry will undergo major changes due    11
5   to the many natural disasters the United States has seen in   23
6   the last few years in places like California and Florida.     34


7        The recent earthquakes in San Francisco, Northridge,     11
8   and Loma Prieta cost thousands of dollars.  Faults like       22
9   the San Andreas are being watched carefully for activity.     33


10       Some tropical storms are spawned in the West Indies      11
11  and move from the Caribbean Sea into the Atlantic Ocean.      22
12  They could affect Georgia, Florida, Alabama, and Texas.       33


13       Some U.S. cities have VHF-FM radio weather stations.     11
14  NASA and NOAA are agencies that launch weather satellites     22
15  to predict the locations, times, and severity of storms.     34
    |  1  |  2  |  3  |  4  |  5  |  6  |  7  |  8  |  9  |  10  |  11  |  12
```

C. DIAGNOSTIC PRACTICE: ALPHABET

Turn to the Diagnostic Practice: Alphabet routine beginning on page SB-2. Type one of the Pretest/Posttest paragraphs and identify any errors made. Then type the corresponding drill lines 2 times for each letter on which you made 2 or more errors and 1 time for each letter on which you made only 1 error. Finally, repeat the same Pretest paragraph and compare your performance.

D. PROOFREADING YOUR DOCUMENTS

D. Study the proof-reading techniques at the right.

Proofreading and correcting errors are an essential part of document processing. To become an expert proofreader:

1. Use the spelling feature of your word processing software to check for spelling errors; then read the copy aloud to see if it makes sense.
2. Proofread for all kinds of errors, espe-cially repeated, missing, or transposed words; grammar and punctuation; and numbers and names.
3. Use the appropriate software com-mand to see an entire page of your document to check for formatting errors such as line spacing, tabs, mar-gins, and bold.

E. PROOFREADING

E. Compare this para-graph with the 3-minute timing on page 41. Edit the paragraph to correct any errors.

```
 8      Once you learn too use a variety of software programs
 9   you will feel confidant and comfortable when you are using
10   a computr.  All you have to do is take a first step and
11   decide to strive for excellence.
```

FORMATTING

F. WORD PROCESSING

Study Lesson 23 in your word processing manual. Complete all of the shaded steps while at your computer.

Lesson 24   Simple Reports

GOALS: To type 29 wam/3'/5e; to format simple reports.

A. Type 2 times.

A. WARMUP

```
1      The experts quickly realized that repairs could cost      11
2   "$985 million" and might exceed 60% of their budget.  Will    23
3   Valdez & Co. begin work before 12 or just wait until 4:30?    34
    |  1  |  2  |  3  |  4  |  5  |  6  |  7  |  8  |  9  |  10  |  11  |  12
```

SKILLBUILDING

B. PRETEST: COMMON LETTER COMBINATIONS

Pretest
Take a 1-minute timing. Determine your speed and errors.

```
4      He tried to explain the delay in a logical way.  The       11
5   man finally agreed to insure the package and demanded to      22
6   know why the postal worker did not record the total amount.   34
    |  1  |  2  |  3  |  4  |  5  |  6  |  7  |  8  |  9  |  10  |  11  |  12
```

Speed Emphasis: If you made 2 or fewer errors on the Pretest, type each *individual* line 2 times.

Accuracy Emphasis: If you made 3 or more errors, type each *group* of lines (as though it were a paragraph) 2 times.

Posttest
Repeat the Pretest timing and compare performance.

F. Take two 3-minute timings. Determine your speed and errors.

Goal: 29 wam/3'/5e

C. PRACTICE: WORD BEGINNINGS

```
7  re reuse react relay reply return reason record results red
8  in inset inept incur index indeed intend inning insured ink
9  de dents dealt death delay detest devote derive depicts den
   |  1  |  2  |  3  |  4  |  5  |  6  |  7  |  8  |  9  | 10  | 11  | 12
```

D. PRACTICE: WORD ENDINGS

```
10  ly lowly dimly apply daily barely unruly deeply finally sly
11  ed cured tamed tried moved amused busted billed creamed fed
12  al canal total equal local postal plural rental logical pal
```

E. POSTTEST: COMMON LETTER COMBINATIONS

F. 3-MINUTE TIMING

```
13       If you ever feel tired when you are typing, you should    11
14  take a rest.  Question what you are doing that is fatiguing    23
15  your muscles, and you will realize that you can change the    35
16  fundamental source of your anxiety.                           42
17       Take a deep breath, and enjoy the relaxing feeling as    53
18  you exhale slowly.  Check your posture, and be sure that      64
19  you are sitting up straight with your back against your       76
20  chair.  Stretch your neck and back for total relaxation.      87
    |  1  |  2  |  3  |  4  |  5  |  6  |  7  |  8  |  9  | 10  | 11  | 12
```

FORMATTING

G. Because word processing software has a variety of defaults for fonts, the number of returns will be used to express vertical spacing in all documents rather than inches.

G. BASIC PARTS OF A REPORT

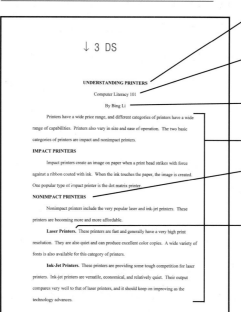

↓ 3 DS

UNDERSTANDING PRINTERS

Computer Literacy 101

By Bing Li

Printers have a wide price range, and different categories of printers have a wide range of capabilities. Printers also vary in size and ease of operation. The two basic categories of printers are impact and nonimpact printers.

IMPACT PRINTERS

Impact printers create an image on paper when a print head strikes with force against a ribbon coated with ink. When the ink touches the paper, the image is created. One popular type of impact printer is the dot matrix printer.

NONIMPACT PRINTERS

Nonimpact printers include the very popular laser and ink-jet printers. These printers are becoming more and more affordable.

Laser Printers. These printers are fast and generally have a very high print resolution. They are also quiet and can produce excellent color copies. A wide variety of fonts is also available for this category of printers.

Ink-Jet Printers. These printers are providing some tough competition for laser printers. Ink-jet printers are versatile, economical, and relatively quiet. Their output compares very well to that of laser printers, and it should keep on improving as the technology advances.

TITLE. Subject of the report; centered; typed in bold and all caps.

SUBTITLE. Secondary or explanatory title; centered; typed in initial caps.

BYLINE. Name of the writer; centered; typed in initial caps.

BODY. Text of the report; double spaced.

SIDE HEADING. Major subdivision of the report; typed at the left margin in bold and all caps.

PARAGRAPH HEADING. Minor subdivision of the report; indented 0.5 inch; typed in bold and initial caps; followed by a bold period and 2 spaces.

H. SIMPLE REPORTS

Spacing: Double-space the entire report. Change to double spacing at the beginning of the report.

Top Margin: After setting double spacing, press Enter 3 times for a top margin of approximately 2 inches.

Side Margins: Default.

Bottom Margin: Default.

Tab: Default.

I. WORD PROCESSING: LINE SPACING AND ALIGNMENT/JUSTIFICATION

Study Lesson 24 in your word processing manual. Complete all of the shaded steps while at your computer. Then format the jobs that follow.

Report 1

Spacing: Double

1. Set the line spacing to double, press Enter 3 times, and change to center alignment/justification.
2. Turn on bold, type the title, and immediately turn off bold.
3. Type the subtitle; then press Enter. Type the byline; then press Enter.
4. Change to left alignment/justification before pressing Tab to indent the first line of the first paragraph.
5. Let the paragraphs word wrap; that is, press Enter only at the end of each paragraph. Your lines may end differently from those shown here.
6. Spell-check, proofread, and preview your document before printing it.

↓ 3 DS

WRITING STYLE

Business Communications 101

By Amy Ho

Today's word processing software makes a variety of powerful and helpful writing tools available to you with the click of a button. You can discover interesting facts about your own style of writing by using these tools.

Many different statistics are automatically gathered as you are typing a document. For example, you can find out how many sentences are in your document and how many words or characters you have used. This information is used to determine details about your writing such as average word length, average number of words in each sentence, and maximum words per sentence.

Average word length and average sentence length determine whether it is easy or difficult for the average person to understand what you have written. Shorter words and sentences usually make writing easier to understand. Word

(continued on next page)

processing software can also analyze the formality of your writing style and suggest ways to make your writing either more formal or perhaps less formal.

If you take advantage of all the tools available in your word processing software, your writing will improve with each document you compose. Think carefully about your reader before you choose a writing style.

Report 2

Spacing: Double

Press Tab to indent paragraphs a full 0.5 inch.

OFFICE TEMP SERVICES
Business Trends Conference

Because of the rising costs of health insurance and other company-paid benefit packages, many businesses are looking to office temp services to help ease the high cost of doing business these days. A company does not have to make a long-term commitment to its temporary workers in terms of salary, benefits, or job stability.

Temp services offer many advantages to prospective employers. Sometimes temp services are available around the clock so that rush jobs can be completed on time. Often a company's reputation depends on its ability to meet deadlines and inspire confidence. Using a temp service can provide the competitive edge necessary for success.

Many temp agencies offer the services of bilingual employees. In major cities like Los Angeles, San Francisco, New York, and Miami, a bilingual employee is a necessity, not a luxury. Also, many foreign companies are based in the United States and have a growing need for bilingual employees in a variety of languages.

Sometimes a client has a need for some specialized service, software, or equipment that will be used immediately or perhaps only once. In this instance, a temporary service is certainly the answer. Because temp services are becoming indispensable for some businesses, many agencies are even sending supervisors to the job site to check on their employees. Clearly, temp services are "here to stay."

Lesson 25   Reports With Side Headings

GOALS: To improve speed and accuracy; to refine language-arts skills in composing; to format reports with side headings.

A. Type 2 times.

A. WARMUP

1   Exactly 610 employees have quit smoking! About 2/3   11
2 of them just quit recently. They realized why they can't   22
3 continue to smoke inside the buildings and decided to stop.   34

| 1 | 2 | 3 | 4 | 5 | 6 | 7 | 8 | 9 | 10 | 11 | 12

SKILLBUILDING

B. Take three 12-second timings on each line. The scale below the last line shows your wam speed for a 12-second timing.

B. 12-SECOND SPEED SPRINTS

4 Today we want to find out if our work will be done on time.
5 Doug will be able to drive to the store if the car is here.
6 Jan will sign this paper when she has done all of the work.
7 This time she will be sure to spend two days with her sons.

| | | |5| | | |10| | | |15| | | |20| | | |25| | | |30| | | |35| | | |40| | | |45| | | |50| | | |55| | | |60

C. Type the paragraph 2 times. Change every masculine pronoun to a feminine pronoun. Change every feminine pronoun to a masculine pronoun.

C. TECHNIQUE PRACTICE: CONCENTRATION

8   She will finish composing the report as soon as he has
9 given her all the research. Her final draft will be turned
10 in to her boss; he will submit it to the company president.

LANGUAGE ARTS

D. COMPOSING

Composing at the keyboard can save you considerable time when you create first drafts of documents. Keep the following points in mind:

1. Type at a comfortable pace as your thoughts come to you. Do not stop to correct errors.

2. Keep your eyes on the screen as you type.

3. Do not be overly concerned with correct grammar. It is more important that you get your thoughts recorded. Any errors you make can be corrected later.

D. Answer each question with a single word.

11 What is your most interesting class?
12 How many miles do you travel to school?
13 Do you have a job?
14 What is your favorite color?
15 In what month were you born?
16 What type of job would you like to have?
17 Do you want to learn more about computers?
18 What day do you set aside for relaxation?
19 How many classes are you taking?

E. REPORTS WITH SIDE HEADINGS

Spacing: Double-space the entire report, including before and after side headings.

Side Headings: Type in bold at the left margin.

Top Margin: After setting double spacing, press Enter 3 times for a top margin of approximately 2 inches.

F. WORD PROCESSING: HELP

Study Lesson 25 in your word processing manual. Complete all of the shaded steps while at your computer. Then format the jobs that follow.

DOCUMENT PROCESSING

Report 3

Spacing: Double

↓ 3 DS

SELECTING A COMPUTER

By Ina Phillips

Before selecting a computer, first consider several factors carefully. Think about what type of work you will be doing, what software is appropriate for your application, and what kinds of budget restrictions you have. Once you have made some thoughtful decisions, you will be prepared to begin shopping.

WORD PROCESSING

The most common application for the personal computer is word processing. If your computer will be used mainly for word processing, you must decide which software would be best suited to the types of documents you produce most often.

SOFTWARE SELECTION

Some word processing software is better at producing graphics that might be used in complicated desktop publishing projects. Some software can create tables with great efficiency. Study your choices, and then make your final selection.

BUDGET RESTRICTIONS

Don't make the mistake of buying the least expensive computer system available. Your primary consideration should always be to buy a system that will run your software. Remember that today's purchase could be tomorrow's mistake. Select a system that can be upgraded as technology changes.

UNDERSTANDING PRINTERS

Computer Literacy 101

By John Sanchez

Printers have a wide range of capabilities. Some print in color and others only in black and white. Some print only one or two pages a minute, while others can print several pages a minute. Their prices will vary with the number of features they offer. The two basic categories of printers are impact and nonimpact.

IMPACT PRINTERS

Impact printers create an image on paper when a print head strikes with force against a ribbon coated with ink. When the ink touches the paper, an image is created. Because the image is created by impact, these printers can be quite noisy.

Dot matrix printers are very popular impact printers for many reasons. They are fairly inexpensive and relatively durable. They can use continuous paper so that paper handling is greatly reduced. However, their output is not letter quality.

NONIMPACT PRINTERS

Nonimpact printers include the very popular laser and ink-jet printers. They are becoming more affordable and can produce a very high-quality output similar to a photocopy. These printers also produce excellent color and can use a wide variety of fonts. Ultimately, the ideal choice for a printer depends on the needs of the user.

Lesson 26	Business Letters

GOALS: To type 30 wam/3'/5e; to format a business letter in block style.

A. Type 2 times.

A. WARMUP

```
1      Mr. G. Yoneji ordered scanners* (*800 dots per inch)    11
2   in vibrant 24-bit color!  He quickly realized that exactly   23
3   31% of the work could be scanned in order to save money.    34
    |  1  |  2  |  3  |  4  |  5  |  6  |  7  |  8  |  9  |  10  |  11  |  12
```

SKILLBUILDING

B. DIAGNOSTIC PRACTICE: ALPHABET

Turn to the Diagnostic Practice: Alphabet routine beginning on page SB-2. Type one of the Pretest/Posttest paragraphs and identify any errors made. Then type the corresponding drill lines 2 times for each letter on which you made 2 or more errors and 1 time for each letter on which you made only 1 error. Finally, repeat the same Pretest paragraph and compare your performance.

C. Take three 12-second timings on each line. The scale below the last line shows your wam speed for a 12-second timing.

C. 12-SECOND SPEED SPRINTS

```
4   She went to the same store to find some good books to read.
5   Frank will coach eight games for his team when he has time.
6   Laura sent all the mail out today when she left to go home.
7   These pages can be very hard to read when the light is dim.
    | | | |5| | |10| | |15| | |20| | |25| | |30| | |35| | |40| | |45| | |50| | |55| | |60
```

D. Take two 3-minute timings. Determine your speed and errors.

Goal: 30 wam/3'/5e

D. 3-MINUTE TIMING

```
8       Holding a good business meeting may require a great      11
9   deal of planning and preparing.  The meeting must be well    22
10  organized and an agenda must be prepared.  It may be hard    34
11  to judge how long a meeting may take or how many people      45
12  will discuss issues raised.                                  51
13      A good moderator is needed to execute the agenda.  He    62
14  or she must know when to move on to the next topic and when  74
15  a point needs more debate.  After a productive meeting,      85
16  you should feel very good.                                   90
    |  1  |  2  |  3  |  4  |  5  |  6  |  7  |  8  |  9  |  10  |  11  |  12
```

E. BASIC PARTS OF A BUSINESS LETTER

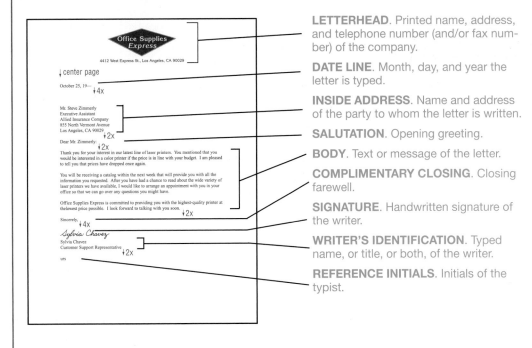

LETTERHEAD. Printed name, address, and telephone number (and/or fax number) of the company.

DATE LINE. Month, day, and year the letter is typed.

INSIDE ADDRESS. Name and address of the party to whom the letter is written.

SALUTATION. Opening greeting.

BODY. Text or message of the letter.

COMPLIMENTARY CLOSING. Closing farewell.

SIGNATURE. Handwritten signature of the writer.

WRITER'S IDENTIFICATION. Typed name, or title, or both, of the writer.

REFERENCE INITIALS. Initials of the typist.

F. BUSINESS LETTERS IN BLOCK STYLE

1. Type all lines beginning at the left margin.
2. Center the letter vertically, and then type the date.
3. After the date, press Enter 4 times and type the inside address. Leave 1 space between the state and the ZIP Code.
4. After the inside address, press Enter twice and type the salutation. Press Enter twice after the salutation.
5. Single-space the body of the letter, but press Enter twice between paragraphs.

Do not indent paragraphs.
6. Press Enter twice after the last paragraph and type the complimentary closing.
7. Press Enter 4 times after the complimentary closing and type the writer's identification.
8. Press Enter twice after the writer's identification and type your reference initials in lowercase letters with no periods or spaces.

G. WORD PROCESSING: CENTER PAGE

Study Lesson 26 in your word processing manual. Complete all of the shaded steps while at your computer. Then format the jobs that follow.

 **DOCUMENT PROCESSING**

Letter 1
Block Style

1. Use standard punctuation: a colon after the salutation and a comma after the complimentary closing.
2. Use word wrap for the paragraphs. Press Enter only at the end of each paragraph. Your lines may end differently from those shown on page 52.
3. Type your initials (not *urs*) for the reference initials.
4. Always spell-check, preview, and proofread your letter when you finish for typing, spelling, and formatting errors.

(continued on next page)

↓center page
October 25, 19--
↓4X

Mr. Steve Zimmerly
Executive Assistant
Allied Insurance Company
855 North Vermont Avenue
Los Angeles, CA 90029
↓2X

Dear Mr. Zimmerly:
↓2X

Thank you for your interest in our latest line of laser printers. You mentioned that you would be interested in a color printer if the price is in line with your budget. I am pleased to tell you that prices have dropped once again.
↓2X

You will be receiving a catalog within the next week that will provide you with all the information you requested. After you have had a chance to read about the wide variety of laser printers we have available, I would like to arrange an appointment with you in your office so that we can go over any questions you might have.
↓2X

Office Supplies Express is committed to providing you with the highest-quality printer at the lowest price possible. I look forward to talking with you soon.
↓2X

Sincerely,
↓4X

Sylvia Chavez
Customer Support Representative
↓2X

urs

Letter 2
Block Style

Open the file for Letter 1 and make the following changes:

1. Change the date to October 23.

2. Change the writer's identification to:
   Agnes Gunderson Customer Service

Letter 3
Block Style

1. Be sure to center the letter vertically.
2. The slash marks in the inside address and closing lines indicate line endings. Do not type the slashes.
3. The ¶ symbol indicates the start of a new paragraph. Do *not* indent paragraphs in a block-style letter. Leave 1 blank line between paragraphs.
4. Spell-check, proofread, and preview your letter when you finish.

November 1, 19— / Ms. Sylvia Chavez / Office Supplies Express / 24133 West Del Monte / Valencia, CA 91355 / Dear Ms. Chavez:
¶Thank you for all the information you sent me on laser printers. I truly appreciate the promptness and courtesy your company has shown, and I feel confident that we will be able to order some printers very soon.

(continued on next page)

¶I am also interested in finding out if your company offers any leasing programs. Our business is interested in a state-of-the-art color copier, and we realize that the price would be prohibitive unless we lease it. Features like duplexing, collating, and size reduction and enlargement are essential.
¶Please call me in a week or so for another appointment. In the meantime, I would appreciate any information you could send regarding color copiers.
Sincerely, / Steve Zimmerly / Executive Assistant / {urs}

Remember to type your initials in place of {urs}.

Lesson 27 | Business Letters

GOALS: To improve speed and accuracy; to refine language-arts skills in capitalization; to format a business letter with an enclosure notation.

A. Type 2 times.

A. WARMUP

```
1        In 7/95 the office will convert to a new phone system.    11
2   A freeze on all toll calls is requested for July.  Account    23
3   #GK23 has a balance of $68 and isn't expected to "pay up."    35
    |  1  |  2  |  3  |  4  |  5  |  6  |  7  |  8  |  9  |  10  |  11  |  12
```

SKILLBUILDING

Pretest
Take a 1-minute timing. Determine your speed and errors.

B. PRETEST: CLOSE REACHES

```
4        The growth in the volume of company assets is due to    11
5   the astute group of twenty older employees.  Their answers    23
6   were undoubtedly the reason for the increase in net worth.    34

    |  1  |  2  |  3  |  4  |  5  |  6  |  7  |  8  |  9  |  10  |  11  |  12
```

Practice
 Speed Emphasis: If you made 2 or fewer errors on the Pretest, type each *individual* line 2 times.
 Accuracy Emphasis: If you made 3 or more errors, type each *group* of lines (as though it were a paragraph) 2 times.

C. PRACTICE: ADJACENT KEYS

```
7   as ashes cases class asset astute passes chased creased ask
8   we weave tweed towed weigh wealth twenty fewest answers wet
9   rt worth alert party smart artist sorted charts turtles art
```

D. PRACTICE: CONSECUTIVE FINGERS

```
10  un undue bunch stung begun united punish outrun untie funny
11  gr grand agree angry grade growth egress hungry group graph
12  ol older solid tools spool volume evolve uphold olive scold
```

Posttest
Repeat the Pretest timing and compare performance.

E. POSTTEST: CLOSE REACHES

F. PACED PRACTICE

Turn to the Paced Practice routine beginning on page SB-14. Take three 2-minute timings, starting at the point where you left off the last time.

G. Study the rules at the right.

≡ sent

≡ prop

≡ time

Edit the paragraph to insert any needed capitalization.

G. CAPITALIZATION

Rule: Capitalize the first word in a sentence.

The exam is scheduled for the last week of the semester.

Rule: Capitalize proper nouns and adjectives derived from proper nouns. (A proper noun is the official name of a particular person, place, or thing.)

The American flag can be seen flying over the White House in Washington.
But: Our country's flag can be seen flying over the government buildings.

Rule: Capitalize the names of the days of the week, months, holidays, and religious days (but do not capitalize the names of the seasons).

Every summer on July 4 we celebrate Independence Day.

```
13      she will graduate in the spring from los angeles city
14   college.  the community college system in the united states
15   provides a quality education for both american and foreign
16   students.  both english and spanish are spoken in several
17   classes, like english 127 and mathematics 105.  on monday,
18   may 30, all classes will be canceled in order to observe
19   memorial day, a national holiday.  on thanksgiving and on
20   christmas, all government offices will be closed to the
21   public.  offices will reopen the following tuesday.
```

FORMATTING

H. ENCLOSURE NOTATION

1. To indicate that an item is enclosed with a letter, type the word *Enclosure* on the line below the reference initials.

Example: urs
        Enclosure
2. If more than one item is being enclosed, type the word *Enclosures.*

I. WORD PROCESSING: DATE INSERT

Study Lesson 27 in your word processing manual. Complete all of the shaded steps while at your computer. Then format the jobs that follow.

DOCUMENT PROCESSING

Letter 4

Block Style

≡ sent

≡ time

Do not type the slashes and do not indent the paragraphs. Whenever you see {Current Date}, type today's date.

≡ sent

{Current Date} / Ms. Denise Bradford / Worldwide Travel, Inc. / 1180 Alvarado, SE / Albuquerque, NM 87108 / Dear Ms. Bradford:

¶Our company has decided to hold its regional sales meeting in Scottsdale, Arizona, during the second week of January. I need information on a suitable conference site.

¶We will need a meeting room with 30 computer workstations, an overhead projector and LCD display, and a microphone and podium. We will also need a fax machine or a computer with a fax modem and on-site secretarial

(continued on next page)

Spell-check, proofread, and preview your document. Be sure you vertically centered the letter.

≡ prop

services. I have enclosed a list of conference attendees and their room preferences.

¶A final decision on the conference site must be made within the next two weeks. Please send me any information you have available for a suitable location in Scottsdale immediately. Thank you for your help.

Sincerely yours, / Bill McKay / Marketing Manager / {urs} / Enclosure

Letter 5

Block Style

Do not indent paragraphs in a block-style letter.

≡ prop

≡ time

≡ sent

{Current Date} / Mr. Bill McKay / Marketing Manager / Viatech Communications / 9835 Osuna Road, NE / Albuquerque, NM 87111 / Dear Mr. McKay:

Thank you for your inquiry regarding a conference site in Scottsdale, Arizona, for 35 people during the second week of January.

I have enclosed several brochures with detailed information on some properties in Scottsdale that provide exclusive service to businesses like yours. All these properties have meeting rooms that will accommodate your needs and also offer additional services you might be interested in using.

Please call me when you have reached a decision. I will be happy to make the final arrangements as well as issue any airline tickets you may be needing.

Yours truly, / Ms. Denise Bradford / Travel Agent / {urs} / Enclosures

Lesson 28   Envelopes

GOALS: To type 31 wam/3'/5e; to format envelopes.

A. Type 2 times.

A. WARMUP

1   At 8:30, Horowitz & Co. will fax Order #V546 to us for   11
2   immediate processing! Just how many additional orders they   23
3   will request isn't known. About 7% of the orders are here.   35

| 1 | 2 | 3 | 4 | 5 | 6 | 7 | 8 | 9 | 10 | 11 | 12 |

B. SUSTAINED PRACTICE: PUNCTUATION

4   Anyone who is successful in business realizes that the   11
5 needs of the customer must always come first. A satisfied   23
6 consumer is one who will come back to buy again and again.   35

7   Consumers must learn to lodge a complaint in a manner   11
8 that is fair, effective, and efficient. Don't waste time   23
9 talking to the wrong person. Go to the person in charge.   34

10   State your case clearly; be prepared with facts and   11
11 figures to back up your claim--warranties, receipts, bills,   23
12 and checks are all very effective. Don't feel intimidated.   34

13   If the company agrees to work with you, you're on the   11
14 right track. Be specific: "I'll expect a check Tuesday,"   23
15 or "I'll expect a replacement in the mail by Saturday."   34

| 1 | 2 | 3 | 4 | 5 | 6 | 7 | 8 | 9 | 10 | 11 | 12

C. PROGRESSIVE PRACTICE: ALPHABET

Turn to the Progressive Practice: Alphabet routine beginning on page SB-7.

Take six 30-second timings, starting at the point where you left off the last time.

D. Take two 3-minute timings. Determine your speed and errors.

Goal: 31 wam/3'/5e

D. 3-MINUTE TIMING

16   Credit cards can make shopping very convenient, and   11
17 they frequently help you record and track your spending.   22
18 However, many card companies impose high fees for using   33
19 their credit cards.   37
20   You must realize that it may be better to pay in cash   48
21 and not use a credit card. Examine all your options. Some   60
22 card companies do not charge yearly fees. Some may offer   71
23 free extended warranties on goods you buy with their credit   83
24 cards. Judge all details; you may be surprised.   93

| 1 | 2 | 3 | 4 | 5 | 6 | 7 | 8 | 9 | 10 | 11 | 12

E. ENVELOPES

A No. 10 envelope (the standard size for business letters) is 9½ by 4⅛ inches. A correctly addressed envelope should include the following:

1. **Return Address.** The sender's name and address typed or printed in the upper left corner with a minimum space of 0.25 inch from the top and side of the envelope.

2. **Mailing Address.** The receiver's name and address typed at least 2 inches from the top and 4 inches from the left edge of the envelope. The mailing address may also be typed in all caps and no punctuation for postal sorting purposes.

Trend Electronics
2206 31st Street
Minneapolis, MN 55407-1911

Mr. Charles R. Harrison
Reliable Software, Inc.
5613 Brunswick Avenue
Minneapolis, MN 55406

Standard large envelope, No. 10, is 9½ × 4⅛ inches.

F. FOLDING LETTERS

To fold a letter for a No. 10 envelope:

1. Place the letter face up, and fold the bottom third of the page up toward the top of the page.
2. Fold the top third of the page down to approximately 0.5 inch from the bottom edge of the page.
3. Insert the last crease into the envelope first with the flap facing up.

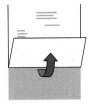 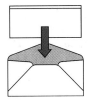

G. WORD PROCESSING: ENVELOPES

Study Lesson 28 in your word processing manual. Complete all of the shaded steps while at your computer. Then format the jobs that follow.

Envelope 1

Do not print any of these documents unless you are sure that your printer is properly set up to print envelopes.

1. Create an envelope with the following mailing address: *Mr. Charles Goldstein / Software Solutions, Inc. / 2981 Canwood Street / Roselle, IL 60172.*
2. Insert the following return address: *Shannon Stone / Data Systems, Inc. / 2201 South Street / Racine, WI 53404.*
3. Append/add the envelope to a blank document.

Envelope 2

1. Open the file for Letter 1 and create an envelope for the letter.
2. Do not insert a return address.
3. Append/add the envelope to the letter.

Envelope 3

1. Open the file for Letter 2 and create an envelope for the letter.
2. Type the following return address: *Agnes Gunderson / Office Supplies*

Express / 24133 West Del Monte / Valencia, CA 91355.

3. Append/add the envelope to the document.

Letter 6

Block Style With Envelope

1. Type the following business letter, and then create an envelope for the letter.
2. Do not insert a return address.

3. Append/add the envelope to the document.

{Current Date} / Ms. Dorothy Turner / Global Moving and Storage / 6830 Via Del Monte / San Jose, CA 95119 / Dear Ms. Turner:

Thank you for registering your PC Fax software so promptly. As a registered user, you are entitled to free technical support 24 hours a day. The enclosed brochure will explain in detail how you can reach us either by fax or by phone whenever you need help.

All our PC Fax users will receive our monthly newsletter, which is filled with tips on using your new software and other material we know you will be interested in receiving. You can now use your fax modem to access a wealth of information on a wide variety of topics.

Please call me if you have any questions or would like to receive any additional information. Your satisfaction is our number one priority.

Sincerely, / Nicholas Moore / Sales Representative / {urs} / Enclosure

---

Lesson 29　Memos

GOALS: To improve speed and accuracy; to refine language-arts skills in spelling; to format interoffice memos.

A. Type 2 times.

A. WARMUP

```
1      Will the package arrive at 11:29 or 3:45?  The exact     11
2  answer to this question could mean the difference between    22
3  losing or saving their account; Joyce also realizes this.    34
   | 1 | 2 | 3 | 4 | 5 | 6 | 7 | 8 | 9 | 10 | 11 | 12
```

B. 12-SECOND SPEED SPRINTS

B. Take three 12-second timings on each line. The scale below the last line shows your wam speed for a 12-second timing.

4 Mary will not be able to meet them at the game later today.
5 The class is not going to be able to meet if they are gone.
6 They could not open that old door when the chair fell over.
7 This very nice piece of paper may be used to print the job.

| | | |5| | | |10| | | |15| | | |20| | | |25| | | |30| | | |35| | | |40| | | |45| | | |50| | | |55| | | |60

C. DIAGNOSTIC PRACTICE: NUMBERS

Turn to the Diagnostic Practice: Numbers routine beginning on page SB-5. Type one of the Pretest/Posttest paragraphs and identify any errors made. Then type the corresponding drill lines 2 times for each number on which you made 2 or more errors and 1 time for each number on which you made only 1 error. Finally, repeat the same Pretest paragraph and compare your performance.

D. PROGRESSIVE PRACTICE: ALPHABET

Turn to the Progressive Practice: Alphabet routine beginning on page SB-7. Take six 30-second timings, starting at the point where you left off the last time.

LANGUAGE ARTS

E. SPELLING

E. Type these frequently misspelled words, paying special attention to any spelling problems in each word.

8 personnel information its procedures their committee system
9 receive employees which education services opportunity area
10 financial appropriate interest received production contract
11 important through necessary customer employee further there
12 property account approximately general control division our

Edit the sentences to correct any misspellings.

13 All company personel will recieve important information.
14 Are division has some control over there financial account.
15 There comittee has received approximately three contracts.
16 The employe and the customer have an oportunity to attend.
17 There was no farther interest in the property or it's owner.
18 When it was necessary, apropriate procedurs were followed.

FORMATTING

F. INTEROFFICE MEMOS

An interoffice memo is usually sent from one person to another in the same organization. Follow these steps to format a memo on plain paper or on letterhead stationery:

1. Press Enter 6 times for a top margin of approximately 2 inches.

2. Type the headings (including the colons) in all caps and bold: ***MEMO TO:***, ***FROM:***, ***DATE:***, and ***SUBJECT:***.

3. Tab once after typing the colon to reach the point where the heading entries begin.

(continued on next page)

4. Leave 1 blank line between the heading lines and between the heading lines and the body of the memo.
5. Leave 1 blank line between paragraphs. Most memos are typed with blocked paragraphs (no indentions).
6. Leave 1 blank line between the body and the reference initials.

DOCUMENT PROCESSING

Memo 1

Spell-check, proofread, and preview your memo for errors.

Words underlined in green are spelling words from the language arts activities.

↓6X

MEMO TO: All Salaried Employees ↓2X

FROM: Linda Vigil, Human Resources ↓2X

DATE: November 2, 19-- ↓2X

SUBJECT: Health Care Benefit Plan ↓2X

Effective January 1, Allied Aerospace Industries will contract with MedNet to begin a new health benefits program for all eligible salaried personnel. A brochure outlining important program information will be mailed to you soon. ↓2X

An open enrollment period will be in effect during the entire month of January. If you and your family are interested in one of the MedNet health plan options, you may transfer yourself and your dependents into any appropriate plan. All applications must be received no later than midnight, January 31. ↓2X

If you have any questions or need any help understanding your options, please call me at Ext. 213. I will be happy to help you select the plan that is best for you. ↓2X

{urs}

Memo 2

MEMO TO: Linda Vigil, Human Resources / **FROM:** Dan Lopez / **DATE:** November 23, 19— / **SUBJECT:** MedNet Benefit Plan

¶Thank you for the brochure detailing the various options for employees under the MedNet plan. I would like clarification on some of the services included in the plan.

¶Because both my wife and I are employees of Allied Aerospace Industries, do we have the choice of enrolling separately under different options? In our present plan, I know that this is possible.

¶We have two dependents. Is it possible to enroll both dependents under different options of the plan, or do they both fall under either one option or the other? I know that in the past you have asked for evidence of dependent status and dates of birth.

¶If you need any further information, please let me know. Thank you very much for your help.

{urs}

Lesson 30   Memos

GOALS: To type 32 wam/3'/5e; to format memos with italics, underline, and attachment notations.

A. Type 2 times.

A. WARMUP

1   Did Zagorski & Sons charge $876 for the renovation?   11
2 The invoice isn't quite right; the exact amount charged in   23
3 July is smeared. Pam will try her best to get the figures.   34

| 1 | 2 | 3 | 4 | 5 | 6 | 7 | 8 | 9 | 10 | 11 | 12

SKILLBUILDING

B. PROGRESSIVE PRACTICE: NUMBERS

Turn to the Progressive Practice: Numbers routine beginning on page SB-11.   Take six 30-second timings, starting at the point where you left off the last time.

C. Type the paragraph 2 times. Use the caps lock key to type a word or series of words in all caps. Reach to the caps lock with the A finger.

C. TECHNIQUE PRACTICE: SHIFT KEY AND CAPS LOCK

4   The new computer has CD-ROM, PCI IDE HDD controller,
5 and an SVGA card. Mr. J. L. Jones will order one from PC
6 EXPRESS out of Orem, Utah. IT ARRIVES NO LATER THAN JULY.

D. Take two 3-minute timings. Determine your speed and errors.

Goal: 32 wam/3'/5e

D. 3-MINUTE TIMING

7   If you want to work in information processing, you   10
8 must realize that there are steps that you must take to   22
9 plan for such an exciting career. First, you must decide   33
10 whether or not you have the right personality traits.   44
11   Then you must be trained in the technical skills you   55
12 will need in such an important field. The technology is   66
13 changing each day. You must stay focused on keeping up   77
14 with these changes. Also, you must never quit learning new   89
15 tasks each day you are on the job.   96

| 1 | 2 | 3 | 4 | 5 | 6 | 7 | 8 | 9 | 10 | 11 | 12

FORMATTING

E. ATTACHMENT NOTATION

Attachment (rather than *Enclosure*) is typed below the reference initials when material is physically attached (stapled or clipped) to a memo.

Example:
urs
Attachment

F. WORD PROCESSING: ITALICS AND UNDERLINE

Study Lesson 30 in your word processing manual. Complete all of the shaded steps while at your computer. Then format the jobs that follow.

Memo 3

Remember to type an attachment notation rather than an enclosure notation.

Spell-check, proofread, and preview your memo for errors.

MEMO TO: All Executive Assistants / **FROM:** Barbara Azar, Staff Development Coordinator / **DATE:** {Current Date} / **SUBJECT:** Standardizing Document Formats

¶Last month we received our final shipment of new laser printers. The installation of these printers in your offices marked the final phaseout of all dot matrix printers.

¶Because all of us can now use italicized fonts in our correspondence, please note the following change: from now on <u>all book and journal titles should be italicized rather than underlined</u> as was done in the past. This new procedure will help us to standardize our documents.

¶The latest edition of *Quick Reference for the Automated Office* has two pages of helpful information on laser printers, which I have attached. Please read them carefully, and we will discuss them at our next meeting.

{urs} / Attachment

Memo 4

MEMO TO: Barbara Azar, Staff Development Coordinator / **FROM:** Sharon Hearshen, Executive Assistant / **DATE:** {Current Date} / **SUBJECT:** Laser Printer Workshop

¶The new laser printers we received are <u>fabulous</u>! I know that you worked very hard to get these printers for us, and all of us in the Sales and Marketing Department certainly appreciate your effort.

¶Several of us would be very interested in seeing the printers demonstrated. Would it be possible to have a workshop with some hands-on training? We are particularly interested in learning about font selection, paper selection, and envelopes and labels.

¶I have attached an article on laser printers from the latest issue of *Office Technology.* It is very informative, and you might like to include it as a part of the workshop. Please let me know if I can help you in any way.

{urs} / Attachment

Letter 7

Progress Check
Block Style

1. Type the following business letter, and then create an envelope for the document.
2. Do not include a return address.
3. Do not append the envelope to the letter.

October 1, 19— / Mrs. Ruzanna Avetisyan / 844 Lincoln Boulevard / Santa Monica, CA 90403 / Dear Mrs. Avetisyan:

¶The League of Women Voters is looking for volunteers to work at the various polling places during the upcoming elections.

¶If you think you will be able to volunteer your time, please fill out and mail the enclosed card. After I receive your card, I will contact you to confirm a location, time, and date.

¶Your efforts are greatly appreciated, Mrs. Avetisyan. Concerned citizens like you make it possible for the public to have a convenient place to vote. Thank you for your interest in this very worthy cause! / Sincerely yours, / Stephanie Holt / Public Relations Volunteer / {urs} / Enclosure

Lesson 31　Simple Tables

GOALS: To improve speed and accuracy; to refine language-arts skills in proofreading; to format simple tables.

A. Type 2 times.

A. WARMUP

```
1      You can save $1,698 when you buy the 20-part video    10
2   series!  Just ask for Series #MX5265 in the next 7 days;  22
3   ordering early qualifies you for a sizable discount of 5%. 34
    |  1  |  2  |  3  |  4  |  5  |  6  |  7  |  8  |  9  |  10  |  11  |  12
```

SKILLBUILDING

Pretest
Take a 1-minute timing. Determine your speed and errors.

B. PRETEST: DISCRIMINATION PRACTICE

```
4      Steven saw the younger, unruly boy take flight as he   11
5   threw the coin at the jury.  The brave judge stopped the   22
6   fight.  He called out to the youth, who recoiled in fear.  34
    |  1  |  2  |  3  |  4  |  5  |  6  |  7  |  8  |  9  |  10  |  11  |  12
```

Practice
　Speed Emphasis: If you made 2 or fewer errors on the Pretest, type each *individual* line 2 times.
　Accuracy Emphasis: If you made 3 or more errors, type each *group* of lines (as though it were a paragraph) 2 times.

C. PRACTICE: LEFT HAND

```
7   vbv verb bevy vibes bevel brave above verbal bovine behaves
8   wew west weep threw wedge weave fewer weight sewing dewdrop
9   fgf gulf gift fight fudge fugue flags flight golfer feigned
```

D. PRACTICE: RIGHT HAND

```
10  uyu buys your usury unity youth buoys unruly untidy younger
11  oio coin lion oiled foils foist prior recoil iodine rejoice
12  jhj jury huge enjoy three judge habit adjust slight jasmine
```

Posttest
Repeat the Pretest timing and compare performance.

E. POSTTEST: DISCRIMINATION PRACTICE

F. Take three 12-second timings on each line. The scale below the last line shows your wam speed for a 12-second timing.

F. 12-SECOND SPEED SPRINTS

```
13  The book that is on top of the big desk will be given away.
14  Bill must pay for the tape or he will have to give it back.
15  They left the meeting after all of the group had gone away.
16  The third person to finish all of the work today may leave.
    |  |  |  5  |  |  |10|  |  |15|  |  |20|  |  |25|  |  |30|  |  |35|  |  |40|  |  |45|  |  |50|  |  |55|  |  |60
```

G. PROOFREADING

G. Edit this paragraph to correct any typing or formatting errors.

17   It doesnt matter how fast you can type or how well
18 you now a software program if you produce documents taht
19 are filled with errors. You must learn to watch for errors
20 in spelling punctuation, and formatting. Look carefully
21 between words and sentences. Make sure that after a period
22 at the end of a sentence, you see two spaces. Sometime it
23 helps to look at the characters in the sentence justabove
24 the one you are proofreading to ensure accuracy.

FORMATTING

H. BASIC PARTS OF A TABLE

1. Tables consist of vertical columns and horizontal rows. A cell, or "box," is created where a column and a row intersect.

2. Tables formatted with horizontal and vertical lines (as shown in the illus-tration) are called boxed tables. Those formatted with no lines are called open tables.

3. If a table appears alone on the page, it should be centered vertically.

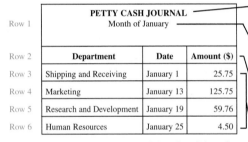

TITLE. Center and type in all caps and bold. If there is no subtitle, insert 1 blank line after the title.

SUBTITLE. Center on the line below the title, and type in initial caps. Insert 1 blank line after the subtitle.

COLUMN HEADINGS. Column headings may be centered or aligned at the left or right, depending on the table. Type column headings in initial caps and bold.

BODY. Left-justify (left-align) text columns; right-justify (right-align) number columns.

I. WORD PROCESSING: TABLE—CREATE AND LINES

go TO

Study Lesson 31 in your word processing manual. Complete all of the shaded steps while at your computer. Then format the jobs that follow.

DOCUMENT PROCESSING

Table 1
2-Column Boxed Table

Simple tables such as this often do not have titles, subtitles, or column heads.

Follow these steps to format Table 1:

1. Center the table vertically on the page.
2. Create a 2-column, 4-row table.
3. Format this table as a boxed table (with lines).

Jose Robledo, President	Administration, Room 210
Carol Seinfeld, Vice President	Administration, Room 304
Martin Hashibe, Dean	Admissions and Records, Room 203
Karine Erkatyan, Associate Dean	Student Services, Room 101

Table 2
3-Column Open Table

The vertical space between table rows differs depending on the word processing software being used to create the table.

Follow these steps to format Table 2:

1. Center the table vertically.
2. Create a 3-column, 3-row table.
3. Format this table as an open table (without lines).

Linda Scher	Office Administration	Da Vinci Hall
Gary Finkle	Dental Technology	Franklin Hall
Gloria Hernandez	Political Science	Holmes Hall

Table 3
3-Column Boxed Table

Follow these steps to format Table 3:

1. Open the file for Table 2.
2. Reformat the table as a boxed table.

Table 4
3-Column Boxed Table

Follow these steps to format Table 4:

1. Center the table vertically.
2. Create a 3-column, 3-row table.
3. Format this table as a boxed table (with lines).

Thomas Freidman	Executive Editor	Los Angeles, California
Dawn Seidman	Associate Editor	St. Louis, Missouri
Martin Gonzalez	Art Director	Seattle, Washington

Lesson 32 Tables With Column Headings

GOALS: To type 33 wam/3'/5e; to format tables with column headings.

A. Type 2 times.

A. WARMUP

```
1      Sales by two travel agencies (Quill, Virgil, & Johnson    11
2  and Keef & Zane) exceeded all prior amounts.  Total sales     23
3  for that year were as follows:  $1,540,830 and $976,223.      34
   |  1  |  2  |  3  |  4  |  5  |  6  |  7  |  8  |  9  |  10 |  11 |  12
```

SKILLBUILDING

B. PROGRESSIVE PRACTICE: ALPHABET

Turn to the Progressive Practice: Alphabet routine beginning on page SB-7.

Take six 30-second timings, starting at the point where you left off the last time.

C. Take two 3-minute timings. Determine your speed and errors.

Goal: 33 wam/3′/5e

C. 3-MINUTE TIMING

4   To create documents that are easy to read, you may   10
5   want to include tables. Joining complex data in a table   22
6   makes the facts clear and quick to understand. Tables   33
7   include rows, columns, and cells.   40
8   Another way to make your reports easy to read is to   50
9   use color. Note how the quality of a document improves   61
10   when you add a zippy color to such features as headings.   73
11   As you try several new formats, you will find that your   84
12   writing comes alive. People who read your reports will   95
13   like your efforts.   99

| 1 | 2 | 3 | 4 | 5 | 6 | 7 | 8 | 9 | 10 | 11 | 12

FORMATTING

D. FORMATTING COLUMN HEADINGS

Column headings are used to describe the information contained in the columns. To format column headings:

1. Type the column headings in initial caps and bold.
2. Align column headings at the left over text columns, at the right over number columns, or centered over all columns.
3. When a column contains dollar amounts or percents, you may include the dollar sign or the percent sign as part of the column heading or add them to each of the column entries.

E. WORD PROCESSING: TABLE—JOIN CELLS

Study Lesson 32 in your word processing manual. Complete all of the shaded steps while at your computer. Then format the jobs that follow.

DOCUMENT PROCESSING

Table 5
2-Column Boxed Table With Centered Column Headings

Format Table 5 as follows:

1. Center the table vertically.
2. Create a table structure with 2 columns and 5 rows.
3. Center the column headings, and type them in bold with initial caps.
4. Type the column text aligned at the left.
5. Join the cells in Row 1; then center and type the title in bold and all caps.
6. Press Enter once to insert 1 blank line after the title.

WORLDWIDE LIFE INSURANCE COMPANY	
Investment Portfolio	**Degree of Risk**
Aggressive Stock Portfolio	Very high risk
Global Portfolio	Moderate to high risk
Common Stock Portfolio	Moderate risk

Table 6
3-Column Open Table With Left-Aligned Column Headings

Format Table 6 as follows:

1. Center the table vertically.
2. Create a table structure with 3 columns and 5 rows.
3. Type the column headings aligned at the left in bold with initial caps.
4. Type the column text aligned at the left.
5. Join the cells in Row 1; then center and type the title in bold and all caps.
6. Press Enter once to insert 1 blank line after the title.

SCHOLARSHIP RECIPIENTS

Student Name	College Department	Community College
Steven Fernandez	Office Administration	Los Angeles City College
Chin Lee	Information Management	College of the Canyons
Anthony West	Computer Science	Saddleback College

Table 7
3-Column Boxed Table With Left-Aligned Column Headings

HOMEOWNERS' INSURANCE RATINGS		
Company	**Overall Satisfaction**	**Speed of Payment**
Allied Insurance	Completely satisfied	Very fast
Coast Casualty	Somewhat satisfied	Moderate to fast
Citywide Insurance	Completely dissatisfied	Slow to moderate

Lesson 33   Tables With Number Columns

GOALS: To improve speed and accuracy; to refine language-arts skills in composing; to format tables with number columns.

A. Type 2 times.

A. WARMUP

```
1      Does Quentin know if 1/2 of the January order will be    11
2  ready?  At 5:30 about 46% of the orders still hadn't been    23
3  mailed!  Mr. Gray expects a very sizable loss this month.    34
   | 1 | 2 | 3 | 4 | 5 | 6 | 7 | 8 | 9 | 10 | 11 | 12
```

B. SUSTAINED PRACTICE: ALTERNATE-HAND WORDS

4   When eight of them began a formal discussion on some   11
5 of the major issues, the need for a chair was very evident.   23
6 A chair would be sure to handle the usual work with ease.   34

7   The eight people in that group decided that the work   11
8 would get done only if they selected one person to be chair   23
9 of their group. They began to debate all the major issues.   35

10   One issue that needed to be settled right up front was   11
11 the question of how to handle proxy votes. It seemed for a   23
12 short time that a fight over this very issue would result.   35

13   The group worked diligently in attempting to solve the   11
14 issues that were being discussed. All of the concerns that   23
15 were brought to the group were reviewed in depth by them.   35

| 1 | 2 | 3 | 4 | 5 | 6 | 7 | 8 | 9 | 10 | 11 | 12

C. TECHNIQUE PRACTICE: ENTER KEY

16 Debit the account. Balance the checkbook. Add the assets.
17 Take the discount. Send the statement. Compute the ratio.
18 Review the account. Credit the amount. Figure the total.
19 Prepare the statement. Send the catalog. Call the client.

D. COMPOSING

20 Have you ever learned a word processing program before?
21 Have you ever been on an interview?
22 Do you own a computer?
23 Do you have a CD-Rom drive?
24 How many blank lines do you leave after the title of a table?
25 Do you enjoy typing tables?
26 Do you know how to center a table vertically?
27 Have you ever had a job before?

E. FORMATTING TABLES WITH NUMBER COLUMNS

1. Columns of numbers should be aligned or justified at the right.
2. The column heading over a column of numbers should be aligned or justified at the right also, except when all of the column headings are centered.
3. Because number columns are often much narrower than text columns, you may need to adjust the width of the number columns so that the table appears balanced.
4. Always adjust column widths *before* joining any cells to ensure that the column widths are adjusted correctly.
5. Adjusting the column widths will reposition the table horizontally on the page. You must issue a command to horizontally center the table.

F. WORD PROCESSING: TABLE—FORMAT AND RESIZE CELLS

Study Lesson 33 in your word processing manual. Complete all of the shaded steps while at your computer. Then format the jobs that follow.

Table 8
3-Column Boxed
Table With Number
Columns

1. Center the table vertically.
2. Create a table structure with 3 columns and 6 rows.
3. Center and type the column headings in initial caps and bold.
4. Type the column text left-aligned and right-align the number columns.
5. Automatically adjust the column widths for all columns.
6. Join the cells in Row 1.
7. Center and type the title in all caps and bold. Center and type the subtitle in initial caps.
8. Press Enter once to insert 1 blank line after the subtitle.
9. Center the table horizontally.

COLOR PRINTERS Inventory		
Type	**Total**	**Sold**
Laser	194	94
Ink-jet	117	37
Bubble-jet	9	2
Dot matrix	29	110

Table 9
3-Column Boxed
Table With Number
Columns

1. Center the table vertically.
2. Create a table structure with 3 columns and 6 rows.
3. Center and type the column headings in initial caps and bold.
4. Type the column text left-aligned and right-align the number columns.
5. Automatically adjust the column widths for all columns.
6. Join the cells in Row 1.
7. Center and type the title in all caps and bold. Center and type the subtitle in initial caps.
8. Press Enter once to insert 1 blank line after the subtitle.
9. Center the table horizontally.

PAYROLL SUMMARY Week Ending December 31, 19--		
Name	**Gross Pay ($)**	**Tax ($)**
Ferguson, Ruth	932	204
Chen, Robert	354	84
Prior, David	93	9
James, Michael	356	37

Table 10
3-Column Boxed
Table With Number
Columns

1. Open the file for Table 9.
2. Change the title to **EMPLOYEE EARNINGS**.

3. Delete the words *Week Ending* from the subtitle and change the first column heading to *Employee.*

Lesson 34   Tables With Totals

GOALS: To type 34 wam/3'/4e; to format tables with totals.

A. Type 2 times.

A. WARMUP

```
 1        This series* (*6 films, 28 minutes) by J. Zeller goes      11
 2   beyond the "basics" of computers.  Viewers keep requesting      23
 3   an extension on the dates; this includes 3/2, 5/5, and 8/9.     35
     |  1  |  2  |  3  |  4  |  5  |  6  |  7  |  8  |  9  | 10  | 11  | 12
```

SKILLBUILDING

B. DIAGNOSTIC PRACTICE: ALPHABET

Turn to the Diagnostic Practice: Alphabet routine beginning on page SB-2. Type one of the Pretest/Posttest paragraphs and identify any errors made. Then type the corresponding drill lines 2 times for each letter on which you made 2 or more errors and 1 time for each letter on which you made only 1 error. Finally, repeat the same Pretest paragraph and compare your performance.

C. Take two 3-minute timings. Determine your speed and errors.

Goal: 34 wam/3'/4e

Note: The error limit has been lowered from 5 errors to 4 errors.

C. 3-MINUTE TIMING

```
 4        Job security is an important factor for most students      11
 5   who expect to have a bright future in the world of work.        23
 6   Those who have computer training will have a much easier        34
 7   time.  Jobs that require computer skills will pay more than     46
 8   those that do not need these very critical skills.              56
 9        If you can learn one or more word processing programs,     67
10   you are almost guaranteed a good job.  If you have a good       79
11   job right now, acquiring more computer skills could lead        90
12   to a big promotion or perhaps a sizable raise in your pay.     102
     |  1  |  2  |  3  |  4  |  5  |  6  |  7  |  8  |  9  | 10  | 11  | 12
```

D. WORD PROCESSING: TABLE—NUMBER FORMAT AND FORMULAS

Study Lesson 34 in your word processing manual. Complete all of the shaded steps while at your computer. Then format the jobs that follow.

DOCUMENT PROCESSING

Table 11
2-Column Open Table With Number Column and Total

1. Center the table vertically.
2. Create a table structure with 2 columns and 5 rows.
3. Type the text in the columns including the word *TOTAL* in the last row, but leave the total amount blank.
4. Format the number column with dollar signs and two places after the decimal point.
5. With the insertion point in the total amount cell, insert the SUM command to get a total amount. (Do not type the question mark.)
6. Automatically adjust the column widths.
7. Join the cells in Row 1 and type the title in all caps and bold. Type the subtitle in initial caps.
8. Center the table horizontally.

UNITED CASUALTY
Liabilities

Net policy reserves	$44,726,719.00
Policy claims	$111,909.00
Other liabilities	$30,551.00
TOTAL	?

Table 12
2-Column Boxed Table With Number Column and Total

1. Center the table vertically.
2. Create a table structure with 2 columns and 7 rows.
3. Type the column headings in bold, then type the information in the columns.
4. Right justify/align the number column, including the column heading.
5. Format the number column with dollar signs and two places after the decimal point.
6. Use the SUM command to total the column.
7. Automatically adjust the column widths.
8. Join the cells in Row 1, type the title in all caps and bold, then center the table horizontally.

OPERATING EXPENSES	
Utilities	**Amount**
Electricity	$19,000.00
Gas	$18,500.00
Telephone	$1,475.00
Water	$7,500.00
TOTAL UTILITIES	?

Table 13
2-Column Open Table
With Number Column
and Total

1. Open the file for Table 12.
2. Change the table from a boxed table to an open table.

3. Add the subtitle *Homeowners' Association.*

Lesson 35 Formatting Review

GOALS: To improve speed and accuracy; to refine language-arts skills in spelling; to practice basic word processing commands.

A. Type 2 times.

A. WARMUP

1   Item #876 won't be ordered until 9/10. Did you gather   11
2 all requests and input them exactly as they appeared? Jack   23
3 will never be satisfied until a profit has been realized.   35

| 1 | 2 | 3 | 4 | 5 | 6 | 7 | 8 | 9 | 10 | 11 | 12

SKILLBUILDING

B. PACED PRACTICE

Turn to the Paced Practice routine beginning on page SB-14. Take three 2-minute timings, starting at the point where you left off the last time.

C. DIAGNOSTIC PRACTICE: NUMBERS

Turn to the Diagnostic Practice: Numbers routine beginning on page SB-5. Type one of the Pretest/Posttest paragraphs and identify any errors made. Then type the corresponding drill lines 2 times for each number on which you made 2 or more errors and 1 time for each number on which you made only 1 error. Finally, repeat the same Pretest paragraph and compare your performance.

 **LANGUAGE ARTS**

D. SPELLING

D. Type this list of frequently misspelled words, paying special attention to any spelling problems in each word.

4 prior activities additional than faculty whether first with
5 subject material equipment receiving completed during basis
6 available please required decision established policy audit
7 section schedule installation insurance possible appreciate
8 benefits requirements business scheduled office immediately

Edit the sentences to correct any misspellings.

9   We requierd the office to schedule all prior activities.
10 The business scheduled the instalation of the equipment.
11 The decision established the basis of the insurance policy.
12 Please audit any additionl material available to faculty.
13 If possible, we would appreciate recieving it immediately.
14 The section requirements to receive benefits were completed.

DOCUMENT PROCESSING

Report 5

BENEFITS PROGRAM OPTIONS
Insurance Alliance of America
By Martin VanWagner

Beginning January 1, our company has contracted with Insurance Alliance of America for a new benefits program for all employees. Please review the information below carefully before you reach any decision.

ENROLLMENT INFORMATION

The open enrollment period for the new benefits program will begin on January 1 and end on January 31. During this time, you are required to submit a completed application for enrollment in either the contributory or noncontributory policy plan. Any dependents must be enrolled in the same plan.

If you do not enroll in a medical insurance plan on or before January 31, you will automatically be enrolled in the noncontributory plan. Your new plan will become effective on the first of the month following your enrollment.

CHANGING BENEFIT PLANS

During the open enrollment period, it is possible to transfer to any available medical plan for which you are eligible. After the open enrollment period ends, you may not change plans again until the next scheduled open enrollment period.

Letter 8
Block Style

December 1, 19--

Mrs. Yvonne Spillotro
105 Northfield Avenue
Edison, NJ 08837

Dear Mrs. Spillotro:

Open enrollment for your medical insurance plan is scheduled to begin the first day of January. I hope it was possible for you to review the material you received last week.

Selecting the right benefit plan for you and your family can be an overwhelming

(continued on next page)

task. To make this decision a little easier, I have enclosed a brochure with this letter summarizing the key features of each policy. Please call me if I can help in any way.

Thank you for choosing Insurance Alliance of America.

Sincerely yours,

Keith Richards
Customer Support

{urs}

Enclosure

Envelope 4

1. Open the file for Letter 8 and create an envelope for the document.

2. Do not insert a return address.
3. Append the envelope to the letter.

Table 14
Progress Check

2-Column Boxed Table With Centered Column Headings, a Number Column, and a Total

1. Center the column headings.

2. Follow standard table format for the rest of this table.

OPERATING INCOME	
West Valley Homeowners' Association	
Category	**Amount**
Homeowner Dues	$207,090.00
Interest Income	$2,750.00
Late-Charges Income	$1,500.00
Prior-Year Excess Funds	$9,986.00
TOTAL INCOME	?

Lesson 36   Multipage Rough-Draft Reports

GOALS: To type 35 wam/3′/4e; to learn basic proofreaders' marks; to format multipage rough-draft reports.

A. Type 2 times.

A. WARMUP

```
1       A plain paper reader/printer must be ordered; it must      11
2   accept jackets and have a footprint of 15 × 27* (*inches).     23
3   Please ask Gary to request Model Z-340 whenever he arrives.    35
    |  1  |  2  |  3  |  4  |  5  |  6  |  7  |  8  |  9  |  10  |  11  |  12
```

SKILLBUILDING

B. Take three 12-second timings on each line. The scale below the last line shows your wam speed for a 12-second timing.

B. 12-SECOND SPEED SPRINTS

```
4   Blake was paid to fix the handle on the bowls that he made.
5   Alan led the panel of four men until the work was all done.
6   Jan will sign this paper when she has done all of the work.
7   They will focus on their main theme for the last six weeks.
    | | | |5| | | |10| | |15| | |20| | |25| | |30| | |35| | |40| | |45| | |50| | |55| | |60
```

C. Type the paragraph 2 times. Every time a number appears in the paragraph, replace it with a number that is two higher. For example, replace *two* with *four* and *five* with *seven*.

C. TECHNIQUE PRACTICE: CONCENTRATION

```
8        The two clerks placed an order for two computers, two
9   printers, three monitors, and four scanners.  The last
10  time he called, two people told him three different things.
```

D. Take two 3-minute timings. Determine your speed and errors.

Goal: 35 wam/3′/4e

D. 3-MINUTE TIMING

```
11       The use of videotapes for training company employees     11
12  is an exciting trend in the business world.  The range of     22
13  topics is wide and varied.  These tapes are designed to       34
14  instruct and entertain.  You can learn anything from office   46
15  etiquette to how and when to hire an office temp.             56
16       Most tapes are sold for a fair price when you stop to    67
17  realize just how many ways you could use these tapes.  One    78
18  use might be to launch a lively debate on some key topics     90
19  during a meeting.  Your prospects are limited only by your    102
20  own imagination.                                              105
    |  1  |  2  |  3  |  4  |  5  |  6  |  7  |  8  |  9  |  10  |  11  |  12
```

E. BASIC PROOFREADERS' MARKS

1. Proofreaders' marks are used to indicate changes or corrections to be made in a document (called a rough draft) that is being revised for final copy.

2. Study the chart to learn what each proofreaders' mark means.

Proofreaders' Marks		Draft	Final Copy
⌒	Omit space	data base	database
∨ or ∧	Insert	if he's not going	if he's not going,
≡	Capitalize	Maple street	Maple Street
ⱨ	Delete	a final draft	a draft
#	Insert space	allready to	all ready to
when / if	Change word	and if you	and when you
/	Use lowercase letter	our President	our president
¶	Paragraph	¶Most of the	Most of the

F. MULTIPAGE REPORTS

To format a multipage report:

1. Use the same side margins for all pages of the report.
2. Leave an approximate 2-inch top margin on page 1.
3. Leave an approximate 1-inch bottom margin on all pages. When you reach the end of a page, a soft page break will automatically be inserted by your software.
4. Leave a 1-inch top margin on continuing pages.
5. Do not number the first page. However, number all continuing pages at the top right.

G. WORD PROCESSING: PAGE NUMBERING AND PAGE BREAK

Study Lesson 36 in your word processing manual. Complete all of the shaded steps while at your computer. Then format the jobs that follow.

Report 6
Multipage, Rough-Draft Report

1. Insert the page numbers at the top right, and suppress the page number on the first page.
2. Change line spacing to double; then press Enter 3 times.
3. Center and type the title in all caps and bold.
4. Center and type the subtitle and byline in initial caps.

(continued on next page)

Paragraph headings are minor subdivisions of a report. They are indented 0.5 inch, are typed in initial caps and bold (including the period), and are followed by 2 spaces.

LEASING OFFICE EQUIPMENT

Hi-tech Research Inc.

by Deborah Springer

Many companies are facing a dilemma these days. In order to remain competitive businesses must use equipment that is state-of-the-art, technologically speaking. They must decide whether to invest their dollars in buying or in leasing their equipment.

Advantages of Leasing

For businesses that are simply not large enough to afford a major capital outlay, leasing can offer many advantages. **Avoid Technological Obsolescence.** Technology is making very dramatic and sweeping changes almost daily. As new products come on the market, they are very expensive initially. Over time, prices tend to drop dramatically and features continue to improve. It just doesn't make sense to make a major huge investement in an item that will likely become obsolete in a short period of time.

Upgrade Easily. If using state-of-the-art equipment it is critical to a company's success, leasing would allow the company to upgrade faster and with reduced cost. The short-term cost of leasing a lease must be compared with the long-term cost of investing in equipment that will not be used any longer when it becomes outdated. A company will not be locked into using hardware that is second-rate because too much money was invested when it was purchased bought. Innovation will be encouraged rather than inhibited.

Option to Buy. if a company leases with an option to buy, the money used to lease could end up being used to help purchase the equipment. If the item being leased ends up being undesirable, the company is not locked into buying it. This option could surely result in some significant savings.

DISADVANTAGES OF LEASING

If the equipment being leased is likely to be used over a long period of time, leasing it could end up costing much more than buying it over the long run. Also, if leasing rates are very high, the cost could be prohibitive or unreasonable when compared with the cost of buying. Sometimes leasing does not include a contract to service the equipment. If a service contract is considered an

(continued on next page)

additional expense, the cost of leasing might be too high. Leasing is an

important alternative in today's business world. The pros and cons must be

weighed carefully before ~~making~~ any final decisions are made.

Report 7
Multipage Report

Open the file for Report 6 and make the following changes:

1. Change the title to *OFFICE EQUIP-MENT: LEASING VS. BUYING*.
2. Use your name in the byline.

3. Change the sideheadings to:
   LEASING ADVANTAGES
   LEASING DISADVANTAGES
4. Delete the last sentence in the paragraph headed *Option to Buy*.

Lesson 37   Bulleted and Numbered Lists

GOALS: To improve speed and accuracy; to refine language-arts skills in punctuation; to format bulleted and numbered lists.

A. Type 2 times.

A. WARMUP

```
1      The check for $432.65 wasn't mailed on time!  Late        10
2  charges of up to 10% can be expected.  To avoid a sizable      22
3  penalty, just mail the check quickly before it is too late.    34
   |  1  |  2  |  3  |  4  |  5  |  6  |  7  |  8  |  9  |  10  |  11  |  12
```

SKILLBUILDING

B. DIAGNOSTIC PRACTICE: ALPHABET

Turn to the Diagnostic Practice: Alphabet routine beginning on page SB-2. Type one of the Pretest/Posttest paragraphs and identify any errors made. Then type the corresponding drill lines 2 times for each letter on which you made 2 or more errors and 1 time for each letter on which you made only 1 error. Finally, repeat the same Pretest paragraph and compare your performance.

C. PACED PRACTICE

Turn to the Paced Practice routine beginning on page SB-14. Take three 2-minute timings, starting at the point where you left off the last time.

D. APOSTROPHES

D. Study the rules at the right.

'sing

Rule: Use *'s* to form the possessive of singular nouns.

My secretary's office is being painted.

'plur

Rule: Use only an apostrophe to form the possessive of plural nouns that end in *s*.

The students' grades were posted in the hall.

'pro

Rule: Use *'s* to form the possessive of indefinite pronouns (such as *someone's* or *anybody's*); do not use an apostrophe with personal pronouns (such as *hers, his, its, ours, theirs,* and *yours*).

It is anybody's guess whether or not the car is hers.

Edit the sentences to insert any needed punctuation.

4 The womans purse was stolen as she held her childs hand.
5 If the book is yours, please return it to the library now.
6 The girls decided to give the parents donations to charity.
7 The childs toy was forgotten by his mothers good friend.
8 The universities presidents submitted the joint statement.
9 The four secretaries salaries were raised just like yours.
10 One boys presents were forgotten when he left the party.
11 If these blue notebooks are not ours, they must be theirs.
12 The plant was designed to recycle its own waste products.

 FORMATTING

E. BULLETED AND NUMBERED LISTS

1. Use bullets or numbers to call attention to items in a list. If the sequence of the items is important, use numbers rather than bullets.
2. Bullets and numbers appear at the left margin and are followed by an indent.
3. Carryover lines indent to align with the text in the previous line, not the bullet or number.

F. WORD PROCESSING: BULLETS AND NUMBERING

go **to**

Study Lesson 37 in your word processing manual. Complete all of the shaded steps while at your computer. Then format the jobs that follow.

 **DOCUMENT PROCESSING**

Report 8
Bulleted List

1. Read the information in Report 8 carefully before you type the report.
2. Type the report using the standard report format.
3. Use the bullet command to add bullets to the list as you type.

(continued on next page)

BULLETED LISTS

- To make items in a list easier to read, use either bullets or numbers.

- When the items' order is not important, use bullets instead of numbers.

- The software command for automatically inserting bullets positions the bullet at the left margin and sets the indent for the list's first line as well as any turnover (second and succeeding) lines.

- The circle you see at the left of this sentence is just one example of a bullet. Large circles, diamonds, squares, or triangles may also be used as bullets.

- A list that is part of the body of a double-spaced document (such as a report) should be double spaced.

- A list that is part of a single-spaced document (such as a letter) should be single spaced with a blank line before and after it.

- If additional text follows the bulleted list, press Enter after typing the bulleted item, then issue the command to end automatic bulleting. If a bulleted item is the last line of a report, do not press Enter.

Report 9
Numbered List

1. Carefully read the information in Report 9 before you type the report.
2. Type the report using the standard report format.
3. Use the numbering command to add numbers to the list as you type.

NUMBERED LIST

1. A numbered list's format is similar to a bulleted list's format. When the sequence of items in a list is important, use numbers instead of bullets.

2. The numbering command automatically inserts the number at the left margin and sets the indent for the first line of the list as well as any turnover lines.

3. A numbered list that is part of a double-spaced document should be double spaced.

4. A numbered list that is part of a single-spaced document should be single spaced with a blank line before and after it.

5. The numbering feature enables you to rearrange the items in your list without having to retype the numbers. As you move items, they will be

(continued on next page)

automatically renumbered in the correct sequence.

6. *If additional text follows the numbered list, press Enter after typing the last numbered item; then issue the command to end automatic numbering. If a numbered item is the last line of a report, do not press Enter.*

Report 10
Bulleted List

1. Open the file for Report 8.
2. Make the changes to the report as indicated by the proofreaders' marks.
3. Add this additional item to the end of the list: *When additional items are added to a list, position the insertion point at the end of the last item, press Enter, and type the new item.*

BULLETED LISTS

- To make items ~~in a list~~ easier to read, use either bullets or numbers. [a list's]

- When the ~~items~~ order is not important, use bullets instead of numbers. [of the items]

- The software command for automatically inserting bullets positions the bullet at the left margin and sets the indent for the ~~list's~~ first line as well as any turnover (second and succeeding) lines. [bullets] [of the item]

- The circle you see at the left of this sentence is ~~just one~~ example of a bullet. Large circles, diamonds, squares, or triangles may also be used as bullets. [an]

- A list ~~that is part of the body of~~ a double-spaced document (such as a report) should be double spaced. [within]

- A list ~~that is part of~~ a single-spaced document (such as a letter) should be single spaced with a blank line before and after it. [within]

- If additional text follows the bulleted list, press Enter after typing the bulleted item, then ~~issue the command to~~ end automatic bulleting. If a bulleted item is the last line of a report, do not press Enter.

Lesson 38 Rough-Draft Reports With Numbered Lists

GOALS: To type 35 wam/3'/4e; to learn more proofreaders' marks; to format rough-draft reports with numbered lists.

A. Type 2 times.

A. WARMUP

```
1        Jerry wrote a great article entitled "Interviewing      10
2   Techniques" on pp. 78 and 123!  A & B Bookstore expected a    22
3   sizable number of requests; thus far, 65% have been sold.     34
    |  1  |  2  |  3  |  4  |  5  |  6  |  7  |  8  |  9  |  10  |  11  |  12
```

SKILLBUILDING

B. Take three 12-second timings on each line. The scale below the last line shows your wam speed for a 12-second timing.

B. 12-SECOND SPEED SPRINTS

```
4   They used about two cubic feet of dirt to fill the planter.
5   The rocks she dug up made the work much harder than before.
6   Nancy will spend as much time as she must to fix the signs.
7   The men kept the keys to the town hall inside the blue box.
    | | | 5 | | | 10 | | | 15 | | | 20 | | | 25 | | | 30 | | | 35 | | | 40 | | | 45 | | | 50 | | | 55 | | | 60
```

C. DIAGNOSTIC PRACTICE: NUMBERS

Turn to the Diagnostic Practice: Numbers routine beginning on page SB-5. Type one of the Pretest/Posttest paragraphs and identify any errors made. Then type the corresponding drill lines 2 times for each number on which you made 2 or more errors and 1 time for each number on which you made only 1 error. Finally, repeat the same Pretest paragraph and compare your performance.

D. Take two 3-minute timings. Determine your speed and errors.

Goal: 35 wam/3'/4e

D. 3-MINUTE TIMING

```
8         Telecommuting is a word you may have heard before but    11
9   don't quite understand.  Very simply, it means working at      23
10  home instead of driving in to work.  Many people like the      34
11  convenience of working at home.  They realize they can save    46
12  money on expenses like gas, clothes, and child care.           57
13        Most home office workers use a computer in their job.    68
14  When their work is completed, they can just fax it to the      80
15  office.  If they need to communicate with other employees,     91
16  they can route calls to a fax or phone and never have to       103
17  leave home.                                                    105
    |  1  |  2  |  3  |  4  |  5  |  6  |  7  |  8  |  9  |  10  |  11  |  12
```

E. MORE PROOFREADERS' MARKS

1. Review the most frequently used proofreaders' marks introduced in Lesson 36.
2. Study the additional proofreaders' marks presented here.
3. Learn what each proofreaders' mark means before typing Report 11.

Proofreaders' Marks		Draft	Final Copy
SS	Single-space	SS ⌐first line / second line⌐	first line second line
ds	Double-space	ds ⌐first line / second line⌐	first line second line
...	Don't delete	a ~~true~~ story	a true story
◯	Spell out	the only ①	the only one
⌐	Move right	⌐Please⌐ send	Please send
⌐	Move left	⌐May I	May I
~~	Bold	Column Heading	**Column Heading**
ital	Italic	*ital* Time magazine	*Time* magazine
u/l	Underline	u/l Time magazine	<u>Time</u> magazine readers
↗	Move as shown	(readers) will see	will see
∽	Transpose	they all see	they see all

F. WORD PROCESSING: CUT, COPY, AND PASTE

Study Lesson 38 in your word processing manual. Complete all of the shaded steps while at your computer. Then format the jobs that follow.

Report 11
Report With List

1. Type this report following the standard report format. If necessary, refer to the illustration on page 44 in Lesson 24.
2. Use the numbering command to type the numbered list.
3. After typing the last item in the list, remember to end the automatic numbering.

(continued on next page)

ds [**CONTROLLING COPIER COSTS**
By Yong Lee

Controlling how and when the copier is used is one of the most difficult

challenges facing an office manager. The office copier is an essential tool that

u/l must be convenient and accessible. However, it is also one of the most

misused pieces of office equipment. Here are ⑥ guidelines for controlling

copier costs:

1. Monitor copier use by installing a system # of accountability such as a

    keypad unit. This unit identifies both the user and the ∧ number of copies

    made.

    ital
2. If a keypad unit is not convenient, ∧ use a card with a magnetic stripe that

    performs the same accountability functions as a keypad.

3. Use a debit # card system to limit the number of copies if excessive

    copying is the main concern.

    Begin
4. ~~Implement~~ a Records Management program to educate employees about

    the basic principles of controlling records ~~in an office~~. Records ital

    ital Management Quarterly should be required reading.

5. Implement a ~~paper~~ recycling plan to raise awareness of wasted paper

    caused by
    ~~through~~ excessive, ∧ unnecessary copying.

6. Encourage employees to store and exchange data electronically using

         s
    their computer ~~systems~~.

    If these methods are implemented ~~and enforced~~, copier costs ~~will~~ should drop

significantly. Ultimately, the goal is to provide employees with convenient and

                                    while
reasonable access to a copier ~~and~~ keeping costs as low as possible.

Report 12
Report With List

Open the file for Report 11 and make the following changes:

1. Change the title to **COPIER COST MANAGEMENT**.

2. Delete the last sentence in Item 1.

3. Add the words *for all employees* to the last sentence in Item 4.

4. Transpose the two sentences in the last paragraph.

Lesson 39   Bound Reports With Bulleted Lists

GOALS: To improve speed and accuracy; to refine language-arts skills in number expression; to format bound reports with bulleted lists.

A. Type 2 times.

A. WARMUP

```
1      Does Xavier know that at 8:04 a.m. his July sales      10
2 quota was realized?  Invoice #671 indicates a 9% increase!  22
3 Several of the employees weren't able to regain their lead. 34
```
| 1 | 2 | 3 | 4 | 5 | 6 | 7 | 8 | 9 | 10 | 11 | 12

SKILLBUILDING

B. Take a 1-minute timing on the first paragraph to establish your base speed. Then take four 1-minute timings on the remaining paragraphs. As soon as you equal or exceed your base speed on one paragraph, advance to the next, more difficult paragraph.

B. SUSTAINED PRACTICE: SYLLABIC INTENSITY

```
4      Taking care of aging parents is not a new trend.  This   11
5 issue has arisen more and more, since we are all now living   23
6 longer.  Companies are now trying to help out in many ways.   35

7      Help may come in many ways, ranging from financial aid   11
8 to sponsoring hospice or in-home respite care.  Employees may 23
9 find it difficult to work and care for aging parents.         34

10     Why are employers so interested in elder care?  Rising   11
11 interest is the result of a combination of several things.    23
12 The most notable is a marked increase in life expectancy.     34

13     Another trend is the increased participation of women,    11
14 the primary caregivers, in the workforce.  Businesses are     23
15 recognizing that work and family life are intertwined.        34
```
| 1 | 2 | 3 | 4 | 5 | 6 | 7 | 8 | 9 | 10 | 11 | 12

C. PROGRESSIVE PRACTICE: ALPHABET

Turn to the Progressive Practice: Alphabet routine beginning on page SB-7. Take six 30-second timings, starting at the point where you left off the last time.

LANGUAGE ARTS

D. Study the rules at the right.   # gen

D. NUMBER EXPRESSION

Rule: In general, spell out numbers 1 through 10, and use figures for numbers above 10.

Only nine copies of the report were mailed, even though 17 people requested a copy.

Rule: Use figures for dates (use *st, d,* or *th* only if the day precedes the month); all numbers if two or more related numbers both above and below ten are used in the same sentence; measurements (time, money, distance, weight, and percent); mixed numbers.

(continued on next page)

fig

On July 1 at 10 a.m., she ordered 2 printers, 3 keyboards, and 12 printer cartridges. The monthly budget allows 12 percent for office supplies.

On the 4th of July, we spent $65 to buy 20 pounds of meat for the picnic, which was held 4 3/5 miles away.

Rule: Spell out numbers used as the first word in a sentence; the smaller of two adjacent numbers; the words *million* and *billion* in even amounts (do not use decimals with even amounts); fractions.

Two million votes were counted, thereby assuring the two-thirds majority needed.

word

On Wednesday three 5-page reports were presented to the assembly.

Edit the sentences to correct any errors in number expression.

```
16  On the third of June, when she turns 60, 2 of her annuities
17  will have earned an average of 10 3/4 percent.
18  Seven investors were interested in buying 2 15-unit condos
19  if they were located within fifteen miles of each other.
20  The purchase price will be over $3,000,000.00 at 11 percent
21  interest; escrow will close on June 3d before five p.m.
22  The agent sent 7 ten-page letters to all the investors.
23  The parcel weighed two pounds.  She also mailed three post-
24  cards, twelve packages, and twenty-one letters on June 4.
```

FORMATTING

E. BOUND REPORTS

1. A left-bound report requires a wider left margin to allow for binding so that text is not hidden.

2. To format a bound report, add additional space to the left margin by increasing the margin by 0.5 inch.

F. WORD PROCESSING: MARGINS

Study Lesson 39 in your word processing manual. Complete all of the shaded steps while at your computer. Then format the jobs that follow.

DOCUMENT PROCESSING

Report 13
Multipage Bound Report With Bulleted List

1. Position the page number at the top right, and suppress the page number on the first page.

2. Change the left margin to add an extra

0.5 inch.

3. Set double spacing, and follow the standard report format to complete the report.

EMPLOYEE HEALTH CARE

By Peggy Stevens

gen

Health care reform has been hotly debated in Congress for at least 18 months in an effort to curb the rising cost of health care. Businesses are

fig, # word

spending more than $800 billion a year on health care. Although it is unlikely that Congress will ever reach a unanimous decision regarding health care

(continued on next page)

reform, it is clear that companies are going to have to take an active role in controlling their health care costs if they are to survive financially.

WELLNESS PROGRAMS

fig

gen

word

fig

fig

Every year on January 1 at exactly 12 a.m., a new year begins. For most people, this means at least one or two resolutions for making the coming year a healthful one. Businesses are realizing that if they implement innovative employee wellness programs, such resolutions can translate into substantial savings in health care costs. Three examples of innovative approaches are as follows:

- Some businesses offer employees as much as a 40 percent reduction in their health care premium as an incentive to participate in a wellness program.

- Some businesses are giving employees cash rebates of $100 or more if they show improvement in things like blood pressure and cholesterol.

- Educating employees about topics such as how to manage stress and quit smoking has been an effective approach.

Health care costs should be reduced because a healthier employee will need fewer visits to the doctor and fewer medications and treatments. Also, if employees are healthier, it makes sense that they will have fewer sick days. A healthier body should also lead to more productivity and energy on the job.

PROGRAM IMPLEMENTATION

Clearly, there is a great incentive for both employers and employees to be interested in implementing some type of wellness program. With proper planning, such innovative programs could be a positive and productive answer to reducing health care costs for everyone involved.

Report 14
Multipage Bound
Report With Bulleted
List

Open the file for Report 13 and make the following changes:

1. Change the title to **HEALTH CARE REFORM**.
2. Add the subtitle *Business Alliance Symposium*.
3. Change the byline to *Elaine Shibata*.
4. Move the last sentence of the first paragraph (*Although it is unlikely . . .*)

to the end of the report directly after the last sentence.

5. Add this sentence to the end of the first paragraph: *Some companies cannot afford to wait for Congress to act and have devised their own solutions to health care.*
6. Delete both side headings.

Lesson 40   Reports With Displays

GOALS: To type 36 wam/3'/4e; to format reports with displays.

A. Type 2 times.

A. WARMUP

```
1        On July 15, a check for exactly $329.86 was mailed to    11
2  Zak & Quinn, Inc.; they never received Check #104.  Does       22
3  Gary know if the check cleared the company's bank account?     34
   |  1  |  2  |  3  |  4  |  5  |  6  |  7  |  8  |  9  |  10  |  11  |  12
```

SKILLBUILDING

Pretest
Take a 1-minute timing. Determine your speed and errors.

Practice
Speed Emphasis: If you made 2 or fewer errors on the Pretest, type each *individual* line 2 times.
Accuracy Emphasis: If you made 3 or more errors, type each *group* of lines (as though it were a paragraph) 2 times.

Posttest
Repeat the Pretest timing and compare performance.

F. Take two 3-minute timings. Determine your speed and errors.

Goal: 36 wam/3'/4e

B. PRETEST: HORIZONTAL REACHES

```
4        The chief thinks the alarm was a decoy for the armed    11
5  agent who coyly dashed away.  She was dazed as she dodged      22
6  a blue sedan.  He lured her to the edge of the high bluff.     34
   |  1  |  2  |  3  |  4  |  5  |  6  |  7  |  8  |  9  |  10  |  11  |  12
```

C. PRACTICE: IN REACHES

```
7  oy foyer loyal buoys enjoy decoy coyly royal cloy ploy toys
8  ar argue armed cared alarm cedar sugar radar area earn hear
9  lu lucid lunch lured bluff value blunt fluid luck lush blue
```

D. PRACTICE: OUT REACHES

```
10  ge geese genes germs agent edges dodge hinge gear ages page
11  da daily dazed dance adapt sedan adage panda dash date soda
12  hi hints hiked hired chief think ethic aphid high ship chip
```

E. POSTTEST: HORIZONTAL REACHES

F. 3-MINUTE TIMING

```
13        Employee complaints are often viewed as a negative    10
14  power in a workforce.  In fact, these complaints should      22
15  be viewed as a chance to communicate with an employee and    34
16  improve morale.  Ignoring complaints does not make them      46
17  go away.  Listening to complaints objectively can help to    57
18  solve a small problem before it turns into a big one.        68
19        Often workers expect a chance to be heard by a person  79
20  who is willing to listen quite openly.  You must learn to    91
21  recognize when a person wants to remain unknown so that      102
22  he or she will be free to talk.                              108
    |  1  |  2  |  3  |  4  |  5  |  6  |  7  |  8  |  9  |  10  |  11  |  12
```

G. REPORTS WITH INDENTED DISPLAYS

1. A paragraph that is quoted or needs special emphasis in a report may be made to stand out from the rest of the report by displaying it single-spaced and indented 0.5 inch from both the left and the right margins (instead of enclosing it in quotation marks).

2. Use the indent commands in your word processing software to display a paragraph.

H. WORD PROCESSING: INDENT AND WIDOWS AND ORPHANS

Study Lesson 40 in your word processing manual. Complete all of the shaded steps while at your computer. Then format the jobs that follow.

DOCUMENT PROCESSING

Report 15
Multipage Report
With Displayed
Paragraph

1. Position the page number at the top right, and suppress the page number on the first page.

2. Follow the standard report format.

3. Change to single spacing at the start of the displayed paragraph, and indent the displayed paragraph 0.5 inch from both margins.

4. After typing the displayed paragraph, press Enter twice; then change to double spacing.

TRAVEL POLICY

Effective July 1, 19—

Rockmart International

As of July 1, 19— the travel policy guidelines will be changed to adhere to Rockmart Internationals limited-expenditures position that was mandated at the board meeting on June 1, 19—. This travel policy will apply to all employees of Rockmart International and will cover in-state and out-of-state travel both.

The new travel policy, as stipulated by the board on June 1 and to become effective on July 1, is as follows:

All Rockmart International employee travel will be restricted to an amount not greater than $500 per month for in-state travel and $1,000 per month for out-of-state travel. This dollar amount will apply to meals, transportation, lodging, and miscellaneous expenses.

(continued on next page)

Travel budgets for each division vary during the months of the year. Because of this variation, division managers may request that their travel moneys be "banked" so that the months of ~~excessive~~ extensive travel can be accommodated by this policy. Any banked travel moneys remaining at the end of the fiscal year will be reallocated.

Divisions are requested to submit quarterly travel reports to the Albuquerque office no later than 14 days prior to the quarter during which travel is anticipated. Travel form A94-022 is to be used for all requests submitted after July. The form should be sent via E-mail to the office ~~in~~ Albuquerque.

Form A94-022 requires that all transportation costs, lodging expenses, and meals be filed with the division--and subsequently with ~~regional~~ headquarters--no later than 7 days after completion of the travel. These expenses will be individually itemized for each trip. Related expenses (duplicating, telephone, and similar expenses) are to be included on Page 2 of the travel form. This policy supersedes Policy A90-324, dated March 1994, and will be in effect until further notice.

ds

Report 16

Progress Check
Multipage Bound
Report With List

1. Format this report as a multipage bound report with a numbered list.

2. Make all changes as indicated by the proofreaders' marks.

ERGONOMICS ~~IN THE~~ OFFICE

By Joyce Moore

How many times have you sat down in front of the computer only to find that after a few minutes of work your neck ~~hurts~~ aches and your wrists are stiff? Unfortunately, this condition is more often the norm rather than the exception as repetitive stress injuries ~~are increasing~~ continue to increase at an alarming rate. So far, the Government is doing very little to provide any guidelines for work place standards. Clearly, office ergonomics will ~~continue to~~ become increasingly important to corporations as they struggle with ~~lowered~~ decreased productivity and increased health care costs. ¶Ergonomics is a broad term that includes adjusting the work environment to suit the comfort and needs of the employee rather than having the employee adjust to the work environment.

(continued on next page)

Most people associate ergonomics primarily with office furniture--for example, adjustable chairs and desks. however, it also includes things like lighting, air quality, and noise control. Providing a workstation that is sound ergonomically is the responsibility of the employer. ⑤guidelines can help an employer design such a workstation:

1. Choose lighting that is adjustable such as swivel-based, swing-arm lamps that can be relocated.

2. Choose office furniture that is adjustable. Chair and desk heights should be adjustable for both height and angle.

3. Provide wrist rests on keyboards to avoid carpal tunnel syndrome injuries.

4. use air filtration systems to screen out allergens and pollutants.

5. Provide noise shields on all printers and carpeting in all work areas to reduce noise pollution.

Clearly, each employee has individual needs that must be considered in the planning of an ergonomically sound work station. Corporate leaders must continue to focus on providing a work station that is comfortable and safe for everyone. In doing so, they will fulfill their responsibility to their employees and in turn find a workforce that is more productive, happier, and healthier.

ds

Test 2-A
3-Minute Timing

1	You need to give yourself a huge pat on the back right	11
2	now. You have just finished learning about letters, memos,	23
3	reports, and tables. You have also increased your speed	35
4	and accuracy well beyond the first day of class. All of	46
5	this hard work is quite an amazing accomplishment.	56
6	You have seen that you can learn a wide range of word	67
7	processing commands and master them. You can expect even	79
8	more progress if you will just continue to learn as much	90
9	as you can each day. Ask questions and keep moving toward	102
10	a new goal each and every day.	108

| 1 | 2 | 3 | 4 | 5 | 6 | 7 | 8 | 9 | 10 | 11 | 12 |

Test 2-B

Letter 9

Block Style

February 14, 19— / Ms. Rose Garcia / Dean, Patten, & Epstein / 2700 Mission Boulevard / Santa Clara, CA 95052 / Dear Ms. Garcia:

Each year the Office Administration Department honors students who will graduate at the end of the semester. These students have worked long and hard to reach their goals, and the Certificates and Awards Program is very important to them.

Your presentation at our last Advisory Committee Meeting was very impressive! I have enclosed a copy of the minutes for you. Because of your outstanding reputation in the legal field, I would like to invite you to be the keynote speaker for our annual Certificates and Awards Program to be held on April 12.

I know that you began your higher education here at our community college. Having you return as a successful attorney with a promising future would be an inspiration to the students. I will be calling you in the next few days so that we can discuss the program in more detail.

Sincerely, / Janet McKay / Chairperson / {urs} / Enclosure

1. Center the table vertically.
2. Center column headings and adjust the column widths.
3. Center the table horizontally.

ADVISORY COMMITTEE MEMBERS		
Name	**Title**	**Company**
Stacey Erranova	Vice President	Office Temps, Inc.
William Zimmerman	Attorney at Law	Baird & Findling
Brenda Chandler	Account Manager	Worldwide Surety

PARKING POLICY

Fall semester

Please read these following guide lines regarding the rules and regulations governing the parking of vehicles on school property:

FACULTY AND STAFF PARKING

Certain lots have been reserved and designated specifically for use by the Faculty and Staff. These lots require a key card to gain entry. A valid and current parking permit must be prominently displayed on the dashboard of all vehicles. If such permits are missing, the vehicle will be cited and could be towed.

Student parking

Several parking lots and parking structures have been assigned designated for Student parking. A valid, current student parking permit must be affixed to the rear bumper of all vehicles. If such permits are missing, the vehicles may be cited. The following lots have been designated for student use:

- Lot 1 on the corner of Melrose Blvd. and Vermont Ave.
- Lot 3 on the corner of Heliotrope and Santa Monica Blvd. This lot will also accommodate 9 disabled parking spaces.

The city of Los Angeles maintains the streets on a regular basis. Please check all signs before parking in any location.

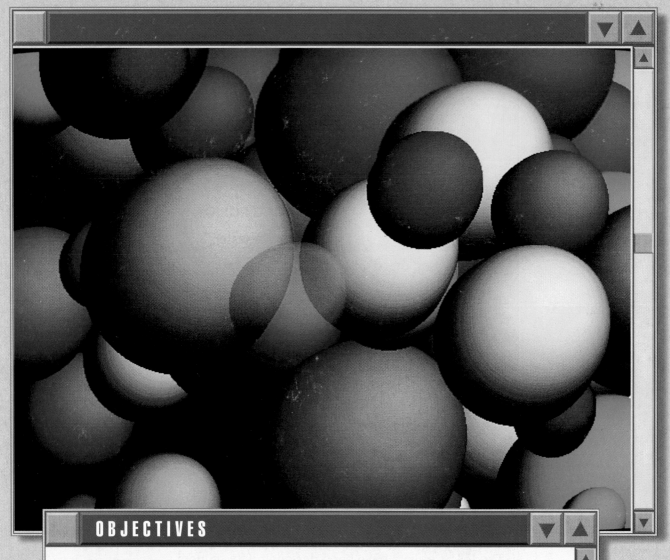

OBJECTIVES

KEYBOARDING
- To type 40 wam/5'/5e.

LANGUAGE ARTS
- To refine proofreading skills and correctly use proofreaders' marks.
- To correctly capitalize, punctuate, and spell.
- To recognize subject/verb agreement and refine composing skills.

WORD PROCESSING
- To use the word processing

commands necessary to complete the document processing activities.

DOCUMENT PROCESSING
- To format modified-block style and personal business letters; memos; tables; reports with special features; employment documents; and lists.

TECHNICAL
- To answer correctly at least 90 percent of the questions on an objective test.

Lesson 41	# Business Letters

GOALS: To improve speed and accuracy; to refine language-arts skills in the use of commas; to format business letters.

A. Type 2 times.

A. WARMUP

```
1        Quite a night!  All sixty senior citizens (including    11
2   the handicapped) really enjoyed that play.  Over 3/4 of      22
3   the tickets were sold; most had been sold by Jeff's group.   34
    |   1   |   2   |   3   |   4   |   5   |   6   |   7   |   8   |   9   |   10   |   11   |   12
```

SKILLBUILDING

B. Take three 12-second timings on each line. The scale below the last line shows your wam speed for a 12-second timing.

B. 12-SECOND SPEED SPRINTS

```
4   Many of the men were at the auction when the vase was sold.
5   Some of the women were also there to buy some old antiques.
6   Jan was hoping to buy two chairs and a lamp at the auction.
7   Len was one of the six people who found an old wooden desk.
    |  |  |  5  |  |  |  10  |  |  |  15  |  |  |  20  |  |  |  25  |  |  |  30  |  |  |  35  |  |  |  40  |  |  |  45  |  |  |  50  |  |  |  55  |  |  |  60
```

C. PROGRESSIVE PRACTICE: ALPHABET

Turn to the Progressive Practice: Alphabet routine beginning on page SB-7. Take six 30-second timings, starting at the point where you left off the last time.

LANGUAGE ARTS

D. Study the rules at the right.

,date

,place

Edit the sentences to correct any errors in the use of commas.

D. COMMAS

Rule: Use a comma before and after the year in a complete date.

On December 7, 1996, the *Tribune* reviewed the Pearl Harbor events.
But: The *News Monthly* dated December 1996 reviewed the same events.

Rule: Use a comma before and after a state or country that follows a city (but not before a ZIP Code).

Sioux City, Iowa, is a lovely place in which to live.
But: Sioux City, Iowa 51102, is where she was born.

```
8    The warehouse building will be ready in September, 1998.
9    The attorney told a clerk to use June 30, 1994 as the date.
10   The report was sent to Nagoya, Japan on March 14, 1996.
11   The move to Toledo, Ohio, was scheduled for November, 1996.
```

E. TITLES IN CORRESPONDENCE

1. Always use a courtesy title before a person's name in the inside address of a letter; for example, *Mr., Mrs.,* or *Dr.*
2. In the closing lines, do not use a courtesy title before a man's name. A courtesy title may be included in a woman's typed name or her signature.
3. Type a person's title on the same line with the name (separated by a comma) if the title is short, or on the line below.
4. When possible, use a person's name in the salutation. The correct form for the salutation is the courtesy title and the last name. If you do not know the name of the person, use a job title or *Ladies and Gentlemen.*

INSIDE ADDRESSES	CLOSING LINES
Mrs. Rose E. Nebel, Owner Nebel Financial Services	Sincerely yours,
Dr. Prayad Chayapruks Executive Director Foy Memorial Hospital	*Mildred D. King* Miss Mildred D. King Adjunct Instructor
Mr. Craig R. Weiger Manager, Dahlke Oil Co.	Cordially,
Waynesville Printing Company	*(Ms.)Evelyn Marketto* Evelyn Marketto Senior Programmer Analyst
SALUTATIONS	Respectfully yours,
Dear Ms. Nebel:	*Jose R. Minuego* Jose R. Minuego Service Representative
Dear Dr. Chayapruks:	
Dear Mr. Weiger:	
Dear Sales Manager:	
Ladies and Gentlemen:	

F. COMPLIMENTARY CLOSINGS

Every letter should end with a complimentary closing. Some frequently used complimentary closings are *Sincerely,* *Sincerely yours, Yours truly, Cordially,* and *Respectfully yours.*

DOCUMENT PROCESSING

Letter 10
Business Letter in Block Style

,place

,date

{Current Date} / Mrs. Phyllis Fenske / 4304 Keller Lane / Mount Vernon, WA 98273-4156 / Dear Mrs. Fenske:

¶We at Garner Homes feel that your selection of a Suncourt town house is just the right choice for you.

¶All units at the Timber Creek site in Mount Vernon, Washington, have been built since March 1993. The Suncourt was awarded three national awards.

¶Thank you, Mrs. Fenske. If you have questions, please let us know.

Sincerely, / Alfred A. Long / Sales Director / {urs}

Letter 11
Business Letter in Block Style

,place

,date

{Current Date} / Mr. Lawrence S. Alwich / 1800 East Hollywood Avenue / Salt Lake City, UT 84108 / Dear Mr. Alwich:

¶Our radio station would like you to reply to our editorial about the proposed airport site that aired from Provo, Utah, on May 15.

¶Of the more than 100 request letters for equal time, we selected yours because you touched on most of the relevant points of this topic.

¶We will contact you further about taping your rebuttal on June 4.

Sincerely, / Karin L. Londgren / General Manager / {urs}

Letter 12
Business Letter in Block Style

Open the file for Letter 10 and revise it to be sent to Mr. and Mrs. Tony L. Carravetti, who live at 2906 28th Avenue South in Lilliwaup, WA 98555. They recently purchased a Delcourt town house, which has received two national awards.

Lesson 42 Personal-Business Letters

GOALS: To type 37 wam/3′/3e; to format personal-business letters.

A. Type 2 times.

A. WARMUP

```
1      B & Z requested 4 boxes at $37/box.  The items they     11
2  wanted were #6 and #7.  A discount of 20% would bring the   22
3  total to approximately $950.  Will you verify the order?    33
   |  1  |  2  |  3  |  4  |  5  |  6  |  7  |  8  |  9  | 10  | 11  | 12
```

SKILLBUILDING

Pretest
Take a 1-minute timing. Determine your speed and errors.

B. PRETEST: VERTICAL REACHES

```
4      Kim knew that her skills at the keyboard made her a     11
5  top rival for the job.  About six persons had seen her race  23
6  home to see if the mail showed the company was aware of it.  34
   |  1  |  2  |  3  |  4  |  5  |  6  |  7  |  8  |  9  | 10  | 11  | 12
```

C. PRACTICE: UP REACHES

Practice
   Speed Emphasis: If you made 2 or fewer errors on the Pretest, type each *individual* line 2 times.
   Accuracy Emphasis: If you made 3 or more errors, type each *group* of lines (as though it were a paragraph) 2 times.

```
7  se seven reset seams sedan loses eases serve used seed dose
8  ki skids kings kinks skill kitty kites kilts kite kids kick
9  rd board horde wards sword award beard third cord hard lard
```

D. PRACTICE: DOWN REACHES

```
10  ac races pacer backs ached acute laced facts each acre lace
11  kn knave knack knife knows knoll knots knelt knew knee knit
12  ab about abide label above abode sable abbey drab able cabs
```

Posttest
Repeat the Pretest timing and compare performance.

E. POSTTEST: VERTICAL REACHES

F. Take two 3-minute timings. Determine your speed and errors.

Goal: 37 wam/3′/3e

F. 3-MINUTE TIMING

```
13      The size of their first paychecks after they finish     11
14  college seems quite high to some young men and women.  They  23
15  then rent a place to live that is just too expensive, or     35
16  they may buy a new car with a huge monthly payment.  For     47
17  some it takes a while to learn that there are other items    58
18  in the monthly budget.                                       63
19      Some of these items are food, student loans, renters'    74
20  insurance, credit cards, car insurance, health insurance,    86
21  utilities, and miscellaneous expenses.  One further goal     97
22  should be to start a savings plan by putting a small amount 109
23  aside from each paycheck.                                   114
   |  1  |  2  |  3  |  4  |  5  |  6  |  7  |  8  |  9  | 10  | 11  | 12
```

G. PERSONAL-BUSINESS LETTERS

Personal-business letters are prepared by individuals to conduct their personal business affairs. To format a personal-business letter:

1. Type the letter on plain paper or personal stationery, not letterhead.
2. Include the writer's address in the letter directly below the writer's name in the closing lines. (Another acceptable format is to type the return address before the date at the top of the letter.)
3. Since the writer of the letter usually types the letter, reference initials are not used.

DOCUMENT PROCESSING

Letter 13
Personal-Business
Letter in Block Style

↓center vertically
{Current Date}
↓4X

Mr. Phillip M. Fesmire, Director
City Parks and Recreation Department
4507 Renwick Avenue
Syracuse, NY 13210-0475

Dear Mr. Fesmire:

Thank you for the excellent manner in which your department accommodated our family last summer. About 120 Fensteins attended the reunion at Rosedale Park on July 28.

I should like to again request that Shelter 5 be reserved for our next year's family reunion on July 27, 19--. A confirmation of the date from your office will be appreciated.

The facilities at Rosedale are in very good condition. The new kitchen area is excellent. Please express our appreciation to those who help make it an exemplary facility.

Sincerely,
↓4X

Miss Vivian L. Fenstein
2410 Farnham Road
Syracuse, NY 13219

Personal-business letter in block style with (a) all lines beginning at the left margin and (b) standard punctuation.

Letter 14
Personal-Business
Letter in Block Style

This personal-business letter is from Walter G. Halverson, who lives at 482 22d Street East in Lawrence, KS 66049. Use today's date, and supply the appropriate salutation. The letter is to be sent to Mr. Robert A. Sotherden, Administrator / Glencrest Nursing Home / 2807 Crossgate Circle / Lawrence, KS 66047.

(continued on next page)

¶Thanks to you and dozens of other people, the fall crafts sale at Glencrest was highly successful. I am very appreciative of the ways in which you helped.

¶I particularly wish to thank you for transporting the display tables and chairs to Glencrest and back to the community center. Many people from the community center attended the sale and commented about how nice it was of you and your staff to support such an activity.

¶Having a parent who is a resident of the home, I am grateful that so many people from the Lawrence area volunteer their services to help make life more pleasant for the residents. Please accept my special thanks to you and your staff for supporting the many activities that benefit all Glencrest residents.

Letter 15
Personal-Business
Letter in Block Style

Open the file for Letter 14 and revise it as follows: Send the letter to Mrs. Diana Hagedon / Hagedon Associates / 2014 30th Street West / Lawrence, KS 66047. Replace the second paragraph with the following: *I particularly wish to thank you and your team for handling the financial transactions for residents in need of help. Their day was brighter because of you and the others who helped. Thank you for your kindness.*

Lesson 43   Memos

GOALS: To improve speed and accuracy;
to refine language-arts skills in proofreading;
to format memos.

A. Type 2 times.

A. WARMUP

```
1       "Rex analyzed the supply," Marge said.  Based on the      11
2  results, a purchase request for 7# at $140 (2% of what we      22
3  needed) was issued.  Was Jack surprised by this?  Vi was!      34
   |  1  |  2  |  3  |  4  |  5  |  6  |  7  |  8  |  9  |  10  |  11  |  12
```

SKILLBUILDING

B. Take three 12-second timings on each line. The scale below the last line shows your wam speed for a 12-second timing.

B. 12-SECOND SPEED SPRINTS

```
4  Nine of those new women were on time for the first session.
5  She could see that many of those old memos should be filed.
6  Forty of the men were at the game when that siren went off.
7  The line at the main hall was so long that I did not go in.
   | | | |5| | | |10| | | |15| | |20| | |25| | |30| | |35| | |40| | |45| | |50| | |55| | |60
```

C. PROGRESSIVE PRACTICE: NUMBERS

Turn to the Progressive Practice: Numbers routine beginning on page SB-11. Take six 30-second timings, starting at the point where you left off the last time.

D. Type the columns 2 times. Press Tab to move from column to column.

D. TECHNIQUE PRACTICE: TAB

8	J. Barnes	P. Varanth	S. Childers	M. Christenson
9	F. Gilsrud	J. Benson	D. Bates	M. Jordan
10	B. Harringer	J. Suksi	J. Lee	P. North
11	V. Hill	A. Budinger	T. Gonyer	S. Kravolec

 **LANGUAGE ARTS**

E. Compare this paragraph with the 3-minute timing on page 102. Edit the paragraph to correct any errors.

E. PROOFREADING

12 Some type of insurance of this kind are straight life
13 for single and children, student health, dread disease,
14 and hospitable indemnity. Others are home morgage, credit
15 card, rental-car, job-loss, and contact-lens loss. A study
16 of policies may save you money every year.

 **DOCUMENT PROCESSING**

Memo 5

Most memos are typed with blocked paragraphs (no indentations) and 1 blank line between paragraphs.

The use of *MEMO TO:* eliminates the need to type the word *MEMO-RANDUM* at the top of the document.

After typing the colon at the end of each bold heading, tab once to reach the point where the heading entries begin.

Type your own reference initials.

MEMO TO: Charles A. Cornelius, President

FROM: Alfred A. Long, Sales Director

DATE: October 20, 19—

SUBJECT: Marketing of Deer Run site

¶The Deer Run project continues to be a high priority venture. Curtis Marlowe and his staff assure me that the ~~the~~ models have been designed to attract first-time homes buyers. I am asking Melissa Sampson to assume total marketing responsibility for the project. A tentative plan for media exposure will be due with in ten days of her appointment. She will likely have some quite imaginative strategies in her plan. I am confident that the fine reputation of Cornelius Homes, Inc., will be further enchanced by the Deer Run project. A schedule of progress reports for the next year is attached.

{urs}

Attachment

Memo 6

MEMO TO: Melissa Sampson, Sales Associate / **FROM:** Alfred A. Long, Sales Director / **DATE:** October 20, 19— / **SUBJECT:** Deer Run Model Homes

¶The first model homes at the Deer Run site will be ready for showing by January 1. On the basis of your sales performance during the past year, I would like to have you assume total marketing responsibility for the project.

¶This may well come as a complete surprise to you. For that reason, please delay your decision until November 1. You likely will want to think through the nature of this assignment and discuss implications with your family.

¶I know that you can do a fine job with this project; I hope your answer will be "Yes!" / {urs}

Memo 7

The use of nicknames and the omission of middle initials and courtesy titles reflect the informal nature of memos as compared with letters.

The word *RE* is sometimes used in place of the word *SUBJECT* in a memo or letter.

Remember, do not indent the paragraphs in a memo.

Remember to type your own reference initials.

MEMO TO: Pat Fillmore

FROM: Hank Swanson, Personnel Director

DATE: October 20, 19--

RE: Promotion to Department Head

You will be pleased to learn that on November 1 you will be promoted to the position of head of the Housewares Department. This is a reflection of the confidence we have in you based on your performance at Layton's Department Store over the past 18 months.

The Housewares Department plays a big role in achieving the objectives of our anchor store in downtown Lowell. There is a need for someone with broad experience in the retail field who can provide leadership in this department.

Pat, I am confident that as head of the Housewares Department you will fit in well as a member of the Layton management team. Congratulations!

Lesson 44 — Business Letters

GOALS: To type 37 wam/3'/3e; to format business letters.

A. Type 2 times.

A. WARMUP

```
1        Three travel agencies (Jepster & Vilani, Quin & Bott,    11
2  and Zeplin & Wexter) sold the most travel tickets for the     23
3  past 6 months.  They sold 785, 834, and 960 total tickets.    34
   |  1  |  2  |  3  |  4  |  5  |  6  |  7  |  8  |  9  |  10  |  11  |  12
```

 SKILLBUILDING

B. DIAGNOSTIC PRACTICE: ALPHABET

Turn to the Diagnostic Practice: Alphabet routine beginning on page SB-2. Type one of the Pretest/Posttest paragraphs and identify any errors made. Then type the corresponding drill lines 2 times for each letter on which you made 2 or more errors and 1 time for each letter on which you made only 1 error. Finally, repeat the same Pretest paragraph and compare your performance.

C. SUSTAINED PRACTICE: NUMBERS AND SYMBOLS

4	The proposed road improvement program was approved	10
5	by the county commissioners at their last meeting. There	22
6	were about ten citizens who spoke on behalf of the project.	34
7	The plan calls for blacktopping a 14-mile stretch on	11
8	County Road #235. This is the road that is commonly called	23
9	the "roller coaster" because of all the curves and hills.	34
10	There will be 116 miles blacktopped by J & J, Inc.	10
11	(commonly referred to as the Jones Brothers*). J & J's	22
12	office is at 1798 30th Avenue past the 22d Street bridge.	33
13	Minor road repair costs range from $10,784 to a high	11
14	of $63,450 (39% of the total program costs). The "county	22
15	inspector" is to hold the project costs to 105% of budget!	34

| 1 | 2 | 3 | 4 | 5 | 6 | 7 | 8 | 9 | 10 | 11 | 12

D. Take two 3-minute timings. Determine your speed and errors.

Goal: 37 wam/3'/3e

D. 3-MINUTE TIMING

16	Many people would be quite amazed to find out that	10
17	they are buying insurance which has the same coverage they	22
18	already have or which is too expensive for what one may get	34
19	back after a loss. We should all take time to check our	46
20	policies to ensure that we do not make this mistake.	56
21	Some types of insurance of this kind are straight life	67
22	for singles and children, student health, dread-disease,	79
23	and hospital indemnity. Others are home mortgage, credit	90
24	card, rental-car, job-loss, and contact-lens loss. A study	102
25	of policies might save you money each year.	111

| 1 | 2 | 3 | 4 | 5 | 6 | 7 | 8 | 9 | 10 | 11 | 12

FORMATTING

E. COPY NOTATIONS

Making file copies of all documents you prepare is a good business practice. At times you may also need copies to send to people other than the addressee of the original document.

A copy notation is typed on a document to indicate that someone else besides the addressee is receiving a copy. (See the illustration on page 103.)

1. Type the copy notation on the line below the reference initials or below the attachment or enclosure notation.
2. At the left margin type a lowercase *c* followed by a colon.
3. Press Tab and type the name of the person receiving the copy.
4. If more than one person is receiving a copy, list the names, single spaced, one beneath the other and aligned at the tab.

(continued on next page)

Sincerely,

Lester A. Fagerlie

Lester A. Fagerlie
Superintendent

urs
Enclosure
c: Mrs. Coretta D. Rice
       Dr. Thomas Moore

DOCUMENT PROCESSING

Letter 16
Business Letter in Block Style

{Current Date} / Mr. and Mrs. Richard Belson / 783 Wellcourt Lane / Mount Vernon, WA 98273-4156 / Dear Mr. and Mrs. Belson:

¶Marian Dickenson has informed me of the visits that she has had with you, and we are pleased that you have made a decision to purchase a home from Garner Homes. We can understand your indecision about purchasing a town house or a one-family house.

¶Your decision likely will be based on these basic differences. With a one-family house you will have the responsibility for the maintenance of both the interior and the exterior. With a town house, of course, you will have responsibility for only the interior. However, you will share the building with one, two, or three other families. Also, you must pay monthly fees to the homeowners' association and abide by their policies.

¶Either Marian or I will be happy to discuss your concerns with you at a time that is convenient. We shall look forward to your call.

Sincerely, / Alfred A. Long / Sales Director / {urs} / c: Marian Dickenson

Letter 17
Business Letter in Block Style

Prepare another letter from Mr. Long (Letter 16). Use the current date and send the letter to Miss Allison E. Grinager / 2408 12th Street / Ellenburg, WA 98926. Use the appropriate salutation and add a copy notation to Marian Dickenson.

¶Thank you for making the decision to purchase a Garner home. Marian Dickenson and I both think that the Delcourt model was the right choice for you. You will enjoy your beautiful new town house for many years.

¶As we agreed, the closing date has been set for November 27 at our office. The interior is completely finished, and the remaining landscaping work will be completed early in the spring of next year.

¶Again, thank you for selecting the Delcourt from Garner Homes. We will have pleasant memories of our several planning sessions.

Letter 18
Business Letter in Block Style

Open the file for Letter 17 and revise it as follows:
1. Send the letter to Ms. Lois Peterson, who lives at 1900 Madison Street in Mount Vernon, WA 98273-0456.
2. Change the closing date to December 1.
3. Delete the last sentence of the letter.

Lesson 45 Letters in Modified-Block Style

GOALS: To improve speed and accuracy; to refine language-arts skills in composing; to format modified-block-style letters.

A. Type 2 times.

A. WARMUP

```
1       Lex was quite pleased with his travel plans; the trip    11
2   to Bozeman was on Flight #578 on July 30, and the return is   23
3   on August 12 on Flight #64.  The ticket will cost $1,090.     34
    | 1  | 2  | 3  | 4  | 5  | 6  | 7  | 8  | 9  | 10 | 11 | 12
```

SKILLBUILDING

B. PACED PRACTICE

Turn to the Paced Practice routine beginning on page SB-14. Take three 2-minute timings, starting at the point where you left off the last time.

LANGUAGE ARTS

C. Answer each question with a complete sentence.

C. COMPOSING

4   What are your best traits that you will bring to your job when you graduate?
5   What are the best traits that you will want to see in your new boss?
6   Would you like to work for a small company or a large company?
7   How much money will you expect to earn each month in your first job?
8   Would you like that first job to be in a small town or a large city?
9   As you begin your first job, what career goal will you have in mind?

FORMATTING

D. MODIFIED-BLOCK-STYLE LETTERS

The modified-block style is one of the most commonly used formats for business letters.

1. Center the letter vertically.
2. Type the date beginning at the centerpoint of the page.
3. Press Enter 4 times and type the inside address at the left margin.
4. Insert 1 blank line before and after the salutation.
5. Type the paragraphs blocked at the left margin (the preferred style) or indented 0.5 inch. Leave 1 blank line between paragraphs.
6. Press Enter twice after the body of the letter and type the complimentary closing at the centerpoint.

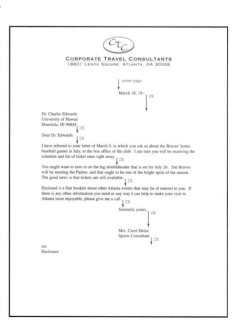

(continued on next page)

7. Press Enter 4 times and type the writer's identification beginning at the centerpoint.

8. Double-space and type your reference initials.

E. WORD PROCESSING: TAB SET AND RULER

Study Lesson 45 in your word processing manual. Complete all of the shaded steps while at your computer. Then format the jobs that follow.

Letter 19
Business Letter in Modified-Block Style

↓ center vertically

November 29, 19—
↓4X

Mr. and Mrs. Arvey Gates-Henderson

2308 Hannegan Road

Bellingham, Wa 9822~~5~~ 6
≡ Gates-↓2X

Do not indent the paragraphs.

Dear Mr. and Mrs. ^Henderson:
↓2X

Delores Matlon, who hosted our Ridgeway open house last Saturday, has referred your unanswered questions to me. We are pleased that you are interested in a Garner home.
↓2X

The usual payment/down is 20 per cent of the total selling price, but some lending agencies require a smaller amount in certain situations. Garner Homes is not itself involved in home financing, but we work with the financial institutions shown on the enclosed list.
↓2X

Yes, the lot you prefer can accommodate a walk out basement. Delores will be in touch with you soon. We can have your new ridgeway ready for occupancy within 90 days.
≡
↓2X

Sincerely,
↓4X

ss ⌐ Alfred A. Long

Sales Director
↓2X

urs

Enclosure

Use November 30, 19—, as the date as you format this personal-business letter to be sent to the Sales Manager at Bachmann's Nursery and Landscaping / 3410 Oneta Avenue / Youngstown, OH 44500-2175. The letter is from Marvin L. Norgaard / 4782 Saranac Avenue / Youngstown, OH 44505-6207. Use the automatic numbering feature for the numbered paragraphs.

If necessary, reset a tab for the numbered list.

Dear Sales Manager:

As you requested on the telephone, I am providing the following list of events relating to my tree problem.

1. On April 15 my wife and I purchased four silver maples at your branch in Warren.

2. We purchased four Japanese red maples at your branch in Niles later that afternoon.

3. After about three months one silver maple and one red maple had died. I phoned both the Warren and Niles branches several times, but no one returned my messages.

As these trees were expensive, I fully expect that you will replace them next spring. I shall look forward to hearing from you.

Sincerely yours,

Letter 21

Progress Check
Business Letter in
Modified-Block Style

Set tabs where necessary.

{Current Date} / Mr. Marvin L. Norgaard / 4782 Saranac Avenue / Youngstown, OH 44505-6207 / Dear Mr. Norgaard:

¶This is in response to your recent letter:

¶1. Your two trees will be replaced without cost next spring. The new trees will match the others in both size and color. A copy of our warranty is enclosed.

¶2. The survival rate for trees cannot be perfect; however, we are indeed sorry that you have had to have this temporary setback.

¶3. The communication breakdown with our two branch offices should not have occurred. We will take steps to ensure that this will not happen in the future.

¶You can be confident that the appearance of your yard will be restored as soon as conditions are right next spring.

Yours truly, / Mrs. Alice G. Schmidt, Co-owner / {urs} / Enclosure / c: Mr. George Lambrecht, Co-owner

Reset a 0.5 inch tab for the copy notation.

Lesson 46   Reports With Author/Year Citations

GOALS: To type 38 wam/3'/3e; to format reports with author/year citations.

A. Type 2 times.

A. WARMUP

1   The giant-size trucks, all carrying over 600 bushels,   11
2 were operating "around the clock"; quite a few of them had   23
3 dumped their boxes in Jenks during the last 18 to 20 hours.   35

   | 1 | 2 | 3 | 4 | 5 | 6 | 7 | 8 | 9 | 10 | 11 | 12

 SKILLBUILDING

B. DIAGNOSTIC PRACTICE: ALPHABET

Turn to the Diagnostic Practice: Alphabet routine beginning on page SB-2. Type one of the Pretest/Posttest paragraphs and identify any errors made. Then type the corresponding drill lines 2 times for each letter on which you made 2 or more errors and 1 time for each letter on which you made only 1 error. Finally, repeat the same Pretest paragraph and compare your performance.

C. Type the paragraph 2 times, using your right thumb to press the space bar in the center.

C. TECHNIQUE PRACTICE: SPACE BAR

4   Dee is it.   Abe is here.   Cal is home.   Bev was lost.
5 Edna can see.   Faye can knit.   Gail can fly.   Hal can type.
6 Fly the kite.   Swim a mile.   Hit that ball.   Shut the door.

D. Take two 3-minute timings. Determine your speed and errors.

Goal: 38 wam/3'/3e

D. 3-MINUTE TIMING

7   The most common type of mortgage for most people over   11
8 the past years has been the fixed-rate mortgage. With this   23
9 type of loan, the amount of the payment is the same each   34
10 month through the length of the loan period. This is true   46
11 even if the period of the loan, for example, is as long as   58
12 thirty years.   61
13   Some lenders will quickly point out that for a lot of   72
14 people there may be a better mortgage. Depending on the   83
15 economy, the size of the monthly payment varies up or down   95
16 each year for an adjustable-rate mortgage. A cap is set on   107
17 any increases to protect the buyer.   114

   | 1 | 2 | 3 | 4 | 5 | 6 | 7 | 8 | 9 | 10 | 11 | 12

E. AUTHOR/YEAR CITATIONS

Any information taken from other sources and used in a report must be documented or cited. The author/year method of citation includes the source information in parentheses at the appropriate point within the text.

1. If a source has one author, give the author's last name followed by a comma, the year of publication fol-

lowed by a comma, and the page number. Example: (Smith, 1995, p. 52).

2. If the author's name appears within the text, give only the year and the page number in parentheses.
3. If a source has two authors, give both last names joined by &.
4. If a source has three or more authors, give the last name of the first author followed by *et al.*

DOCUMENT PROCESSING

Report 18
Two-Page Unbound
Report

JUDGING A COMPUTER SYSTEM

By Marilyn Clark

Judging the effectiveness of a computer system has taken on a new dimension in the past few years, if for no ~~particular~~ reason other than the wide range of computer systems from which the user can select. It is important, therefore, that we investigate the criteria that should be considered in making this important decision.

CRITERION 1: SPEED

This is probably the most ~~critical~~ obvious criterion considered when one purchases a computer system. The value of a computer is directly related to its speed, and a computer's speed is typically measured in megahertz (MHz). A MHz is one million cycles per second, and many of today's microcomputers run in the range of 90 to 100 MHz (Crenshaw, 1996, p. 173).

CRITERION 2: FLEXIBILITY This second criterion is ~~now~~ especially important because of the rapid turn over of hardware and software in the computer ~~industry.~~ The flexibility of a computer system is important for two general reasons:

To accommodate a variety of programs. Hundreds and possibly thousands of software packages are available today to meet the needs of computer users. The computer you purchase must be able to accommodate this variety of soft ware and be flexible enough to change with the increasing sophistication of software packages.

To Permit Expandability. Because of the substantial investment you make in a computer, you do not want to commit your resources to a computer that cannot be expanded to handle (1) newer, more powerful operating systems; (2) "memory-hungry" software packages; (3) network interfaces; and (4) additional users (Hartung and Kallock, 1996, p. 239)

ds

(continued on next page)

CRITERION 3: CONVENIENCE

A third consideration is convenience. It is easy to learn ~~how to~~ operate your computer? Does the manufacturer stand by it's waranty, and is it difficult to obtain repairs? How convenient is it to buy parts for your computer (such as memory boards and drives) if you want to expand your system? these questions need to be answered, and the answers should be weighed before you purchase a computer system new. carefully

Report 19

Open the file for Report 18 and make the following changes:

1. Change the title to *JUDGING COMPUTER EFFECTIVENESS.*
2. Use your name in the byline.
3. Change the side headings to the following:
   COMPUTER OPERATING SPEED
   SYSTEM FLEXIBILITY
   OVERALL CONVENIENCE

4. Transpose the two paragraphs that begin with paragraph headings (Paragraphs 4 and 5).
5. Replace the final question in the **Convenience** section with the following: *How far would you have to travel to secure replacement parts (if needed), or how many days would you have to wait if you ordered them from the dealer?*

Lesson 47   Reports With Footnotes

GOALS: To improve speed and accuracy; to refine language-arts skills in the use of quotation marks and italics (or the underline); to format reports with footnotes.

A. Type 2 times.

A. WARMUP

```
1     Tag #357X was attached to a black jug that was 1/3        10
2  full of a creamy liquid.  Tags #491Z and #478V were both     22
3  attached to beautiful large lamps (crystal and porcelain).   34
   | 1 | 2 | 3 | 4 | 5 | 6 | 7 | 8 | 9 | 10 | 11 | 12
```

SKILLBUILDING

B. PACED PRACTICE

Turn to the Paced Practice routine beginning on page SB-14. Take three 2-minute timings, starting at the point where you left off the last time.

C. DIAGNOSTIC PRACTICE: NUMBERS

Turn to the Diagnostic Practice: Numbers routine beginning on page SB-5. Type one of the Pretest/Posttest paragraphs and indentify any errors made. Then type the corresponding drill lines 2 times for each number on which you made 2 or more errors and 1 time for each number on which you made only 1 error. Finally, repeat the same Pretest paragraph and compare your performance.

LANGUAGE ARTS

D. QUOTATION MARKS AND ITALICS (OR UNDERLINE)

D. Study the rules at the right.

Rule: Use quotation marks around the titles of newspaper articles, magazine articles, chapters in a book, reports, conferences, and similar items.

"title

The next assignment is to read the chapter entitled "The Kennedy Years."
Kurt read and reread the article, "An Interview With Joe Montana."

Rule: Use quotation marks around a direct quotation.

"quot

The officer replied, "The fingerprints are in the lab for analysis."
"All books are to be returned within one week," the statement reads.

Rule: Italicize (or underline) the titles of books, magazines, newspapers, and other complete published works.

____title

The Fifties by David Halberstam has an excellent coverage of the decade.
The article in Sports Illustrated covered the new basketball rules changes.

Edit the sentences to correct any errors in the use of quotation marks and the underline (or italics).

4 The interest rates were discussed in the November 24 "Tribune."
5 *Types of Life Insurance* is an excellent chapter.
6 His reply was very short and to the point: Definitely!
7 Her proposed title for the report was "Reactions to GATT."
8 The December 2 issue of "Newsweek" had an excellent coverage.
9 The Realtor replied, "The first thing to consider is location."

FORMATTING

E. REPORTS WITH FOOTNOTES

Footnote references indicate the sources of facts or ideas used in a report. Although the footnotes may be formatted in a variety of ways, they have many things in common:

1. Footnotes are indicated in the text by superior figures.

2. Footnotes are numbered consecutively throughout the report.

3. Footnotes appear at the bottom of the page on which the references appear.

4. A footnote should include the name of the author, the title of the book or article, the publisher, the place of publication, the year of publication, and the page number(s).

(continued on next page)

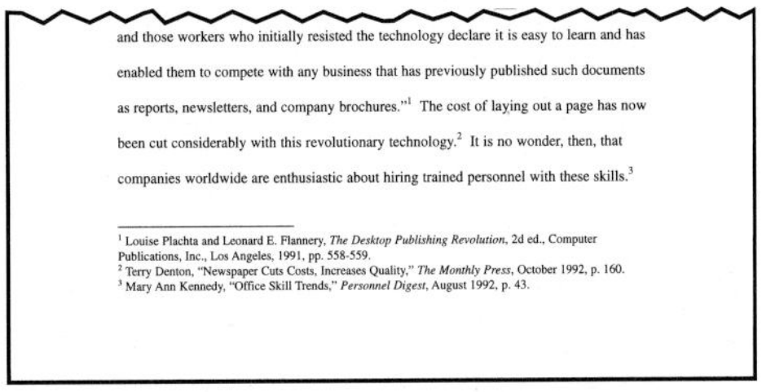
and those workers who initially resisted the technology declare it is easy to learn and has enabled them to compete with any business that has previously published such documents as reports, newsletters, and company brochures."[1] The cost of laying out a page has now been cut considerably with this revolutionary technology.[2] It is no wonder, then, that companies worldwide are enthusiastic about hiring trained personnel with these skills.[3]

[1] Louise Plachta and Leonard E. Flannery, *The Desktop Publishing Revolution*, 2d ed., Computer Publications, Inc., Los Angeles, 1991, pp. 558-559.
[2] Terry Denton, "Newspaper Cuts Costs, Increases Quality," *The Monthly Press*, October 1992, p. 160.
[3] Mary Ann Kennedy, "Office Skill Trends," *Personnel Digest*, August 1992, p. 43.

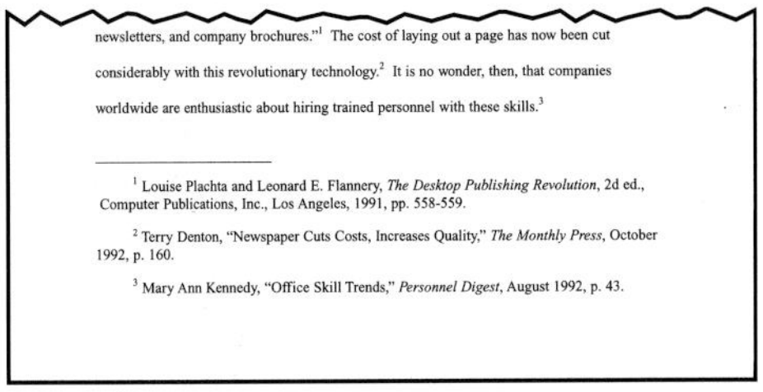
newsletters, and company brochures."[1] The cost of laying out a page has now been cut considerably with this revolutionary technology.[2] It is no wonder, then, that companies worldwide are enthusiastic about hiring trained personnel with these skills.[3]

[1] Louise Plachta and Leonard E. Flannery, *The Desktop Publishing Revolution*, 2d ed., Computer Publications, Inc., Los Angeles, 1991, pp. 558-559.

[2] Terry Denton, "Newspaper Cuts Costs, Increases Quality," *The Monthly Press*, October 1992, p. 160.

[3] Mary Ann Kennedy, "Office Skill Trends," *Personnel Digest*, August 1992, p. 43.

F. LONG QUOTATIONS

A paragraph that is quoted or considered essential to a report may be "highlighted" or displayed by using single spacing and indenting the paragraph 0.5 inch from both the left and right margins to make it stand out from the rest of the report.

G. WORD PROCESSING: FOOTNOTES

go TO

Study Lesson 47 in your word processing manual. Complete all of the shaded steps while at your computer. Then format the jobs that follow.

DOCUMENT PROCESSING

Report 20
One-Page Unbound Report With Footnotes

"quot

SHOPPING FOR A HOME

(Part I)

Buying a home is a proces that many of us will go through in our life time. If we are like many prospective buyers, we will experience this decision three or four major times in our working years. A home is typically the largest purchase we will make, and it deserves therefore our careful attention.

"Most people think that the important criteria in shopping for a home is its site."1

The site should be on land that is well drained and free from ~~from~~ flooding ~~that can cause extensive damage.~~ Check the ~~area~~ city zoning plan to determine if you have choosen a site that is free from flooding and highwater levels ~~that can cause extensive damage.~~ You should also check to see if the ground is stable. Ground that shifts can cause cracks in foundations and walls.

Moreau suggests that a ~~home~~ survey be undertaken in the early stages:

> Key problems are encroachments-tees, buildings, or additions to the house that overlap the property line or may violate zoning regulations. The solution can be as simple as moving or removing trees or bushes.2

The buying of a house is a major under taking with a long list of items that must be investigated. To ensure that the building is structurally sound, many prospective buyers use the services of a building inspector.

(continued on next page)

[1]"Building a Home for Tomorrow," *homes & gardens,* (Apr.) 27, 1992, pp. 17-24.
[2]Dan Moreau, "Home Buyers: 7 Traps at Settlement," *Kiplinger's Personal Finance Magazine,* July 1994, p. 68.

Report 21
Two-Page Unbound
Report With
Footnotes

Remember to add a
page number.

Open the file for Report 20 and make the following changes.
1. Change the page reference in footnote 1 to p. 19.

2. Add the following paragraphs and references to the end of the report.

¶The walls, ceiling, and floors (if you have a basement) need to be checked for proper insulation. "Both the depth and 'R' factor need to be checked for proper levels."[3] In addition, cross braces should have been used between the beams supporting a floor.

¶Finally, a thorough check should be made of the heating, cooling, and electrical systems in the home. "These features are often overlooked by prospective homeowners; nevertheless, they are as critical as any others to be examined."[4]

_____

[3]"Home Construction in the '90s," *Family Living,* October 9, 1992, p. 75.
[4]Randall Evans and Marie Alexander, *Home Facilities Planning,* Bradshaw Publishing, Salt Lake City, Utah, 1992, p. 164.

Lesson 48   Reports With Endnotes

GOALS: To type 38 wam/3'/3e; to format reports with endnotes.

A. Type 2 times.

A. WARMUP

```
1      "Baxter & Heimark, Inc., sold 63 new vehicles (47 cars    11
2   and 16 trucks) during June," the sales manager reported.     23
3   This is 41.2% of quarterly sales, an amazing achievement!     34
       |  1  |  2  |  3  |  4  |  5  |  6  |  7  |  8  |  9  |  10  |  11  |  12
```

SKILLBUILDING

Pretest
Take a 1-minute timing.
Determine your speed
and errors.

B. PRETEST: ALTERNATE- AND ONE-HAND WORDS

```
4       The chair of the trade committee served notice that      11
5   the endowment grant exceeded the budget.  A million dollars   23
6   was the exact amount.  The greater part will be deferred.     34
       |  1  |  2  |  3  |  4  |  5  |  6  |  7  |  8  |  9  |  10  |  11  |  12
```

Practice
Speed Emphasis: If you made 2 or fewer errors on the Pretest, type each *individual* line 2 times.
Accuracy Emphasis: If you made 3 or more errors, type each *group* of lines (as though it were a paragraph) 2 times.

C. PRACTICE: ALTERNATE-HAND WORDS

7 visible signs amendment visual height turndown suspend maps
8 figment usual authentic emblem island clemency dormant snap
9 problem chair shamrocks profit thrown blandish penalty form

D. PRACTICE: ONE-HAND WORDS

10 trade poplin greater pumpkin eastward plumply barrage holly
11 exact kimono created minikin cassette opinion seaweed union
12 defer unhook reserve minimum attracts million scatter plump

E. POSTTEST: ALTERNATE- AND ONE-HAND WORDS

Posttest
Repeat the Pretest timing above and compare performance.

F. 3-MINUTE TIMING

F. Take two 3-minute timings. Determine your speed and errors.

Goal: 38 wam/3'/3e

13   Many people are quite amazed to learn that through   10
14 the years there have been large differences in the average   22
15 annual incomes of those who live in rich states and those   34
16 who live in poorer regions of the country. However, during   46
17 the past decade the states with low per capita incomes have   58
18 pulled closer to the national norm. At the same time some   70
19 of the high-income states have fallen back.   78
20   A reason is that there is now a better-paying mix of   89
21 jobs in the rural states. Many industrial firms have moved   101
22 to these states in an effort to keep down their operating   113
23 costs.   114

| 1 | 2 | 3 | 4 | 5 | 6 | 7 | 8 | 9 | 10 | 11 | 12 |

FORMATTING

G. REPORTS WITH ENDNOTES

Like footnotes, endnotes indicate sources of facts or ideas used in a report. However, endnotes appear at the end of a report on the last page. Although endnotes may be formatted in a variety of ways, they also have many things in common:

1. Endnotes are indicated in the text by superior figures.

2. Endnotes are numbered consecutively throughout the report.

3. Endnotes appear at the end of the report, either on the last page or on a separate page.

4. Endnotes should include the name of the author, the title of the book or article, the publisher, the place of publication, the year of publication, and the page number(s).

(continued on next page)

The format of your endnote references may not look like those shown here.

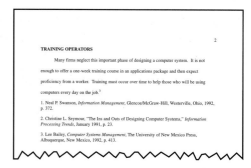

H. WORD PROCESSING: ENDNOTES

Study Lesson 48 in your word processing manual. Complete all of the shaded steps while at your computer. Then format the jobs that follow.

Report 22
Two-Page Unbound Report With Endnotes

DESIGNING A COMPUTER SYSTEM

Designing a computer system involves a variety of different operations such as word processing, data processing, communications, printing, and other office-related functions. These areas can be integrated into a very powerful computer system.

DESIGNING THE SYSTEM

One of the first steps is to determine what information is going to be computerized and what personnel will need these resources.[i] This decision should involve all departments in the planning stage of system design. If necessary, you may have to invite input from those departments which are going to be closely involved in computer use after the system has been designed.

There may also be a need to acquire the systems design experience of outside experts—people whose careers consist primarily of planning and developing computer systems for management.[ii]

SELECTING HARDWARE AND SOFTWARE

Bailey believes that "the selection of software precedes any hardware choices. Too many people, however, select the hardware first and then try to match their software with the computer."[iii] After the software has been selected, a decision must be made as to whether hardware should be purchased or leased. Although many firms decide to purchase their own hardware, others have taken the route of time-sharing or remote processing whereby the costs of processing data can be shared with other users.

TRAINING OPERATORS

Many firms neglect this important phase of designing a computer system. It is not enough to offer a one-week training course in an applications package and then expect proficiency from a worker. Training must occur over time to help those who will be using computers every day on the job.

(continued on next page)

Your endnotes may not look like those shown here.

[i]Neal Swanson, *Information Management,* Glencoe/McGraw-Hill, Westerville, Ohio, 1992, p. 372.

[ii]Christine L. Seymour, "The Ins and Outs of Designing Computer Systems," *Information Processing Trends,* January 1991, p. 23.

[iii]Lee Bailey, *Computer Systems Management,* The University of New Mexico Press, Albuquerque, New Mexico, 1992, p. 413.

Report 23
Two-Page Unbound
Report With Endnotes

Open the file for Report 22, and add the following paragraph, as well as the accompanying endnote, as the final paragraph and the final endnote in the report.

Finally, it should be recognized that training is an ongoing responsibility. As technology, software, hardware, and procedures change, training must occur regularly and on a continuing basis.[4]

4. Paula Blair, *Administrative Management,* Southern Publishing Company, Atlanta, Georgia, 1992, p. 420.

Lesson 49   Bibliography and Reference Lists

GOALS: To improve speed and accuracy; to refine language-arts skills in spelling; to format a bibliography and a reference list.

A. Type 2 times.

A. WARMUP

```
1        The prize troop received the following extra gifts:      11
2   $20 from Larson's Bakery; $19 from Calsun, Ltd.;* $50 from    22
3   some judges; and quite a number of $5 gift certificates.      34
    |  1  |  2  |  3  |  4  |  5  |  6  |  7  |  8  |  9  |  10 |  11 |  12
```

SKILLBUILDING

B. Take three 12-second timings on each line. The scale below the last line shows your wam speed for a 12-second timing.

B. 12-SECOND SPEED SPRINTS

```
4   Joe must try to type as fast as he can on these four lines.
5   The screens were very clear, and the print was easy to see.
6   We will not be able to print the copy until later on today.
7   The disk will not store any of the data if it is not clean.
    | | | 5 | | |10| | |15| | |20| | |25| | |30| | |35| | |40| | |45| | |50| | |55| | |60
```

C. SUSTAINED PRACTICE: ROUGH DRAFT

8	Various human responses are asymmetrical. This means	11
9	that we ask more from one side of the body than the other	23
10	each time we wave, wink, clap our hands, or cross our legs.	34

11	Each one of these actions demands a clear decision,	11
12	usually (unconscious and instantaneous), to ~~start~~ begin the process	23
13	of moving two parts of the body in very different directions.	34

14	¶ All infants ~~children~~ go though remarkably involved stages as they	12
15	develop their preferrence. As a child ~~children~~ grows (she or he)may	24
16	favor the right hand, the left, or both the same at times.	35

17	¶ By the time most kids are (eight or seven) stability occurs,	12
18	and one hand is permanently dominant over the other. For	24
19	some unknown reason, nine out of ten choose the right hand.	36

| 1 | 2 | 3 | 4 | 5 | 6 | 7 | 8 | 9 | 10 | 11 | 12 |

LANGUAGE ARTS

D. SPELLING

20	per provided international receipt commission present other
21	questions maintenance industrial service following position
22	management absence proposal corporate mortgage support well
23	approval recommendations facilities balance experience upon
24	premium currently because procedure addition paid directors

25	The international comission provided a list of proceedures.
26	That industrial maintainance proposal is curently in place.
27	The directers and management supported the recomendations.
28	Those present raised a question about a corperate morgage.
29	Six of the folowing persons have now given their aproval.
30	In adition, Kris has premium experience at the facilitys.

FORMATTING

E. BIBLIOGRAPHIES

A bibliography is an alphabetic listing of sources typed on a separate page at the end of a report. To format a bibliography:

1. Use the same side margins as the report pages.

2. Center and type the title in all caps and bold approximately 2 inches from the top of the page followed by a double space (press Enter twice).

(continued on next page)

3. Type the first line at the left margin and indent carry over lines 0.5 inch (a hanging indent).

4. Arrange book entries in this order: author (last name first), title (in italics), publisher, place of publication, and year.

5. Arrange journal articles in this order: authors (last name first), article title (in quotation marks), journal title (in italics), series number, volume num-

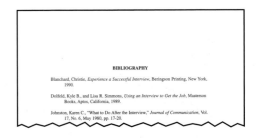

ber, issue number, date, and page number(s).

F. REFERENCE LISTS IN APA FORMAT

Reference lists also indicate sources of ideas or facts used in a report. To format an APA (the American Psychological Association) reference list:

1. Use the same side margins as the report and double spacing.

2. Center and type the title with initial caps approximately 1 inch from the top of the page followed by a double space.

3. Indent the first line of each entry.

4. Arrange book entries in this order: author (last name first), publication date in parentheses, chapter title with only the first word capitalized (no quotation marks or underline), book title (underlined), publisher's city and 2-letter state abbreviation, publisher's name.

5. Arrange periodical entries in this order: author (last name first), publication date in parentheses, article title with only the first word capitalized (no quotation marks or underline), periodical title and volume number underlined, page numbers.

DOCUMENT PROCESSING

Report 24
Bibliography

BIBLIOGRAPHY

Bilanski, Charles R., "Corporate Structures in the Year 2000," *Modern Management,* Vol. 34, July 1994, pp. 21-24.

Calhoun, Josten C., "Warehouse Facilities Needs," *Realty Services Reports,* November 1995, pp. 82-86.

Dahlman, Leland, and Joyce C. Fahler, "Trends for Boards of Directors," *International Press,* Vol. 19, November 1993, pp. 38-47.

Hammersmith Institute, *Bold Positions of the New Administration,* Hammersmith Institute Press, Baltimore, Maryland, 1992.

Jefferson, R. C., *Challenges for Industrial Commissions,* Sampson Books, Des Moines, Iowa, 1994.

Lowell, James T., et al., "Mortgage Experiences of Three Entrepreneurs," *Journal of Free Enterprise,* No. 28, June 1992, pp. 53-56.

Report 25
Reference List in APA Format

Be sure to underline titles. Do not type them in italics.

References

Bilanski, Charles R. (1994, July). Corporate structures in the year 2000. Modern Management, 34, 21-24.

Calhoun, Josten C. (1995, November). Warehouse facilities needs. Realty Services Reports, 82-86.

Dahlman, Leland, & Fahler, Joyce C. Trends for boards of directors. International Press, 19, 38-47.

Hammersmith Institute. (1992). Bold positions of the new administration. Baltimore, MD: Hammersmith Institute Press.

Jefferson, R. C. (1994). Challenges for industrial commissions. Des Moines, Iowa: Sampson Books.

Report 26
Bibliography

BIBLIOGRAPHY *ital*

Byers, Ed, "Newsletter Design," Personal Publisher, (Apr.) 1994, pp. 14-15.

Collins, Wanda, "Taking a Journey with DTP, TDP Computeing, May 1993, p. 28.

Hirsh, Mitch, DTP Manual for Executives, Computer Press, Denver, 1995.

Sade, Beth, Desk Top Publishing Comes Of Age, Midwestern book company, Kansas City, p. 48. *1994* *Missouri,*

Lesson 50   Preliminary Report Pages

GOALS: To type 39 wam/3'/3e; to format preliminary report pages.

A. Type 2 times.

A. WARMUP

```
1      Did Jack and Hazel see the first Sox ball game?  I've     11
2  heard there were 57,268 people there (a new record).  Your    23
3  home crowd was quiet when the game ended with a 4-9 loss.     34
   |  1  |  2  |  3  |  4  |  5  |  6  |  7  |  8  |  9  |  10  |  11  |  12
```

B. PROGRESSIVE PRACTICE: ALPHABET

Turn to the Progressive Practice: Alphabet routine beginning on page SB-7. Take six 30-second timings, starting at the point where you left off the last time.

C. 12-SECOND SPEED SPRINTS

4 Some of the new pups will be sold to the men who work here.
5 Most of the boys and girls got to go to the fair last week.
6 She has to take six of the top teams to the games that day.
7 Dick said that the right way to do it is also the easy way.

| | | |5| | | |10| | | |15| | | |20| | | |25| | | |30| | | |35| | | |40| | | |45| | | |50| | | |55| | | |60

D. Take two 3-minute timings. Determine your speed and errors.

Goal: 39 wam/3'/3e

D. 3-MINUTE TIMING

8   Just imagine that you are buying your first house and   11
9 have given notice to your landlord that you will move out   23
10 at the end of the month. Then you are amazed to find out   34
11 that a local plumber has a lien on the property. Both the   46
12 seller and the buyer are involved in the legal closing, but   58
13 the buyer is more likely to run into trouble by being lax.   70
14   Whether you are using an attorney or a real estate   80
15 person to help you, problems can be avoided by acquainting   92
16 yourself well in advance with papers to be signed. The   103
17 title search should be conducted well in advance of the   114
18 final closing.   117

| 1 | 2 | 3 | 4 | 5 | 6 | 7 | 8 | 9 | 10 | 11 | 12

FORMATTING

E. TITLE PAGES

Reports should have a title page, which at the very least shows the report title, the writer's name and identification, and the date. The title (and subtitle, if any) are typed on the top part of the page; the writer's name and identification are typed in the center of the page; and the date is typed on the lower part of the page.

To format a title page, follow these steps:

1. Center the page vertically.
2. Center the title in all caps and bold. Double-space, and center the subtitle with initial caps in regular type.
3. Press Enter 12 times, and center the words *Prepared by* followed by a blank line.
4. Center the writer's name and identification on separate lines, single-spaced.
5. Press Enter 12 times, and center the date.

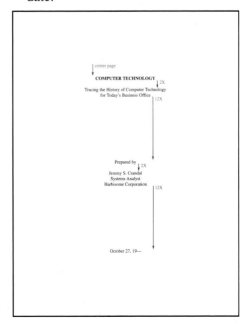

F. TABLE OF CONTENTS

A table of contents (see Report 28) is usually supplied with long reports. The table of contents identifies the major sections of a report and the page numbers where they can be found.

1. Use the same margins that were used for the report.
2. Center and type the word **CONTENTS** approximately 2 inches from the top of the page in all caps and bold, followed by a double space.
3. Type the major headings in all caps; double-space before and after them.
4. Indent subheadings (using default tabs) and type them with initial caps and single spacing.
5. Align page numbers flush right, and type them with dot leaders—a series of periods that helps guide the reader's eye across the page to the page number on the same line.

G. WORD PROCESSING: TAB SET—DOT LEADERS

Study Lesson 50 in your word processing manual. Complete all of the shaded steps while at your computer. Then format the jobs that follow.

Report 27
Title Page

Report 28
Table of Contents

THE SECRETARY IN TODAY'S AUTOMATED OFFICE

Maintaining Traditional Skills While Developing High-Tech Competence

Prepared by
Phyllis G. Browe
Systems Analyst
The Western Office Group

December 9, 19--

↓2 inches **CONTENTS**

(continued on next page)

Report 29

Progress Check
Two-Page Unbound
Report With Endnotes

MANAGING YOUR TIME

The Key to Success in an Office

Using your time efficiently in an office will help you get more work done in less time. Wasted time can never be recovered; therefore, the ideas in this report will help you better manage your time.

PLAN YOUR WORK EACH DAY

Take a few minutes at the beginning of each workday to plan your day's activities.[1] Decide which tasks should be first and which tasks can be completed later.

Obtaining Necessary Materials. Gather all necessary supplies and materials that you will need to accomplish the tasks that must be completed.[2] Have all your paper, pens and pencils, and other materials at your desk and within easy reach whenever you need to use them.

Completing Individual Tasks. Regardless of the work in which you are involved, it is usually better to finish one task before beginning another. However, if your supervisor assigns you a task that must be accomplished immediately, the original task may have to be completed later. If this happens, identify the point of your progress on your original task so that you can resume your work with little hesitation.

Before you begin any task, be sure you have a thorough understanding of what must be done. If you need to ask a question, be sure you have reviewed all of your materials for a possible answer before interrupting someone. If

(continued on next page)

there are several questions, write them down so that you ask them in the proper sequence.

SPEND YOUR TIME WISELY

Although you may want to work from beginning to end on a task, it may be better to take a short break or two when the task is of considerable length. By taking a few minutes to relax both mentally and physically, you likely will finish your task in less time.

1. Dorothy R. Crattburg, *Managing Time Wisely,* Trafton Valley Press, Monterey, California, 1995, p. 7.

2. Donald E. Wilkins and Lila G. Wahlstrom, "Time Is Money," *The New Office,* March 1995, pp. 35-37.

UNIT ELEVEN ▶ Employment Documents

Lesson 51   Resumes

GOALS: To improve speed and accuracy; to refine language-arts skills in the use of commas; to format resumes.

A. Type 2 times.

A. WARMUP

```
1        "Look at them!  Have you ever seen such huge birds?"      11
2   When questioned later on an exam, about 80% to 90% of the      23
3   junior girls were amazed to learn that they were ospreys.      34
    |  1  |  2  |  3  |  4  |  5  |  6  |  7  |  8  |  9  | 10  | 11  | 12
```

SKILLBUILDING

B. DIAGNOSTIC PRACTICE: ALPHABET

Turn to the Diagnostic Practice: Alphabet routine beginning on page SB-2. Type one of the Pretest/Posttest paragraphs and identify any errors made. Then type the corresponding drill lines 2 times for each letter on which you made 2 or more errors and 1 time for each letter on which you made only 1 error. Finally, repeat the same Pretest paragraph and compare your performance.

C. PACED PRACTICE

Turn to the Paced Practice routine beginning on page SB-14. Take three 2-minute timings, starting at the point where you left off the last time.

LANGUAGE ARTS

D. COMMAS

D. Study the rules at the right.

| Rule: | Use a comma between each item in a series of three or more. |

,ser   The invoice, contract, and cashier's check were enclosed.
,ser   Ms. Dolezal, Mr. Kneisl, and Mrs. Sperry signed the document.

| Rule: | Use a comma before and after a transitional expression (such as *therefore* or *however*). |

,tran   They learned, however, that Mrs. Kneisl also had to sign.
,tran   Therefore, the closing will be delayed until November 26.

| Rule: | Use a comma before and after a direct quotation. |

,quot   Ms. Dolezal inquired, "What materials shall we bring along?"
,quot   "We will meet at 3 p.m. at the bank," Ms. Trask informed us.

(continued on next page)

4 Liz sent items to the lawyer, the bank and the courthouse.
5 The abstract, deed, and sales contract were all in order.
6 However Mrs. Sperry's flight was two hours late.
7 Therefore, the closing was also delayed for two hours.
8 "The occupancy date is November 28" replied Ms. Trask.
9 Mrs. Kneisl said, "We want to thank you for your kindness."

FORMATTING

E. RESUMES

When you apply for a job, you may be asked to submit a resume. The purpose of a resume is to convey your qualifications for the position you are seeking. A resume should include the following:

1. Personal information (name, address, telephone number).
2. A summary of your educational background and special training.
3. Previous work experience.
4. Any activities or accomplishments that relate to the position for which you are applying.
5. (Optional) Your career goal.
6. (Optional) References. References

should consist of at least three people who can tell a prospective employer what kind of worker you are.

Often, your resume creates the first impression you make on a prospective employer; be sure it is free of errors.

A variety of styles is acceptable for formatting a resume (see Illustrations 1 and 2 that follow). Choose a style (or design one) that is attractive and which enables you to get all the needed information on one or two pages. A one-page resume should be vertically centered; the first page of a two-page resume should start approximately 2 inches from the top of the page.

Illustration 1

Illustration 2

F. WORD PROCESSING: FONT/FONT SIZE AND LINES

Study Lesson 51 in your word processing manual. Complete all of the shaded steps while at your computer. Then format the jobs that follow.

DOCUMENT PROCESSING

Report 30
Resume

Use a hanging indent at 1.5 inches.

Type the following resume in the same format as Illustration 1 on page 124. Follow these steps:

1. Center the page vertically.
2. Center and type the name in 18-point font size, all caps, and bold.
3. Turn off bold, return to 12-point font size and press Enter three times.
4. Center and type the address and telephone number.
5. At the left margin, type the side heading *EDUCATION* in all caps and bold.
6. Align the remaining text for the section approximately 1.5 inches from the left margin. Type the name of the school and any degrees earned.
7. Press Enter twice and type the course information aligned with the previous text. Press Enter twice and complete the remaining information.
8. Press Enter twice before beginning each new section.
9. Insert a horizontal line below the name.

SHANNON T. ANDREWS

349 Sycamore Terrace, Sioux City, IA 51104
712-555-7256
↓2X

EDUCATION   West Iowa Business College, Sioux City, Iowa
Degree: A.A. in Office Systems, May 1995
↓2X

Courses in accounting, business communication, computer application software (Lotus, dBase, WordPerfect, and Microsoft Word), office systems management, and telecommunications.
↓2X

Wayne High School, Wayne, Nebraska
Graduated: May 1993
↓2X

EXPERIENCE   Computer Systems Technician, June 1993-Present
Kramer & Kramer, Sioux City, Iowa
Duties include reviewing, installing, and updating software programs used for processing legal documents and monitoring computer network system for branch offices of Kramer & Kramer.
↓2X

Salesclerk, May 1991 to May 1993 (part-time)
Blanchard's Department Store, Wayne, Nebraska
Duties included selling sporting goods and operating Panasonic cash register. Assisted sales manager in completing monthly sales reports generated by WordPerfect and Lotus software programs.
↓2X

(continued on next page)

ACTIVITIES	President, FBLA Chapter, 1992
	Spanish Honor Society, 1993
	Academic Scholarships, 1994-1995
	Member, Intramural Soccer Team, 1994-1995
	Captain, American Legion Softball Team, 1994

↓2X

| **REFERENCES** | References available on request. |

Report 31
Resume

Open the file for Report 30 and make the following changes:

1. Change the name to 20-point font size, and change the address to: *927 Dace Avenue, Sioux City, IA 51101.*

2. Change the side headings to 14-point font size, and center them. Press Enter 2 times before and after the headings. Begin all of the section text at the left margin.

3. Add desktop publishing and program-ming (Pascal) to the Education section before telecommunications.

4. Replace the first work experience with *Programmer, June 1993-Present / Teledyne Inc. / Sioux City, Iowa / Duties include writing Pascal programs to monitor quality control within Research and Development.*

5. Delete the Spanish Honor Society and the Softball Team entries in the Activities section.

Lesson 52   Letters of Application

GOALS: To type 39 wam/5'/5e; to format letters of application.

A. Type 2 times.

A. WARMUP

```
1      Mark these quilts down by 25%:  #489, #378, and #460.      11
2  Leave the prices as they are for the remainder of the sizes   23
3  in that section.  Three adjoining sections will be next.      34
    |  1  |  2  |  3  |  4  |  5  |  6  |  7  |  8  |  9  |  10  |  11  |  12
```

SKILLBUILDING

B. Take three 12-second timings on each line. The scale below the last line shows your wam speed for a 12-second timing.

B. 12-SECOND SPEED SPRINTS

```
4  Most of those boys and girls said they would go to college.
5  Some said that they would need to gain some new job skills.
6  Many of them plan to go on to school for two or four years.
7  Most of them do have a good idea what their majors will be.
    | | | 5 | | |10| | |15| | |20| | |25| | |30| | |35| | |40| | |45| | |50| | |55| | |60
```

C. PROGRESSIVE PRACTICE: NUMBERS

Turn to the Progressive Practice: Numbers routine beginning on page SB-11. Take six 30-second timings, starting at the point where you left off the last time.

D. Take two 5-minute timings. Determine your speed and errors.

Goal: 39 wam/5′/5e

D. 5-MINUTE TIMING

8	We hear and read a lot about the importance of being	11
9	conscientious about our jobs. While this cannot be denied,	23
10	it is also important for individuals to learn how to relax	35
11	and enjoy their hobbies, their friends, and their family	46
12	when they are away from their place of work.	55
13	There are dozens of different types of vacations that	66
14	are unique in different parts of the country. But many	77
15	people all over the country elect to take their vacations	89
16	in the fall during the color season. They head north to	101
17	the mountains so that they can experience the breathtaking	112
18	beauty of the tree leaves as they change color. Leaves may	124
19	turn to gold or to orange before they fall from the trees;	136
20	some turn to red or to burgundy.	142
21	These scenes have been described by some as wildfires	153
22	of beauty. In addition to the many mountain ranges across	165
23	the country where fall colors abound, the northern states	177
24	from the west coast to the east coast are favorite sites	188
25	during the prime foliage season.	195

| 1 | 2 | 3 | 4 | 5 | 6 | 7 | 8 | 9 | 10 | 11 | 12

FORMATTING

E. LETTERS OF APPLICATION

A letter of application is sent along with a resume to a prospective employer. Together, the letter and the resume serve to introduce a person to the organization.

The letter of application should be no longer than one page and should include (1) the job you are applying for and how you learned of the job, (2) the highlights of your enclosed resume, and (3) a request for an interview.

DOCUMENT PROCESSING

Letter 22
Modified-Block Style

March 15, 19— / Ms. Kay Brewer, Personnel Director / Blanchard Computer Systems / 2189 Dace Avenue / Sioux City, IA 51107 / Dear Ms. Brewer:

¶Please consider me as an applicant for the position of data records operator advertised in the March 13 edition of the *Sioux City Press*.

¶In May I will graduate with an A.A. degree in Office Systems from West Iowa Business College. My enclosed resume shows that I have completed courses

(continued on next page)

in Lotus, dBase, WordPerfect, Microsoft Word, and office systems. These software packages are used in your Blanchard offices in Sioux City.

¶The position with your company is very appealing to me. If you wish to interview me for this position, please call me at 712-555-7256.

Sincerely, / Shannon T. Andrews / 349 Sycamore Terrace / Sioux City, IA 51104 / Enclosure

Letter 23
Block Style

August 10, 19— / Personnel Director / Arlington Communications / 2403 Sunset Lane / Arlington, TX 76015-3148 / Dear Personnel Director:

Please consider me as an applicant for a position with ~~you~~. [Arlington Communications]

The two part-time jobs I held during the summer months at your company convinced me that ~~arlington~~ [A]rlington ~~comunications~~ [communication] is the place, [where] I want to work. My strengths have always been in the [enclosed] arts, as you can see on the [enclosed] resume, which ~~reveals~~ [lists] a number of courses in English, and speech, [and communication technology] [for any possible openings]

If you would like to interview me [for any possible openings] this summer or fall, [please] call me at 214-~~2~~[5]55-2340. I look forward to hearing from you.

Sincerely yours, / Kenneth R. Talbot / 68~~92~~ Center[ville] Road / Garland, TX 75041-9285 / Enclosure

Letter 24
Block Style

Open the file for Letter 23, and revise it to be sent to Ms. Lila Mae Colbert, of Texas Media, Inc., at 3809 Fourth Street West in Arlington, TX 76013. Delete the second sentence in the second paragraph.

Lesson 53   Employment Test

GOALS: To improve speed and accuracy; to refine language-arts skills in proofreading; to format documents used in employment tests.

A. Type 2 times.

A. WARMUP

```
1      Janice had sales of over $23,000; Kathy's sales were     11
2  only $17,368 for the same quiet period.  They agreed that    22
3  some inventory sizes were wrong and should be exchanged.     34
   |  1  |  2  |  3  |  4  |  5  |  6  |  7  |  8  |  9  |  10  |  11  |  12
```

Pretest
Take a 1-minute timing. Determine your speed and errors.

B. PRETEST: COMMON LETTER COMBINATIONS

4   They formed an action committee to force a motion for   11
5   a ruling on the contract case. This enabled them to comply   23
6   within the lawful time period and convey a common message.   35

| 1 | 2 | 3 | 4 | 5 | 6 | 7 | 8 | 9 | 10 | 11 | 12

Practice
   Speed Emphasis: If you made 2 or fewer errors on the Pretest, type each *individual* line 2 times.
   Accuracy Emphasis: If you made 3 or more errors, type each *group* of lines (as though it were a paragraph) 2 times.

C. PRACTICE: WORD BEGINNINGS

7   for forget formal format forces forums forked forest formed
8   per perils period perish permit person peruse perked pertly
9   com combat comedy coming commit common compel comply comets

D. PRACTICE: WORD ENDINGS

10   ing acting aiding boring buying ruling saving hiding dating
11   ble bubble dabble double enable feeble fumble tumble usable
12   ion action vision lesion nation bunion lotion motion legion

Posttest
Repeat the Pretest timing and compare performance.

E. POSTTEST: COMMON LETTER COMBINATIONS

F. Type the paragraph 2 times, keeping your eyes on the copy so that you do not lose your place as you type these long, difficult words.

F. TECHNIQUE PRACTICE: CONCENTRATION

13   The syncopated rhythm titillated the audience as the
14   musicians performed. The music of Mauritania, Zimbabwe,
15   Guinea, Zaire, Mozambique, Namibia, and Zambia was played.

G. Edit this paragraph to correct any typing or formatting errors.

G. PROOFREADING

16   The Smith were please to learn from their insurance
17   agent that the covrage ona $50,000 life insurance policy
18   policy would be increased by $ 20,000 at no extra cost.
19   The continued to pay the same premum, not knowing that the
20   cash value of thier original policy was being taped each
21   month to pay an adddittional premium for hte new coverage.

DOCUMENT PROCESSING

Employment Test A

Letter 25   ,quot
Block Style

November 14, 19— / Mr. Margin T. Hegman / 182 Bonanza Avenue /

Anchorage, AK 99502 / Dear Mr. Hegman:

¶ I recently told Sid Loft about your Feb. 15th visit. He replied, "That's terrific!"

Your discussion on the future of multi-media presentations with CD-ROM

(continued on next page)

is indeed timely. You can expect from 100 to 150 participants in your session, which will be held from 1:00 [3] to 2:45 p.m. in Conference Room 2 [II R]. Enclosed with this letter is a parking permit that will allow you to park [free of charge] at the hotel Alexander. The permit is good for all 3 days of the Conference.

Please complete and return to me the speaker equipment form, with this letter that is also enclosed [that]. In the event that you have some unique request, we want to be sure that all your equipment needs will be met.

Please be sure to call me at 415-555-3874 if you have questions about the conference. We look forward to seeing you in ~~March~~ February.

Sincerely, / Jane R. Kelley / conference chair / Enc. 2

Employment Test B
Report 32

This is *Page 3* of a company report which contains several errors in punctuation, spelling, and grammar that must be identified and corrected.

Double-space the report, and use standard margins for an unbound report.

¶**Income Stock Fund.** The Income Stock Funds' objective is current income, and the potential for capital appreciation.

¶The first six month's of the fiscal year produced a total return of 25.4%, including a dividend income distribution. Electric utilities petroleum and drugs is the largest holdings in the portfolio. Net assets has grown to $225.7 million from $104.5 million on September 1.

¶**Income fund.** The Income Fund's investment objective are maximum current income without undue risk to principle. Consistant with this objective, the

,ser

fund held 48.3% in mortgage securities, 12.8% in corporate bonds, and 19.9% in electric utility common stocks,

,tran

¶In addition, the fund also has a portion invested in high-yeild common stocks, which have yeilds almost as high as bonds.

¶**Money Market Fund.** The money Market Fund's investment objective is maximum current yield without undue risk to principle. There are no deviation from this policy in order to achieve additional yield. During the past six months the yield advantage increased from 25 basis points to 29 basis points. Net assits of the fund have grown to $1,375.5 milion from $927.5 milion on September 30.

Employment Test C

Table 16
Boxed Table

Prepare a copy of this table, supplying missing information where necessary. Size the table so that Column 1 entries fit on a single line.

STATEMENT OF EXPENSES June 30, 19--			
Expense	Income Stock ($)	Income Fund ($)	Money Market ($)
Management Fees	923,928	232,687	2,418,661
Registration Fees	35,427	11,855	66,121
TOTAL	?	?	?

Lesson 54 Follow-Up Letters

GOALS: To type 39 wam/5'/5e; to format follow-up letters.

A. Type 2 times.

A. WARMUP

```
1        The new firm, Kulver & Zweidel, will be equipped to      11
2   handle from 1/6 to 1/4 of Martin's tax needs after they       22
3   move to the new location at 1970 Gansby, just east of Main.   34
    |  1  |  2  |  3  |  4  |  5  |  6  |  7  |  8  |  9  |  10  |  11  |  12
```

SKILLBUILDING

B. Take three 12-second timings on each line. The scale below the last line shows your wam speed for a 12-second timing.

B. 12-SECOND SPEED SPRINTS

```
4   Pat went back to the store where he had seen the red shirt.
5   The salesclerk acted as though she had not seen him before.
6   There was a huge change when he walked into a second store.
7   Pat was met at the front door with a smile and a handshake.
    | | | |5| | |10| | |15| | |20| | |25| | |30| | |35| | |40| | |45| | |50| | |55| | |60
```

C. PROGRESSIVE PRACTICE: ALPHABET

Turn to the Progressive Practice: Alphabet routine beginning on page SB-7. Take six 30-second timings, starting at the point where you left off the last time.

D. 5-MINUTE TIMING

D. Take two 5-minute timings. Determine your speed and errors.

Goal: 39 wam/5'/5e

8	While most home-repair contractors are trustworthy,	10
9	honest, hardworking people, most of us have heard stories	22
10	about individuals who have been cheated by unscrupulous con	34
11	artists. If you are urged to sign a contract quickly for	46
12	home repairs, that should be a signal that it is time to	57
13	slow down and take a better look at your position.	67
14	It does not make sense to go forward without getting	78
15	an estimate from at least one other contractor or business.	90
16	Most people have been surprised to see the wide range of	102
17	estimates they have received.	108
18	You should not even think of signing a contract with a	119
19	business or any contractor before you check its record of	131
20	performance in the city or town in which you live. You may	143
21	be well rewarded for the extra time that it takes. Ask for	155
22	names of past customers so you can ask about the quality of	167
23	the work and whether or not it was completed on schedule.	178
24	You may even be able to view some jobs that were recently	190
25	finished and then decide.	195

| 1 | 2 | 3 | 4 | 5 | 6 | 7 | 8 | 9 | 10 | 11 | 12

FORMATTING

E. FOLLOW-UP LETTERS

As soon as possible after your interview (preferably the next day), you should send a follow-up letter to the person who conducted your interview.

In the letter, thank the person who conducted the interview, highlight your particular strengths, and restate your interest in working for that organization. A positive tone is very important.

DOCUMENT PROCESSING

Letter 26
Modified-Block Style
With Blocked
Paragraphs

September 12, 19-- / Ms. Carole Rothchild / Personnel Director / Arlington Communications / 2403 Sunset Lane / Arlington, TX 76015-3148 / Dear Ms. Rothchild:

It was a real pleasure meeting with you yesterday and learning of the wonderful career

(continued on next page)

opportunities at Arlington Communications. I enjoyed meeting all the people, especially those working in the Publications Division. Thank you for taking the time to tell me about the interesting start-up history of the company and its location in Arlington.

I believe my experience and job skills match nicely with those you are seeking for a desktop publishing individual, and this position is exactly what I have been looking for. You may recall that I have had experience with all of the equipment and software that are used in your office.

Please let me hear from you when you have made your decision on this position. I am very much interested in joining the professional staff at Arlington Communications.

Sincerely yours, / Kenneth R. Talbot / 6829 Centerville Road / Garland, TX 75041-9285

Letter 27
Block Style

April 7, 19— / Ms. Kay Brewer, Personnel Director / Blanchard Computer Systems / 2189 Dace Avenue / Sioux City, IA 51107 / Dear Ms. Brewer:

Thanks for the opportunity of interviewing you with Blanchard computer Systems yesterday. Please express my appreciation to all of those who were involved.

The interview gave me a very good feeling about the company. The positive description that you shared me with convinced me that blanchard is in deed a company at which I would like to work. I was greatly impressed with the summary of social service programs for citizens throughout the community that are sponsored by Blanchard.

You may recall that I have had experience with all of the equipment that is used. It appears to me that my strengths in software application computer soft ware and office systems would blend in well with your company profile.

I look forward to hearing you from soon regarding your decision on the position of data records operator.

(continued on next page)

Sincerely, / Shannon T. Andrews / 349 Sycamore Terrace / Sioux City, IA 51104

Letter 28
Block Style

Open the file for Letter 27, and revise it to be sent to Mr. William E. Boyd / Personnel Director / Hawkeye Computers, Inc. / 5604 Melrose Avenue / Sioux City, IA 51105. It will be necessary to replace *Blanchard Computer Systems* with *Hawkeye Computers, Inc.* in both the first and the second paragraphs.

Lesson 55 Integrated Employment Project

GOALS: To improve speed and accuracy; to refine language-arts skills in composing; to format employment documents.

A. Type 2 times.

A. WARMUP

1 Prices were quickly lowered (some by as much as 50%) 11
2 at Rich's garage sale. He could see that extra sales would 23
3 not be over the 25%* he had projected to finance the prize. 35

| 1 | 2 | 3 | 4 | 5 | 6 | 7 | 8 | 9 | 10 | 11 | 12

SKILLBUILDING

B. Take a 1-minute timing on the first paragraph to establish your base speed. Then take four 1-minute timings on the remaining paragraphs. As soon as you equal or exceed your base speed on one paragraph, advance to the next, more difficult paragraph.

B. SUSTAINED PRACTICE: CAPITALIZATION

4 There are several different approaches that one can 11
5 take when considering a major purchase. Some people make 22
6 the mistake of simply going to a store and making a choice. 34

7 When one couple decided to buy a chest-type freezer, 11
8 they looked at a consumer magazine in the library. The 22
9 Sears, Amana, and General Electric were shown as best buys. 34

10 That same issue of their magazine compared electric 11
11 ranges. Jonathan and Mary Ann found that the Maytag, Magic 23
12 Chef, Amana, and Gibson were determined to be best buys. 34

13 Best buys for full-size microwave ovens were the Sharp 11
14 Carousel, Panasonic, and GoldStar Multiwave. The midsize 23
15 models were the Frigidaire, Panasonic, and Sears Kenmore. 34

| 1 | 2 | 3 | 4 | 5 | 6 | 7 | 8 | 9 | 10 | 11 | 12

C. PACED PRACTICE

Turn to the Paced Practice routine beginning on page SB-14. Take three 2-minute timings, starting at the point where you left off the last time.

LANGUAGE ARTS

D. COMPOSING

D. Answer each question with a complete sentence.

16 Why do you need to prepare in advance for an interview?

17 What do good grades have to do with getting the right job?

18 How can good communication skills help in the world of work?

19 How might knowledge of a foreign language help on the job?

20 Why are ethics important in business?

21 How can you improve your confidence in speaking before a group?

DOCUMENT PROCESSING

Report 33
Resume

Letter 29
Application Letter

Letter 30
Follow-up Letter

In this unit you have learned how to prepare a resume, an application letter, and a follow-up letter—all of which are frequently used by job applicants.

You will now use these skills in preparing the documents necessary to apply for the job described in the newspaper ad that follows.

Prepare a resume for yourself as though you are applying for the job described in the ad in the next column. Use actual data in the resume. Assume that you have just graduated from a postsecondary program. Include school-related activities, courses you have completed, and any part-time or full-time work experience you may have acquired. Make the resume as realistic as possible, and provide as much information as you can about your background.

Prepare an application letter to apply for the position described in the ad. Date your letter March 10. Emphasize the skills you have acquired during your years in school and while working in any part-time or full-time positions. Use Letters 22 and 23 (pages 127 and 128) as guides for your letter.

Assume that your interview was held on March 25 and that you would very much like to work for Tri-State Publishing. It is now the day after your interview. Prepare a follow-up letter expressing your positive thoughts about working for Tri-State. Use Letters 26 and 27 (pages 132 and 133) as guides for your letter.

COMPUTER APPLICATIONS SPECIALIST

Tri-State Publishing, a New York City-based publisher specializing in trade and industrial titles, has an immediate opening for a Computer Applications Specialist whose primary responsibilities include word processing and desktop publishing.

This is an entry-level position within the Public Relations Department in our Philadelphia office. Applicant must have had training in WordPerfect and desktop publishing (preferably PageMaker or Ventura). Knowledge of computer operating systems is also helpful.

Excellent company benefits available that include a comprehensive medical and dental program, disability insurance, and a company credit union.

If interested, send a letter of application and resume to:

Mr. David E. Frantelli
Personnel Department
Tri-State Publishing
9350 Andover Road
Philadelphia, PA 19114

Tri-State is an Equal Opportunity Employer

Lesson 56   Allwood Publications

GOALS: To type 40 wam/5′/5e; to format various business documents.

A. Type 2 times.

A. WARMUP

1   Kyu Choi jumped at the opportunity to assume 40% of   11
2 the ownership of the restaurant. Alverox & Choi Chinese   22
3 Cuisine will be opening quite soon at 1528 Wayzata Street.   34

| 1 | 2 | 3 | 4 | 5 | 6 | 7 | 8 | 9 | 10 | 11 | 12

SKILLBUILDING

B. PROGRESSIVE PRACTICE: ALPHABET

Turn to the Progressive Practice: Alphabet routine beginning on page SB-7. Take six 30-second timings, starting at the point where you left off the last time.

C. Type the paragraph 2 times, using the caps lock key and the shift key correctly.

C. TECHNIQUE PRACTICE: SHIFT/CAPS LOCK

4   RHONDA KORDICH was promoted on APRIL 1 to SENIOR
5 SECRETARY. The SOLD sign replaced the FOR SALE sign at
6 1904 ELM DRIVE. The trip to DULUTH was on INTERSTATE 35.

D. Take two 5-minute timings. Determine your speed and errors.

Goal: 40 wam/5′/5e

D. 5-MINUTE TIMING

7   All of us have seen too many newspaper articles that   11
8 describe tragic auto accidents on our nation's highways.   22
9 This is true in spite of the efforts of both the government   34
10 and the auto industry to reduce the number of accidents.   46
11 The development of air bags and antilock brakes in recent   58
12 years has been very good. And there will be many more   69
13 momentous safety breakthroughs in the future.   78
14   There will be cruise control that automatically slows   89
15 a car to prevent it from getting too close to the vehicle   100
16 in front. The system will use radar to check the space   112
17 between the cars and will quickly apply the brakes.   122
18   Infrared sensors will be introduced that will extend a   133
19 driver's night vision, enabling the driver to see people or   145
20 objects in the dark. Video cameras will be controlled by   157
21 computers to read lane markings and alert all drivers to   168
22 take corrective action when needed. We will also see autos   180
23 that can sense a skid and apply one brake to keep the car   192
24 straight. All these changes are amazing.   200

| 1 | 2 | 3 | 4 | 5 | 6 | 7 | 8 | 9 | 10 | 11 | 12

Situation: Today is November 25, 19—. You are working as an administrative assistant to Ms. Maridel B. Ash, editorial director of Allwood Publications. The following jobs are to be completed in the order shown.

Letter 31
Block Style

Ms. Victoria F. Eng
85 Holly Drive
Chadron, NE 69337

Dear Ms. Eng:

Thank you very much for your inquiry about Allwood Publications. It is a pleasure to respond.

We publish four magazines. Their names, the names of their editors, and their cost per year are listed on the enclosed table. All are subscription magazines. None are sold at newsstands.

If you would like any other details, please let me know.

Sincerely yours,

M. Ash

Remember to add the enclosure notation.

Table 17
Open Table

ALLWOOD PUBLICATIONS

Title	Editor	Cost Per Year
Parenting Today	Roberta Holt	$19.97
Just for Fun	Greg Harrison	$12.95
Puzzle Quest	Tina Ho	$12.95
Only for Children	Maria Montoya	$17.20
TOTAL		$63.07

Memo 8
Rough Draft

MEMO

TO: All Editors

FROM: Maridel B. Ash, Editorial Director

DATE: November 52, 19—

SUBJECT: Meeting on December 8

A meeting for all editors has been scheduled for 1 p.m. on December 8. We will be discussing the following these topics:

1. The use of eye-catching icons that will highlight the regular features in our monthly magazines.

2. The introduction of a new feature entitled "Small talk" in for Only for Children *ital* as proposed by Maria Montoya.

3. The integration of some of the features that are now used exclusively in Parenting *ital* Today into our other publications.

Lesson 57 — International Marketing

GOALS: To improve speed and accuracy; to refine language-arts skills in the use of hyphens, grammar, and abbreviations; to format various business documents.

A. Type 2 times.

A. WARMUP

```
1     Lex issued an ultimatum:  Quit driving on the lawn or      11
2  I will call the police.  A fine of $50 (or even more) may     22
3  be levied against Kyle who lives at 12549 Zaine in Joplin.    34
   |  1  |  2  |  3  |  4  |  5  |  6  |  7  |  8  |  9  |  10  |  11  |  12
```

B. DIAGNOSTIC PRACTICE: ALPHABET

Turn to the Diagnostic Practice: Alphabet routine beginning on page SB-2. Type one of the Pretest/Posttest paragraphs and identify any errors made. Then type the corresponding drill lines 2 times for each letter on which you made 2 or more errors and 1 time for each letter on which you made only 1 error. Finally, repeat the same Pretest paragraph and compare your performance.

C. PACED PRACTICE

Turn to the Paced Practice routine beginning on page SB-14. Take three 2-minute timings, starting at the point where you left off the last time.

LANGUAGE ARTS

D. HYPHENS, AGREEMENT, AND ABBREVIATION

D. Study the rules at the right.

Rule: Hyphenate compound adjectives that come before a noun (unless the first word is an adverb ending in *ly*).

-adj   The determination of production goals is a high-level decision.
-adj   The reduction in hard-copy files saved the company thousands of dollars.

Rule: Use singular verbs and pronouns with singular subjects and plural verbs and pronouns with plural subjects.

Agr sing   Neither Karla nor Marie must change her computer.
Agr plur   Both Richard and Erik sold their used books at a good price.

Rule: In nontechnical writing, do not abbreviate common nouns (such as *dept.* or *pkg.*), compass points, units of measure, or the names of months, days of the week, cities, or states (except in addresses).

Abb no   Regular department meetings are on the first and third Mondays each month.
Abb no   The proposed office site is 2 miles north of the old one in Los Angeles.

Edit the sentences to correct any errors in the use of the hyphen, verb-pronoun agreement, or abbreviations.

4   The purchasing director was good at locating low-cost software.
5   All newly-hired employees attended three orientation workshops.
6   Either Glenda or Phyllis are handling the payroll this month.
7   The auditor and the treasurer are meeting with the president.
8   The new fleet cars are averaging about 21 miles per gal.
9   The remaining men will be transferred in Jan. to Athens, Ga.

DOCUMENT PROCESSING

Situation: Today is July 16, 19—, and you are the secretary to Mr. Carter B. Phillips, vice president for marketing of Rockford International in Jacksonville, Florida. The company markets electronic products all over the world. Mr. Phillips wants the letter typed first; he prefers the modified-block-style letter with standard punctuation.

Memo 9

MEMO TO: Jim Watters
(Legal Department)
From: Carter B. Phillips
DATE:
Subject: Contract for Rockford-China

(continued on next page)

several
There are still unresolved issues relating to our establishment of a wholly

foreign-owned enterprise in the Peoples Republic of China (PRC).

1. Our first concern is that Rockford-China must be able to accept orders from

any customer within the PRC in either local or foreign currency without

Government interference.

2. Also, Rockford-China must be able to pay duties in local chinese currency

for imported components, sub-assemblies, and complete products in order to

utilize locally generated revenues.

3. Rockford-China must have the freedom to set sales prices in any currency

and to pay dividends without Government interference.

Please incorporate these provisions in the draft agreement, which, it is hoped,

will be ready for signing by Thurs. of next week.

Table 18
Boxed Table

QUOTATION FOR PROPOSED INITIAL ORDER

Kangas-Rockford

Effective on August 1, 19—

Item	Item Price
Temperature Text Station	$184,000.00
Test Strength Fixture	$12,047.00
Oscilloscope	$7,855.00
XBL Transformer	$19.60
4B Resister network	$3.12
2CD Diode	$.89
4DC Capacitor Ceramic	$.65
6D Resister	$.12
mpn Transistor	$.07
TOTAL	

Mr. G. Leland Paulin
Krevitz and Paulin, Attorneys-at-Law
12406 Old Olden Avenue
Trenton, NJ 08610

Dear Mr. Paulin:

(continued on next page)

I have been informed that Talmo & Associates and your firm are now representing Lanmoore Engineering Designs, Inc., with respect to our joint arbitration hearing. The case will be heard before the London Court of International Arbitration on November 15.

Neither Rockford International nor Lanmoore has questioned our actions in the years since we began our business relationship. This is the first time that our marketing efforts have resulted in arbitration.

I look forward to receiving a summary from Jim Watters of our Legal Department after your meeting with him in early August.

Sincerely yours,

Carter B. Phillips
Vice President for Marketing

Lesson 58   Surgical Associates

GOALS: To type 40 wam/5'/5e; to format various business documents.

A. Type 2 times.

A. WARMUP

1   Do you think 1/3 of the contents of the five quart-   10
2 sized boxes would be about right? I do! If not, we can   22
3 adjust the portions by adding 6 or 7 gallons of warm water.   34

| 1 | 2 | 3 | 4 | 5 | 6 | 7 | 8 | 9 | 10 | 11 | 12

Pretest
Take a 1-minute timing. Determine your speed and errors.

Practice
Speed Emphasis: If you made 2 or fewer errors on the Pretest, type each *individual* line 2 times.
Accuracy Emphasis: If you made 3 or more errors, type each *group* of lines (as though it were a paragraph) 2 times.

Posttest
Repeat the Pretest timing and compare performance.

F. Take two 5-minute timings. Determine your speed and errors.

Goal: 40 wam/5'/5e

B. PRETEST: CLOSE REACHES

```
4        Sally took the coins from the pocket of her blouse      10
5   and traded them for fifty different coins.  Anyone could     22
6   see that Myrtle looked funny when extra coins were traded.   34
    |  1  |  2  |  3  |  4  |  5  |  6  |  7  |  8  |  9  |  10  |  11  |  12
```

C. PRACTICE: ADJACENT KEYS

```
7   as asked asset based basis class least visas ease fast mass
8   we weary wedge weigh towel jewel fewer dwell wear weed week
9   rt birth dirty earth heart north alert worth dart port tort
```

D. PRACTICE: CONSECUTIVE FINGERS

```
10  sw swamp swift swoop sweet swear swank swirl swap sway swim
11  gr grade grace angry agree group gross gripe grow gram grab
12  ol older olive solid extol spool fools stole bolt cold cool
```

E. POSTTEST: CLOSE REACHES

F. 5-MINUTE TIMING

```
13       An acquaintance of mine always seems to get her house     11
14  chores completed on time and never seems to be rushed.  So     23
15  I asked her what her special secret was.  She replied that    35
16  the only explanation she could offer was what she refers to   47
17  as her "bonus time."                                          51
18       While waiting in her auto for her son to finish his      61
19  piano lesson or while waiting to visit her dentist, she       73
20  takes a notepad and finalizes her grocery list.  Or she may   85
21  write out some monthly checks and reconcile her checkbook.    97
22  Other things she mentioned were planning the guest list and   109
23  menu for a dinner party and sorting through money-saving      120
24  coupons that she had previously clipped.                      128
25       Picking up on her ideas, I discovered over several       139
26  months that I was adding to her bonus-time list.  My purse    150
27  was cleaned out, and old photographs had been sorted and      162
28  mailed to relatives and friends.  Thank-you notes were in     173
29  the mail early, and my fingernails appeared better than       185
30  they had in years.  And I had listened to a lot of favorite   197
31  cassette tapes.                                               200
    |  1  |  2  |  3  |  4  |  5  |  6  |  7  |  8  |  9  |  10  |  11  |  12
```

Report 34
Surgery Report

Memo 10

Situation: Today is August 4, 19—, and you are a medical office assistant for Ann M. Michaels, M.D., at Surgical Assoc-iates in Bloomington, Illinois. Complete the following jobs.

Please prepare a surgery report for Dr. Michaels. Center **BLOOMINGTON GENERAL HOSPITAL / 2013 MAIN STREET / BLOOMINGTON, IL 61704** in all caps, bold, and single spaced at the top of the page. Press Enter 2 times, and then add the following headings in bold at the left just as you would position them for a memo: **PATIENT:, SURGEON:, DATE:.** The patient is Edna F. Applewick; the surgery was performed on August 4, 19—. Complete the report as follows:

BLOOMINGTON GENERAL HOSPITAL
2013 MAIN STREET
BLOOMINGTON, IL 61704

PATIENT: Edna F. Applewick

SURGEON: Ann M. Michaels, M. D.

DATE: August 4, 19—

The right hip was prepped and draped in the usual sterile fashion. A standard lateral incision was made through skin and subcutaneous tissue down to the tensor fascia, which

¶The right hip was prepped and draped in the usual sterile fashion. A standard lateral incision was made through skin and subcutaneous tissue down to the tensor fascia, which was incised along its length. The vastus lateralis was then reflected away from the lateral femoral cortex.
¶Under image intensification, a guidewire was placed at an angle through the lateral cortex into the femoral head. A 125-mm Ambi nail with four-hole sideplate was then placed over the guidewire and attached to the femur with four bone screws, each appropriately drilled, measured, and placed.
¶The wound was irrigated with lactated Ringer's. The vastus lateralis was closed using interrupted 0 Dexon; the tensor fascia was closed using interrupted 0 Dexon over a medium Hemovac drain. The subcutaneous tissue was closed with 3-0 Dexon, and the skin was closed with staples. A light compression dressing was applied. The patient tolerated the procedure well and left the operating room in satisfactory condition. Estimated blood loss was 250 cc.

MEMO TO: Kate Peterson

FROM: Ann M. Michaels, M.D.

DATE: August 4, 19--

SUBJECT: Supplemental Dental and Optical Insurance Coverage

Welcome to Surgical Associates. I am confident that you are the type of person who will provide the kind of care that our patients need.

(continued on next page)

You indicated on your employment form that you would like to have both supplemental dental and optical coverage under your health insurance coverage. Please provide the necessary information on the attached form.

I want everyone at Surgical Associates to have a positive feeling about our work environment. If at any time you have a concern, please let me know so that remedial action can be taken.

Attachment

Letter 33
Block Style

August 4, 19—

Mrs.
~~Ms.~~ Rebecca F. Pedrin

1244 Mt. Vernon Drive

Normal, IL 61761

Mrs.
Dear ~~Ms.~~ Pedrin :

The post-operative report from the audiologist indicates that there is still a 50

right
per cent loss in hearing in your ear. You may wish to consider the use of a

hearing aid. A copy of an article entitled "Hearing aid update" is enclosed for

your review.

¶ I do recall that you were not pleased with the hearing aid you had about ④
significantly
or ⑤ years ago. However, the new technology has ~~dramatically~~ improved the

quality of these instruments. I would like both you and Mr. Pedrin to read
discuss
the article and ~~dissues~~ the contents.

Sincerely Yours,

Ann M. Michaels, M. D.

Lesson 59 — Valley State Bank

GOALS: To improve speed and accuracy; to refine language-arts skills in spelling; to format various business documents.

A. Type 2 times.

A. WARMUP

```
1       Crowne and Metzner, Inc., employees* joined with 68      10
2  youngsters to repair the brick homes of 13 elderly persons;   22
3  several became very well acquainted with six of the owners.   34
   | 1 | 2 | 3 | 4 | 5 | 6 | 7 | 8 | 9 | 10 | 11 | 12
```

SKILLBUILDING

B. DIAGNOSTIC PRACTICE: NUMBERS

Turn to the Diagnostic Practice: Numbers routine beginning on page SB-5. Type one of the Pretest/Posttest paragraphs and identify any errors made. Then type the corresponding drill lines 2 times for each number on which you made 2 or more errors and 1 time for each number on which you made only 1 error. Finally, repeat the same Pretest paragraph and compare your performance.

C. Take three 12-second timings on each line. The scale below the last line shows your wam speed for a 12-second timing.

C. 12-SECOND SPEED SPRINTS

```
4  Kay Sue is on her way to that new show to take some photos.
5  Most of the ones who go may not be able to make it on time.
6  When they got to their seats, they were glad they had come.
7  Both men and women might take some of their pets with them.
   | | | |5| | |10| | |15| | |20| | |25| | |30| | |35| | |40| | |45| | |50| | |55| | |60
```

LANGUAGE ARTS

D. SPELLING

D. Type this list of frequently misspelled words, paying special attention to any spelling problems in each word.

```
8   complete recent members enclosed determine development site
9   medical facility permanent library however purpose personal
10  electrical implementation representative discussed eligible
11  organization discuss expense minimum performance next areas
12  separate professional changes arrangements reason pay field
```

Edit the sentences to correct any misspellings.

```
13  Members of the medicle and profesional group discussed it.
14  The development of the seperate cite will be completed.
15  A recent represive said the libary facility may be next.
16  A perpose of the electricle organization is to get changes.
17  However, the implimentation of changes will be permenant.
18  Arrangments for the enclosed eligable expenses are listed.
```

Situation: Today is Wednesday, October 1. You are the secretary to Mr. G. A. Lohrsbach, a senior vice president at Valley State Bank in Casper, Wyoming. Mr. Lohrsbach prefers the modified-block-style letter.

Letter 34
Modified-Block Style

Please prepare a letter to be sent to Ms. Lisa B. Dahl-Borg, President / Dahl & Associates / 8420 El Rio Road / Casper, WY 82604 / Dear Ms. Dahl-Borg:

¶Congratulations on making the decision to move your firm to the Mountain View Mall. You and your employees will enjoy the pleasant and modern surroundings as well as the availability of excellent restaurants and shops.
¶Valley State Bank, with a branch located right in the mall, would like to serve your various banking needs. We have been providing banking services for merchants and employees in the mall for over six years.
¶I look forward to visiting with you after your move on December 1 in order to identify the different ways in which we can help you. I am optimistic that we will have a long and mutually beneficial business relationship.
Sincerely,

Table 19
Open Table

Reformat this as an open table.

Press Enter once before typing the column headings in Row 2, Cells A and D to align them correctly.

IMPORTANCE OF BANKING SERVICES Mountain View Mall Employees			
Service	Very Important	Moderately Important	Unimportant
Free checking	96%	4%	0%
Teller machines	74%	18%	8%
Drive-in service	76%	16%	8%
Installment loans	83%	15%	2%
Personal banker	65%	9%	26%
Bank credit card	93%	5%	2%
Trust department	38%	17%	45%
Financial planning	33%	42%	25%
Safe-deposit boxes	74%	20%	6%

Memo 11

MEMO TO: Avis Culpepper, President

DATE: October 1, 19--

FROM: G. A. Lohrsbach, Senior Vice President

SUBJECT: Mountain View Mall survey

The survey of Mountain View Mall Employes was completed on schedule. A table that summarizes the results is attached for your information. A meeting to discuss follow-up strategies will be held inthe conference room at 9:00 a.m. on Oct. 8. Your precense at the meeting will be helpful.

Lesson 60   Metro Security Systems

GOALS: To type 40 wam/5'/5e; to format various business documents.

A. Type 2 times.

A. WARMUP

```
1      "The #6 report shows increases from 2,649 to 3,779      10
2  units," the proud CEO announced.  Ms. Bailey's reaction was  22
3  quite amazing as 80 jobs were validated with checked boxes.  34
      |  1  |  2  |  3  |  4  |  5  |  6  |  7  |  8  |  9  |  10  |  11  |  12
```

SKILLBUILDING

B. Take a 1-minute timing on the first paragraph to establish your base speed. Then take four 1-minute timings on the remaining paragraphs. As soon as you equal or exceed your base speed on one paragraph, advance to the next, more difficult paragraph.

B. SUSTAINED PRACTICE: PUNCTUATION

```
4      The men in the warehouse were having a very difficult   11
5  time keeping track of the inventory.  Things began to go     22
6  much more smoothly for them when they got the new computer.  34

7      Whenever something was shipped out, a computer entry     11
8  was made to show the change.  They always knew exactly what  23
9  merchandise was in stock; they also knew what to order.      34

10     Management was pleased with the improvement.  "We       10
11  should have made the change years ago," said the supervisor 22
12  to the plant manager, who was in full agreement with him.   34

13     This is just one example (among many) of how the work   11
14  area can be improved.  Workers' suggestions are listened    22
15  to by alert, expert managers.  Their jobs go better, too.   34
      |  1  |  2  |  3  |  4  |  5  |  6  |  7  |  8  |  9  |  10  |  11  |  12
```

C. Take two 5-minute timings. Determine your speed and errors.

Goal: 40 wam/5'/5e

C. 5-MINUTE TIMING

16	Compost piles have become more and more common all	10
17	over the country in recent years. Backyard and food wastes	22
18	are turned into humus, which can be applied to vegetable	34
19	gardens, flower gardens, and lawns. When mixed with soil,	46
20	the humus will help break up clay, help hold moisture, and	57
21	encourage the growth of friendly bacteria.	66
22	There are two desirable reasons why people who live in	77
23	houses should have a compost pile in their backyards. The	89
24	first reason is that compostable materials, such as leaves,	101
25	grass, and food waste, are about one-fourth of the rubbish	113
26	in landfills. As most good sites for landfills are quickly	125
27	being used up, the use of a compost pile is an important	136
28	contribution to the environment.	143
29	A second reason is suggested in the first paragraph.	154
30	The use of a free soil conditioner makes a lot of sense.	165
31	However, sizable amounts of food scraps must be joined with	177
32	grass and leaves so there is nitrogen to put composting	189
33	bacteria to work. Also, compost piles must be kept moist.	200

| 1 | 2 | 3 | 4 | 5 | 6 | 7 | 8 | 9 | 10 | 11 | 12

DOCUMENT PROCESSING

Situation: Today is Monday, March 4. You are the administrative assistant to Mrs. Louise Short, the marketing manager for Metro Security Systems, located in St. Louis, Missouri. Mrs. Short wants *Mrs.* used in closing lines of letter.

Report 35
Unbound Report

METRO SECURITY SYSTEMS

Metro Security Systems is pleased to announce the introduction of its newest home security system-- THE OBSERVER, Model 1023!

THE OBSERVER includes such standard features as:

- State-of-the-art infrared motion detectors.
- Built-in microprocessor to eliminate false alarms.
- Eight door and window sensors for maximum security.
- Battery power to keep the system active during power failures!
- Easy-to-use control panel.

Metro Security is pleased to offer a two-year

(continued on next page)

warranty with this new system. The cost of the system to dealers is $850, and the suggested retail price is $1,280. Discounts are available for large orders.

Over 7,000 homes in the St. Louis metropolitan area are now protected with Metro's security systems. Names of satisfied users will be provided on request.

For any technical questions about this new product, call our engineers at 1-800-555-3473. For sales information, call our marketing personnel at 1-800-555-3797.

Letter 35
Block Style

Mr. Alvin R. Schilling / 2437 Barken Avenue, Suite 1506 /

St. Louis, MO 63121 / Dear Mr. Schilling:

Thank you for your letter recently about our Security Systems. We have

carried a full line of residential and industrial security systems for the past

twelve years. As you open your new law office, it is understandable that you

are concerned about the security of your office files. Our sales representative

in your area of St. Louis, Carlos Jiminez, will be contacting you soon to

discuss your needs. Metro security will have a booth at the trade show at the

St. Louis Convention Ctr. on March 14. If you plan to attend, please stop by

and introduce yourself.

Sincerely Yours,
C: Carlos Jiminez

Table 20
Boxed Table

METRO SECURITY SYSTEMS New Industrial Clients in Past Quarter			
Company	**City, State**	**Phone**	**Contact**
ABD Controls	Leadwood, MO	314-555-9042	Donald Guidi
Chester Products	St. Louis, MO	314-555-1565	Thomas Perez
Crane Electronics	Farmington, MO	314-555-1420	Rita Clarke
Datatronics, Inc.	St. Louis, MO	314-555-3148	Vera Crispen
DK Plumbing	Danville, MO	314-555-2731	Richard Cruse

Ask your instructor for the General Information Test on Part 3.

Test 3-A
5-Minute Timing

1	Many people are aware that their eating habits are	10
2	surely not what they should be. All of the various media	22
3	put out so much information that most of us know what we	33
4	need to do to change. There is agreement that the goal	47
5	should be to develop a lifetime eating pattern which is	56
6	low in fat and high in fruits and vegetables.	65
7	If one is really sincere about making a commitment to	76
8	healthy eating routines, the first thing to do is to take	88
9	stock of existing habits. Jot down all of the foods that	99
10	you eat for one week and how much of them you eat. After	111
11	identifying the high-fat foods, look for lower-fat versions	123
12	that you can learn to accept as substitutes. For example,	135
13	pretzels are a preferred choice to chips, and ice milk or	146
14	frozen nonfat yogurt can be substituted for ice cream.	157
15	Good eaters acquaint themselves with food labels and	168
16	watch out for fat content. They also eat on a set schedule	180
17	and limit their snacking. They also change their favorite	192
18	recipes to reduce the fat content in them.	200

| 1 | 2 | 3 | 4 | 5 | 6 | 7 | 8 | 9 | 10 | 11 | 12

Test 3-B

Letter 36
Modified-Block Style

Use the current date and type a letter addressed to Mr. Robert D. Beilow, Director of Athletics / Mountainview Community College / 157 Valley Road / Winslow, AZ 86047.

As you are aware, the eight conferences of the quad states have now agreed to sponsor a basketball tournament to determine a champion from the quad states of Arizona, Colorado, New Mexico, and Utah.

¶1. The tournament will be held on the campus of Farmington Community College in Farmington, New Mexico, on March 19-21.

¶2. Each school must make its own travel arrangements. Lodging and meals will be available at Farmington. (Details are enclosed.)

¶3. On the basis of advertising and ticket revenues, each school participating in the tournament will receive some compensation.

¶Please call me if you have any questions about this invitation.

Sincerely, / Carline J. Wuoka / Administrator / {urs} / Enclosure

BASKETBALL TOURNAMENT

By Charlotte Luna

On March 19, 19—, an exciting new basketball competition will be inaugurated. The eight conference winners in the basketball programs in the community colleges of the quad states of AZ, CO, NM, and UT will meet in farmington, NM.

New Agreement

The community college Athletic Directors in the quad states have agreed that each league will send its conference champion to a tournament during the third week end of March to determine a quad states champion.[1]

Financial Benefits

The raised revenues, after expenses, will be returned to the colleges. Each college's share will be based on its performance in the tournament.[2] Thus the tournament champion will collect the biggest share of revenues.

---

[1] Pat Muranka, "Basketball Tournament Becomes a Reality," *Quad States Community College Newsletter*, July 1994, p. 12.

[2] Ibid.

Use the current date and type this memo to Marvin Palomaki, Athletic Director from Debra Marchant, Tournament Manager. The memo concerns the Quad States Tournament.

¶The participating colleges in the quad states tournament have been sent the packet of information and forms. As this is my first experience in coordinating the activities for an event like this, I am very appreciative of everything that you have done to help me.

¶Housing arrangements have been made at the Manson Inn, and all meals will be provided at the Farmington Community College dining hall. The contracts for the officials (including referees) have all been received. All media personnel are being kept informed of the developments.

¶Please look over the attached list. Have I overlooked anything?

{urs} / Attachment

Skillbuilding

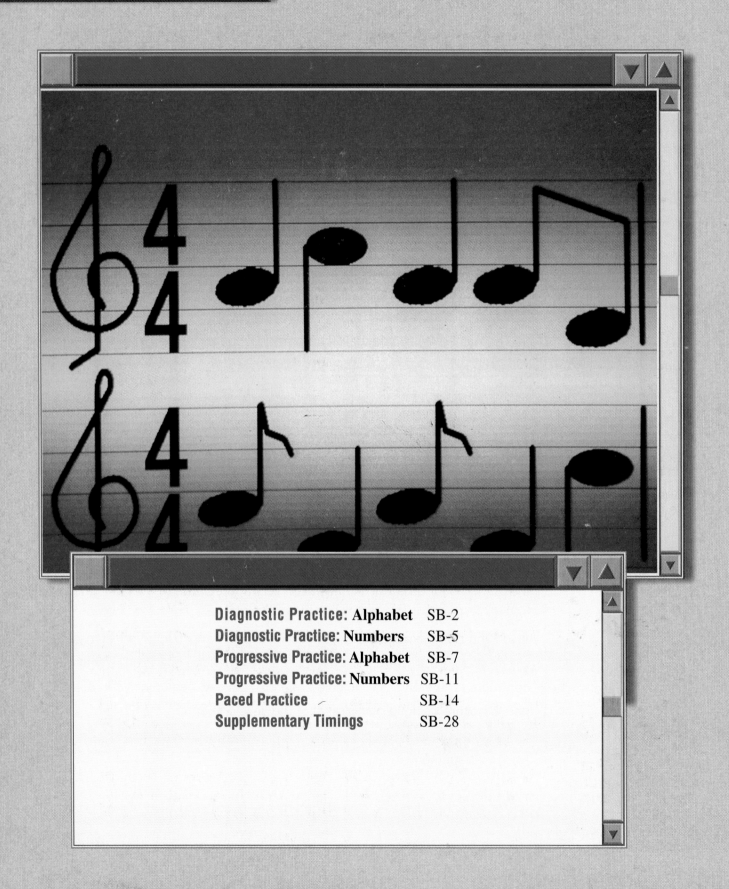

Diagnostic Practice: Alphabet

The Diagnostic Practice: Alphabet program is designed to diagnose and then correct your keystroking errors. You may use this program at any time throughout the course after completing Lesson 9.

Directions

1. Type one of the 3 Pretest/Posttest paragraphs once, pushing *moderately* for speed. Identify your errors.

2. Note your results—the number of errors you made on each key and your total number of errors. For example, if you typed *rhe* for *the*, that would count as 1 error on the letter *t*.

3. For any letter on which you made 2 or more errors, select the corresponding drill lines and type them twice. If you made only 1 error, type the drill once.

4. If you made no errors on the Pretest/Posttest paragraph, type one 3-line set of the Troublesome Pairs on page SB-4.

5. Finally, retype the same Pretest/Posttest, and compare your performance with your Pretest.

PRETEST/POSTTEST

Paragraph 1

    Sylvia and Julia made six quilts that were sold at the bazaar. Several kinds of new craft projects were judged to be quite complex and were given five kinds of prizes. Most sizable quarterly taxes were backed by both boys and girls.

Paragraph 2

    Jacob and Zeke Koufax quietly enjoyed jazz music on my new jukebox. My six or seven pieces of exquisite equipment helped both create lovely music by Richard Wagner; I picked five very quaint waltzes from Gregg Ward's jazz recordings.

Paragraph 3

    A quiet girl seized the black vase and gave it to five judges who examined it carefully. Two quickly gave it high marks. Forty people in the adjoining zone were quite vexed at some lazy judges who were lax about keeping on schedule.

PRACTICE: INDIVIDUAL REACHES

Note that each letter drill provides practice in typing that letter combination with as many other letters as possible. For example, in the A drill, the first word (Isaac) practices *aa*, the second word (badge) practices *ba*, the third word (carry) practices *ca*, and so on, through *za* in Zaire.

```
aa Isaac badge carry dared eager faced gains habit dials AA
aa jaunt kayak label mamma Nancy oasis paint Qatar rapid AA
aa safer taken guard vague waves exact yacht Zaire Aaron AA

bb about ebbed ebony rugby fiber elbow amber unbar oboes BB
bb arbor cubic oxbow maybe abate abbot debit libel album BB
bb embed obeys urban tubes Sybil above lobby webby bribe BB

cc acted occur recap icing ulcer emcee uncle ocean force CC
cc scale itchy bucks excel Joyce acute yucca decal micro CC
cc mulch McCoy incur octet birch scrub latch couch cycle CC
```

```
dd admit daddy edict Magda ideal older index oddly order DD
dd outdo udder crowd Floyd adapt added Edith Idaho folds DD
dd under modem sword misdo fudge rowdy Lydia adept buddy DD

ee aegis beach cents dense eerie fence germs hence piece EE
ee jewel keyed leads media nerve poems penny reach seize EE
ee teach guest verse Wendy Xerox years zesty aerie begin EE

ff after defer offer jiffy gulfs infer often dwarf cuffs FF
ff awful afoul refer affix edify Wolfe infra aloof scarf FF
ff bluff afoot defer daffy fifty sulfa softy surfs stuff FF

gg again edges egged soggy igloo Elgin angel ogled Marge GG
gg outgo auger pygmy agape Edgar Egypt buggy light bulge GG
gg singe doggy organ bugle agree hedge began baggy Niger GG

hh ahead abhor chili Nehru ghost Elihu khaki Lhasa unhat HH
hh aloha phony myrrh shale Ethan while yahoo choir jihad HH
hh ghoul Khmer Delhi hoard photo rhino shake think while HH

ii aired bides cider dices eight fifth vigil highs radii II
ii jiffy kinds lives mired niece oiled piped rigid siren II
ii tired build visit wider exist yield aimed binds cigar II

jj major eject fjord Ouija enjoy Cajun Fijis Benjy bijou JJ
jj banjo jabot jacks jaded jails Japan jaunt jazzy jeans JJ
jj jeeps jeers jelly jerks jibed jiffy jilts joint joker JJ

kk Akron locks vodka peeks mikes sulky links okras larks KK
kk skins Yukon hawks tykes makes socks seeks hiker sulks KK
kk tanks Tokyo jerky pesky nukes gawks maker ducks cheek KK

ll alarm blame clank idled elope flame glows Chloe Iliad LL
ll ankle Lloyd inlet olive plane burly sleet atlas Tulsa LL
ll yowls axles nylon alone blunt claim idler elite flute LL

mm among adman demit pigmy times calms comma unman omits MM
mm armor smell umber axmen lymph gizmo amass admit demon MM
mm dogma imply films mommy omits armed smear bumpy adman MM

nn ankle Abner envoy gnome Johns input knife kilns hymns NN
nn Donna onion apnea angle snore undid owned cynic angle NN
nn entry gnash inset knoll nanny onset barns sneer unfit NN

oo aorta bolts coats dolls peony fouls goofs hoped iotas OO
oo jolts kooky loins moral noise poled Roger soaks total OO
oo quote voter would Saxon yo-yo zones bombs colts doles OO

pp apple epoch flips alpha ample input droop puppy sharp PP
pp spunk soups expel typed April Epsom slips helps empty PP
pp unpin optic peppy corps spite upset types apply creep PP
```

```
qq Iraqi equal pique roque squad tuque aquae equip toque QQ
qq squab squat squid squaw quail qualm quart queen quell QQ
qq query quest quick quiet quilt quirk quota quote quoth QQ

rr array bring crave drive erode freak grain three irate RR
rr kraft honor orate Barry tramp urges liver wrote lyric RR
rr rears armor broth crown drawl erect freer grade throw RR

ss ashen bombs specs binds bares leafs bangs sighs issue SS
ss necks mills teams turns solos stops stirs dress diets SS
ss usury Slavs stows abyss asked stabs cords mares beefs SS

tt attic debts pacts width Ethel often eight itchy alter TT
tt until motto optic earth stops petty couth newts extra TT
tt myths Aztec atone doubt facts veldt ether sight Italy TT

uu audio bumps cured dumps deuce fuels gulps huffy opium UU
uu junta kudos lulls mumps nudge outdo purer ruler super UU
uu tulip revue exult yucca azure auger burns curve duels UU

vv avows event ivory elves envoy overt larva mauve savvy VV
vv avant every rivet Elvis anvil coves curvy divvy avert VV
vv evict given valve ovens serve paves evade wives hover VV

ww awash bwana dwarf brews Gwenn schwa kiwis Elwin unwed WW
ww owner Irwin sweet twins byway awake dwell pewee tower WW
ww Erwin swims twirl awful dwelt Dewey owlet swamp twine WW

xx axiom exile fixed Bronx toxin Sioux Exxon pyxie axman XX
xx exert fixes foxes oxbow beaux calyx maxim exact sixth XX
xx proxy taxes excel mixed boxer axing Texas sixty epoxy XX

yy maybe bylaw cynic dying eying unify gypsy hypos Benjy YY
yy Tokyo hilly rummy Ronny loyal pygmy diary Syria types YY
yy buyer vying Wyatt epoxy crazy kayak ready cycle bawdy YY

zz azure Czech adzes bezel dizzy Franz froze Liszt ritzy ZZ
zz abuzz tizzy hazed czars maize Ginza oozes blitz fuzzy ZZ
zz jazzy mazes mezzo sized woozy Hertz fizzy Hazel Gomez ZZ
```

```
B/V Beverly believes Bob behaved very bravely in Beaverton.
F/G Griffin goofed in figuring their gifted golfer's score.
H/J Joseph joshed with Judith when John jogged to Johnetta.

M/N Many women managed to move among the mounds of masonry.
O/P A pollster polled a population in Phoenix by telephone.
Q/A Quincy acquired one quality quartz ring at the banquet.

U/Y Buy your supply of gifts during your busy July journey.
X/C The exemptions exceed the expert's wildest expectation.
Z/A Liza gazed as four lazy zebras zigzagged near a gazebo.
```

Diagnostic Practice: Numbers

The Diagnostic Practice: Numbers program is designed to diagnose and then correct your keystroking errors. You may use this program at any time throughout the course after completing Lesson 14.

Directions

1. Type one of the 3 Pretest/Posttest paragraphs once, pushing *moderately* for speed. Identify your errors.

2. Note your results—the number of errors you made on each key and your total number of errors. For example, if you typed *24* for *25* that would count as 1 error on the number *5*.

3. For any number on which you made 2 or more errors, select the corresponding drill lines and type them twice. If you made only 1 error, type the drill once.

4. If you made no errors on the Pretest/Posttest paragraph, type one set of the drills that contain all numbers on page SB-6.

5. Finally, retype the same Pretest/Posttest, and compare your performance with your Pretest.

Paragraph 1

The statement dated May 24, 1995, listed 56 clamps, 14 batteries, 160 hammers, 358 screwdrivers, 1,208 pliers, and 2,475 files. The invoice numbered 379 showed 387 hoes, 406 rakes, 92 lawn mowers, 63 tillers, and 807 more lawn items.

Paragraph 2

My inventory records dated May 31, 1994, revealed that we had 458 pints, 2,069 quarts, and 8,774 gallons of paint. We had 2,053 brushes, 568 scrapers, 12,063 wallpaper rolls, 897 knives, 5,692 mixers, 480 ladders, and 371 step stools.

Paragraph 3

Almost 270 hot meals were delivered to the 15 shut-ins in April, 260 in May, and 280 in June. Several workers had volunteered 7,534 hours in 1996, 6,348 hours in 1995, 5,438 in 1994, and 6,277 in 1993. About 80 people were involved.

PRACTICE: INDIVIDUAL REACHES

1 aq aql aqlqa 111 ants 101 aunts 131 apples 171 animals a1
They got 11 answers correct for the 11 questions in BE 121.
Those 11 adults loaded the 711 animals between 1 and 2 p.m.
All 111 agreed that 21 of those 31 are worthy of the honor.

2 sw sw2 sw2ws 222 sets 242 steps 226 salads 252 saddles s2
The 272 summer tourists saw the 22 soldiers and 32 sailors.
Your September 2 date was all right for 292 of 322 persons.
The 22 surgeons said 221 of those 225 operations went well.

3 de de3 de3ed 333 dots 303 drops 313 demons 393 dollars d3
Bus 333 departed at 3 p.m. with the 43 dentists and 5 boys.
She left 33 dolls and 73 decoys at 353 West Addison Street.
The 13 doctors helped some of the 33 druggists in Room 336.

4 fr fr4 fr4rf 444 fans 844 farms 444 fishes 644 fiddles f4
My 44 friends bought 84 farms and sold over 144 franchises.
She sold 44 fish and 440 beef dinners for $9.40 per dinner.
The '54 Ford had only 40,434 fairly smooth miles by July 4.

5 fr fr5 fr5rf 555 furs 655 foxes 555 flares 455 fingers f5
They now own 155 restaurants, 45 food stores, and 55 farms.
They ordered 45, 55, 65, and 75 yards of that new material.
Flight 855 flew over Farmington at 5:50 p.m. on December 5.

6 jy jy6 jy6yj 666 jets 266 jeeps 666 jewels 866 jaguars j6
Purchase orders numbered 6667 and 6668 were sent yesterday.
Those 66 jazz players played for 46 juveniles in Room 6966.
The 6 judges reviewed the 66 journals on November 16 or 26.

7 ju ju7 ju7uj 777 jays 377 jokes 777 joists 577 juniors j7
The 17 jets carried 977 jocular passengers above 77 cities.
Those 277 jumping beans went to 77 junior scouts on May 17.
The 7 jockeys rode 77 jumpy horses between March 17 and 27.

8 ki ki8 ki8ik 888 keys 488 kites 888 knives 788 kittens k8
My 8 kennels housed 83 dogs, 28 kids, and 88 other animals.
The 18 kind ladies tied 88 knots in the 880 pieces of rope.
The 8 men saw 88 kelp bass, 38 kingfish, and 98 king crabs.

9 lo lo9 lo9ol 999 lads 599 larks 999 ladies 699 leaders 19
All 999 leaves fell from the 9 large oaks at 389 Largemont.
The 99 linemen put 399 large rolls of tape on for 19 games.
Those 99 lawyers put 899 legal-size sheets in the 19 limos.

0 ;p ;p0 ;p0p; 100 pens 900 pages 200 pandas 800 pencils ;0
There were 1,000 people who lived in the 300 private homes.
The 10 party stores are open from 1:00 p.m. until 9:00 p.m.
They edited 500 pages in 1 book and 1,000 pages in 2 books.

All numbers   ala s2s d3d f4f f5f j6j j7j k8k 191 ;0; Add 6 and 8 and 29.
That 349-page script called for 10 actors and 18 actresses.
The check for $50 was sent to 705 Garfield Street, not 507.
The 14 researchers asked the 469 Californians 23 questions.

All numbers   ala s2s d3d f4f f5f j6j j7j k8k 191 ;0; Add 3 and 4 and 70.
They built 1,200 houses on the 345-acre site by the canyon.
Her research showed that gold was at 397 in September 1994.
For $868 extra, they bought 15 new books and 62 used books.

All numbers   ala s2s d3d f4f f5f j6j j7j k8k 191 ;0; Add 5 and 7 and 68.
A bank auditor arrived on May 26, 1994, and left on May 30.
The 4 owners open the stores from 9:30 a.m. until 6:00 p.m.
After 1,374 miles on the bus, she must then drive 185 more.

Progressive Practice: Alphabet

This skillbuilding routine contains a series of 30-second timings that range from 16 wam to 104 wam. The first time you use these timings, take a 1-minute timing on the Entry Timing paragraph. Note your speed.

Select a passage that is 2 words a minute higher than your current speed.

Then take six 30-second timings on the passage.

Your goal each time is to complete the passage within 30 seconds with no errors. When you have achieved your goal, move on to the next passage and repeat the procedure.

Entry Timing

Bev was very lucky when she found extra quality in the   11
home she was buying. She quietly told the builder that she   23
was extremely satisfied with the work done on her new home.   35
The builder said she can move into her new house next week.   47

| 1 | 2 | 3 | 4 | 5 | 6 | 7 | 8 | 9 | 10 | 11 | 12

16 wam The author is the creator of a document.

18 wam Open means to access a previously saved file.

20 wam A byte represents one character to every computer.

22 wam A mouse may be used when running Windows on a computer.

24 wam Soft copy is text that is displayed on your computer screen.

26 wam Memory is the part of the word processor that stores information.

28 wam A menu is a list of choices to direct the operator through a function.

30 wam A sheet feeder is a device that will insert sheets of paper into a printer.

32 wam An icon is a small picture that illustrates a function or an object in software.

34 wam A window is a rectangular area with borders that displays the contents of open files.

36 wam To execute means to perform an action specified by an operator or by the computer program.

38 wam Output is the result of a word processing operation. It is in either printed or magnetic form.

40 wam Format refers to the physical features which affect the appearance and arrangement of your document.

42 wam   A font is a style of type of one size or kind which includes all letters, numbers, and punctuation marks.

44 wam   Ergonomics is the science of adapting working conditions or equipment to meet the physical needs of employees.

46 wam   Home position is the starting position of a document; it is typically the upper left corner of the display monitor.

48 wam   The mouse may be used to change the size of a window and to move a window to a different location on the display screen.

50 wam   An optical scanner is a device that can read text and enter it into a word processor without the need to type the data again.

52 wam   Hardware refers to the physical equipment used, such as the central processing unit, display screen, keyboard, printer, or drives.

54 wam   A peripheral device is any piece of equipment that will extend the capabilities of a computer system but is not required for operation.

56 wam   A split screen displays two or more different images at the same time; it can, for example, display two different pages of a legal document.

58 wam   When using Windows, it's possible to place several programs on a screen and to change the size of a window or to change its position on a screen.

60 wam   With the click of a mouse, one can use a Button Bar or a toolbar for fast access to features that are frequently applied when using a Windows program.

62 wam   An active window can be reduced to an icon when you use Windows, enabling you to double-click another icon to open a new window for formatting and editing.

64 wam   Turnaround time is the length of time needed for a document to be keyboarded, edited, proofread, corrected if required, printed, and returned to the originator.

66 wam   A local area network is a system that uses cable or another means to allow high-speed communication among many kinds of electronic equipment within particular areas.

68 wam   To search and replace means to direct the word processor to locate a character, word, or group of words wherever it occurs in the document and replace it with newer text.

70 wam   Indexing is the ability of a word processor to accumulate a list of words that appear in a document, including page numbers, and then print a revised list in alphabetic order.

72 wam   When a program needs information from you, a dialog box will appear on the desktop. Once the dialog box appears, you must identify the option you want and then choose that option.

74 wam   A facsimile is an exact copy of a document, and it is also a process by which images, such as typed letters, graphs, and signatures, are scanned, transmitted, and then printed on paper.

76 wam   Compatibility refers to the ability of a computer to share information with another computer or to communicate with some other machine. It can be accomplished by using hardware or software.

78 wam   Some operators like to personalize their desktops when they use Windows by making various changes. For example, they can change the screen colors and the pointer so that they will have more fun.

80 wam   Wraparound is the ability of a word processor to move words from one line to another line and from one page to the next page as a result of inserting and deleting text or changing the size of margins.

82 wam   It is possible when using Windows to compare the contents of different directories on the screen at the very same time. You can then choose to copy or move a particular file from one directory to another.

84 wam   List processing is an ability of a word processor to keep lists of data that can be updated and sorted in alphabetic or numeric order. A list can also be added to any document that is stored in one's computer.

86 wam   A computer is a wondrous device which accepts data that are input and then processes the data and produces output. The computer performs its work by using one or more stored programs which provide the instructions.

88 wam   The configuration is the components that make up your word processing system. Most systems include a keyboard that is used for entering data, a central processing unit, at least one disk drive, a monitor, and a printer.

90 wam Help for Windows can be used whenever you see a Help button in a dialog box or on a menu bar. Once you finish reading about a topic that you have selected, you may see a list of some related topics from which you can choose.

92 wam When you want to look at the contents of two windows when using Windows, you will want to reduce the window size. Do this by pointing to a border or a corner of a window and dragging it until the window is the size that you want.

94 wam Scrolling means to display a large amount of text by rolling it horizontally or vertically past the display screen. As the text disappears from the top section of the monitor, new text will appear at the bottom section of the monitor.

96 wam The Windows Print Manager is used to install and configure printers, join network printers, and monitor the printing of documents. Windows requires that a default printer be identified, but you can change the designation of it at any time.

98 wam A stop code is a command that makes a printer halt while it is printing to permit an operator to insert text, change the font style, or change the kind of paper in the printer. To resume printing, the operator must use a special key or command.

100 wam A computerized message system is a class of electronic mail that enables any operator to key a message on any computer terminal and have the message stored for later retrieval by the recipient, who can then display the message on his or her terminal.

102 wam Many different graphics software programs have been brought on the market in recent years. These programs can be very powerful in helping with a business presentation. If there is a need to share data, using one of these programs might be quite helpful.

104 wam Voice mail has become an essential service that many people in the business world use. This enables anyone who places a call to your phone to leave a message if you cannot answer it at that time. This special feature helps many workers to be more productive.

Progressive Practice: Numbers

This skillbuilding routine contains a series of 30-second timings that range from 16 wam to 80 wam. The first time you use these timings, take a 1-minute timing on the Entry Timing paragraph. Note your speed.

Select a passage that is 4 to 6 words a minute *lower* than your current alphabetic speed. (The reason for selecting a lower speed goal is that sentences with numbers are more difficult to type.) Take six 30-second timings on the passage.

Your goal each time is to complete the passage within 30 seconds with no errors. When you have achieved your goal, move on to the next passage and repeat the procedure.

Entry Timing

Their bags were filled with 10 sets of jars, 23 cookie	11
cutters, 4 baking pans, 6 coffee mugs, 25 plates, 9 dessert	23
plates, 7 soup bowls, 125 recipe cards, and 8 recipe boxes.	35
They delivered these 217 items to 20487 Mountain Boulevard.	47

| 1 | 2 | 3 | 4 | 5 | 6 | 7 | 8 | 9 | 10 | 11 | 12

16 wam   There were now 21 children in Room 2110.

18 wam   Fewer than 12 of the 121 boxes arrived today.

20 wam   Maybe 12 of the 21 applicants met all 15 criteria.

22 wam   There were 34 letters addressed to 434 West Cranbrooke.

24 wam   Jane reported that there were 434 freshmen and 43 transfers.

26 wam   The principal assigned 3 of those 4 students to Room 343 at noon.

28 wam   Only 1 or 2 of the 34 latest invoices were more than 1 page in length.

30 wam   They met 11 of the 12 players who received awards from 3 of the 4 trainers.

32 wam   Those 5 vans carried 46 passengers on the first trip and 65 on the next 3 trips.

34 wam   We first saw 3 and then 4 beautiful eagles on Route 65 at 5 a.m. on Tuesday, June 12.

36 wam   The 16 companies produced 51 of the 62 records that received awards for 3 of 4 categories.

38 wam   The 12 trucks hauled the 87 cows and 65 horses to the farm, which was about 21 miles northeast.

40 wam She moved from 87 Bayview Drive to 657 Cole Street and then 3 blocks south to 412 Gulbranson Avenue.

42 wam My 7 or 8 buyers ordered 7 dozen in sizes 5 and 6 after the 14 to 32 percent discounts had been bestowed.

44 wam There were 34 men and 121 women waiting in line at the gates for the 65 to 87 tickets to the Cape Cod concert.

46 wam Steve had listed 5 or 6 items on Purchase Order 241 when he saw that Purchase Requisition 87 contained 3 or 4 more.

48 wam Your items numbered 278 will sell for about 90 percent of the value of the 16 items that have code numbers shown as 435.

50 wam The managers stated that 98 of those 750 randomly selected new valves had about 264 defects, far exceeding the usual 31 norm.

52 wam Half of the 625 volunteers received over 90 percent of the charity pledges. Approximately 83 of the 147 agencies will have funds.

54 wam Merico hired 94 part-time workers to help the 378 full-time employees during the 62-day period when sales go up by 150 percent or more.

56 wam Kaye only hit 1 for 4 in the first 29 games after an 8-game streak in which she batted 3 for 4. She then hit at a .570 average for 6 games.

58 wam The mail carrier delivered 98 letters during the week to 734 Oak Street and also took 52 letters to 610 Faulkner Road as he returned on Route 58.

60 wam Pat said that about 1 in 5 of the 379 swimmers had a chance of being among the top 20. The best 6 of those 48 divers will receive the 16 best awards.

62 wam It rained from 3 to 6 inches, and 18 of those 20 farmers were fearful that 4 to 7 inches more would flood about 95 acres along 3 miles of the new Route 78.

64 wam   Those 7 sacks weighed 48 pounds, more than the 30 pounds that I had thought. All 24 believe the 92-pound bag is at least 15 or 16 pounds above its true weight.

66 wam   They bought 7 of the 8 options for 54 of the 63 vehicles last month. They now own over 120 dump trucks for use in 9 of the 15 new regions in the big 20-county area.

68 wam   Andy was 8 or 9 years old when they moved to 632 Glendale Street away from the 1700 block of Horseshoe Lane, which is about 45 miles directly west of Boca Raton, FL 33434.

70 wam   Doug had read 575 pages in the 760-page book by March 30; Darlene had read only 468 pages. Darlene has read 29 of those optional books since October 19, and Doug has read 18.

72 wam   That school district has 985 elementary students, 507 middle school students, and 463 high school students; the total of 1,955 is 54, or 2.84 percent, over last year's grand total.

74 wam   Attendance at last year's meeting was 10,835. The goal for this year is to have 11,764 people. This will enable us to plan for an increase of 929 participants, a rise of 8.57 percent.

76 wam   John's firm has 158 stores, located in 109 cities in the West. The company employs 3,540 males and 2,624 females, a total of 6,164 employees. About 4,750 of those employees work part-time.

78 wam   Memberships were as follows: 98 members in the Drama Guild, 90 members in Zeta Tau, 82 members in Theta Phi, 75 in the Bowling Club, and 136 in the Ski Club. This meant that 481 joined a group.

80 wam   The association had 684 members from the South, 830 members from the North, 1,023 members from the East, and 751 from the West. The total membership was 3,288; these numbers increased by 9.8 percent.

Paced Practice

The Paced Practice skillbuilding routine builds speed and accuracy in short, easy steps, using individualized goals and immediate feedback. You may use this program at any time after completing Lesson 9.

This section contains a series of 2-minute timings for speeds ranging from 16 wam to 96 wam. The first time you use these timings, take the 1-minute Entry Timing.

Select a passage that is 2 wam higher than your current typing speed. Then use this two-stage practice pattern to achieve each speed goal—first concentrate on speed, and then work on accuracy.

Speed Goal. Take three 2-minute timings in total. Your goal each time is to complete the passage in 2 minutes without regard to errors.

When you have achieved your speed goal, work on accuracy.

Accuracy Goal. To type accurately, you need to slow down—just a bit. Therefore, to reach your accuracy goal, drop back 2 wam to the previous passage. Take consecutive timings on this passage until you can complete it in 2 minutes with no more than 2 errors.

For example, if you achieved a speed goal of 54 wam, you should then work on an accuracy goal of 52 wam. When you have achieved 52 wam for accuracy, you would then move up 4 wam (for example, to the 56-wam passage) and work for speed again.

Entry Timing

The judge quietly spoke to the attorneys before asking   11
them to begin. The defendant was in the courtroom, and the   23
court reporter was already there to record the proceedings.   35
The jury was anxious to hear about any evidence discovered.   47

| 1 | 2 | 3 | 4 | 5 | 6 | 7 | 8 | 9 | 10 | 11 | 12

16 wam

We often do not think about the amount of time and effort spent doing a task. If we did, we would realize that many of us work hard even while we are playing.

18 wam

For example, people sweat, strain, and even suffer from discomfort when playing sports. People seem to do this for fun. If someone made them do it, they might not be so willing.

20 wam

Spending time on a job is work. For many people, work is something that they do to stay alive. Today, work means more than merely staying alive. People expect different rewards from their careers.

22 wam Work can be interesting, and more and more workers are now emphasizing that their work should be interesting. Yes, there are some very boring jobs, and every job has some aspects that are not exciting and more routine.

24 wam Today, there are many different types of jobs from which you might choose. These range from the routine to the exotic. If you begin the planning early, you can work at many different types of jobs and learn much from each job experience.

26 wam Workers tend to identify with their careers, and their careers in a real sense give them a feeling of importance and of belonging. People's jobs also help determine how people spend their spare time, who their friends are, and sometimes even where they live.

28 wam Work can take place in school, in a factory, in an office, at home, or outside; it can be done for money or experience or even voluntarily. It should be quite clear that work can be an activity that involves responsibility of some type. That same thing can be said about a job.

30 wam A career relates to work that is done for pay. But it means much more than a particular job; it is the pattern of work done throughout your lifetime. A career deals with looking ahead, planning, setting goals, and then reaching goals. The well-planned career becomes part of a person's lifestyle.

32 wam Whichever career path you select, the degree of pride shown in your work has to be at a very high level. Others will judge you by how well you do the work. Your image is affected by what you believe other people think of you as well as what you think of yourself. The quality of your efforts impacts on both of them.

34 wam

If a matter is important to a supervisor or to a firm, it should also be important to the employee. The competent person can be depended on to place priorities in order. The higher your job-satisfaction level, the greater is the likelihood that you will be pleased with all aspects of your life. Positive attitudes will produce rewards.

36 wam

Whenever people work together, attention has to be given to human relations factors. A quality organization will concern itself with interpersonal skills needed by all workers. Respect, courtesy, and patience are examples of the many words that can blend together to bring about positive human relationships in the office as well as in different situations.

38 wam

My alarm didn't go off. The road was detoured. The baby-sitter was sick. The car wouldn't start. And for some, the list of excuses goes on and on. Be thankful that this list is not yours. You will keep the tardy times to a minimum by planning and anticipating. You will realize that those people who jump the gun to quit work early at the end of each day have a bad habit.

40 wam

Some people take forever to become acquainted with the office routines. Some must have every task explained along with a list of things to be done. Some go ahead and search for new things to do. Initiative is a trait that managers must look for in people who will get promoted while on the job. A prized promotion and a pay raise can be a reward for demonstrating that a person has unique ideas.

42 wam   Newly employed workers are quite often judged by their skills in informal verbal situations. A simple exchange of greetings when being introduced to a customer is an example that illustrates one situation. A new employee might have a very good idea at a small-group meeting. However, unless that idea can be verbalized to other members in a clear, concise manner, the members will not develop a special appreciation.

44 wam   Many supervisors state that they want their workers to use what they refer to as common sense. Common sense tells a person to answer the telephone, to open the mail, and to lock the door at the end of every working day. It is easy to see that this trait equates with the use of sound judgment. The prized employee should desire to capitalize on each new experience that will help him or her to use better judgment when making decisions.

46 wam   Every person should set as a goal the proper balancing of the principal components in one's life. Few people will disagree with the conviction that the family is the most important of the four major ingredients in a human life. Experts in the career education field are quick to say that the family must be joined with leisure time, vocation, and citizenship in order to encompass a full "career." The right balance will result in satisfaction and success.

48 wam   As we increasingly become an information society, there is an ever-increasing awareness of high office costs. Such costs are labor intensive, and those who justify them are very concerned about their workers' use of time management principles. Researchers in the time management field have developed several techniques for examining office tasks and analyzing routines. The realization that time is money is only the beginning and must be followed with an educational program.

50 wam   We all want to work in a pleasant environment where we are surrounded with jovial people who never make a mistake. The realities of the real world tell us, however, that this likely will not happen; the use of corrective action may be required. For the very reason that this quality is so difficult to cultivate, all of us should strive to improve the manner in which we accept constructive criticism. By recognizing the positive intent of a supervisor, each of us will accumulate extra benefits.

52 wam   The worker and the firm might be compared in some ways with a child and the family unit. Just as a child at times disagrees with a parent, the worker might question policies of the organization. In both cases, policies must exist for conflict resolution. One option for a vexed child is to run away from home; an employee may offer a letter of resignation. A much better option in both situations is the discussion of differences. The child remains loyal to the family, and the worker remains loyal to the company.

54 wam   Those people who aspire to a role in management must be equal to the challenge. Individuals who have supervisory responsibilities must make fine judgments as decisions are formed that affect the entire organization. The challenge of managing is trying and lonely. While other labels are sometimes used to explain some of the basic management functions, the concepts remain the same. The four main functions involve actuating, organizing, planning, and controlling of such components as personnel, production, and the sales of products.

56 wam   Going to work has always been a major part of being an adult. Of course, many adolescents also have jobs that can keep them extremely busy. The work one does or the job one holds is a critical factor in determining many other things about the way a person is able to live. Various work habits are as crucial to one's success as the actual job skills and knowledge that one brings to that job. If a person is dependable, organized, accurate, efficient, cooperative, enthusiastic, and understanding, he or she will be quickly recognized by most supervisors.

58 wam   Being dependable is a desirable trait to have. When a worker says that something will be done by a specific time, it is quite assuring to a manager to know that a dependable worker is assigned to it. Workers who are dependable learn to utilize their time to achieve maximum results. This trait is also apparent with workers who have a good record for attendance. If a company is to be productive, it is essential to have workers who are on the job. Of course, the trustworthy employee not only is on the job but also is the worker that can be counted on to be there on time.

60 wam   The ability to organize is one other quality that is necessary to exhibiting good work habits. A worker must have a sense of being able to plan the work that is to be done and then to be able to work that plan to be organized. It is commonly understood that competent workers are well organized. If office workers are organized, requests are handled promptly, letters are answered quickly, and projects do not accumulate on the desk. In addition, the organized office worker returns all phone calls without delay and makes a list of those activities that are to be accomplished on a daily basis.

62 wam   Another trait or work habit essential for success on a job is accuracy. Accurate workers are in much demand. The worker who tallies numbers checks them very carefully to be sure that there are no errors. When reviewing documents, the accurate worker has excellent proofreading skills to locate all errors. Since accuracy is required on all jobs, it is critical that a person possess this trait. Accurate workers are careful in all the work that they undertake or complete. If a worker checks all work that is done and analyzes all steps that are taken, it is likely that a high level of accuracy will be attained.

64 wam   Efficiency is another work habit that is much admired. This means that a worker is quick to complete an assignment and to begin work on the next job. Efficient workers think about saving steps and time when working. For example, one should plan to make one trip to the copier versus going for each individual job. Being efficient means having all the right tools to do the job right. An efficient worker is able to zip along on required jobs, concentrating on doing the job right. Being efficient also means having all needed supplies for every job within reach. This means that a worker can produce more work in a little less time.

66 wam   Cooperation is another desired work habit. This means that an employee is thinking of all the team members when a decision is made. A person who cooperates is willing to do something for the benefit of the entire group. As a member of a work unit or team, it is absolutely essential that you take extra steps to cooperate. Cooperation may mean being a good sport if you have to do something you would rather not do. It could also mean a worker helps to correct an error made by someone else in the office. If a worker has the interests of the organization at heart, it should be a little bit easier to resolve to cooperate with endeavors of the company.

68 wam   Enthusiasm is still another work trait that is eagerly sought by most employers. Being enthusiastic means that an employee has lots of positive energy. This is reflected in actions toward the work as well as toward the employer. It has been noted that enthusiasm can be catching. If workers have enthusiasm, they can reach for the gold. It might pay to examine your own level of enthusiasm for a given job or project. Analyze whether you help to build up people or whether you seem to project a negative or a pessimistic attitude. There will always be lots of job opportunities for workers who are known to possess a wealth of enthusiasm for the work they are assigned to.

70 wam   Understanding is another work habit or trait that is a requirement to be an excellent worker. In this society, the likelihood of working with people who have differences is quite probable. It is essential to have workers who can understand and accept all the differences that are evident in all the other employees who are in a unit or division. On the job, it is imperative that workers realize that employees will have different aptitudes and abilities. The chances are also good that differences in race, ethnicity, religion, work ethic, cultural background, and attitude can be found. With so many possible differences, it is clear that a very high degree of mutual understanding is needed.

72 wam   Reviewing the seven previous Paced Practice exercises, it can be concluded that specific work habits or traits can play a major role in determining the success of a worker at a given job or task. Most managers would be quick to agree on the importance of these traits. These habits would most likely be evaluated on any performance appraisal forms you might see. Of course, while these work habits are critical to the success of an individual on the job, there is also the need for specific competencies and abilities for a given job. A new worker must size up the needed blend of these traits in addition to those required competencies. As will be noted, a worker needs various skills to become a success at work.

74 wam
A major part of an office job is deciding what kinds of equipment will best meet company objectives. One should analyze several systems, checking for easy and flexible usage. The next step is then defining the requirements of each job in terms of work volume, space requirements, and overall budget restrictions. The different function types must then be categorized. An itemized checklist of every task should be used to identify the various tasks performed by every employee. Data may be obtained through the use of interviews, questionnaires, or observation. Some subjects covered may include document creation, worker interaction, scheduling, typing, filing, and telephoning. Technology must then be selected to match job needs.

76 wam
While technology has quite dramatically changed nearly all office procedures in the last decade, the attention to changing human interaction at the workplace because of all of these changes has been largely neglected. Some people have a great deal of enthusiasm for working with different kinds of computers, while others view computers as a great threat, a fearsome complexity. It is expected that most people's jobs will in time be affected by computers. It is imperative to ease employees' qualms about learning to use the new equipment. A good method is to nurture a positive attitude toward the computer by convincing employees of two things. First, office work is made much easier. Second, the workers are much more apt to become highly organized.

78 wam   The ergonomics experts stress the major role furniture plays in the well-being of office workers. Many years ago, we paid little attention to whether our chairs and desks suited our utility and comfort needs. But now we know that various styles, sizes, shapes, and colors have quite an impact on our quality and quantity of work. An informed manager must carefully plan workers' surroundings. Colors in a workplace may produce major effects on one's moods. Studies show that the cool colors, such as blue and green, are quiet and relaxing. Cool colors should be used in offices that are located in warm areas such as south or west sections of the building. The warm colors, such as red, yellow, and orange, are cheerful and add zip to a job, which may help improve morale.

80 wam   Today we hear a great deal about how important human relations are in management. Job-related human interaction is a comparatively new concern. This can be easily seen if we look at the history of leadership theories as they apply to management practice. When people first started to study leadership, it was expected that certain qualities, such as height, could predict effective leaders. Next, exceptional leaders were studied to see if they had similar qualities. However, that proposal was not any more successful than the earlier approaches. Now, it is generally known that many elements combine to make a person an effective leader. A specific leader's proficiency varies from one situation to another. Leaders must develop a personal style that will serve them well while on the job.

82 wam
Do you enjoy your work most of the time? Do you look forward to going to work each day? Though some people say that their work is unpleasant, the majority of both men and women usually will say that they find their work generally satisfying. If it isn't, the problem may be that there is a poor fit between the job and the worker. Quality of life at work is a major concern of both management and labor. When jobs become boring and routine, workers often become less productive because they do not feel challenged. The concept of job enrichment greatly enhances the types of experiences an employee deals with every day by upgrading the responsibilities of the job. Opportunity for growth is the key to job enrichment. All organizations should have some jobs that have great potential for enrichment and growth.

84 wam
More and more women are moving into executive levels in business and industry. Many women who pursue careers in management today have moved into their positions after having gained experience as office support personnel. This background gives them a real appreciation for those myriad contributions made by such workers as file clerks, word processors, and other office support staff members who work in a firm. Some women have acquired their managerial roles after earning degrees and acquiring experience through jobs in such fields as finance, marketing, accounting, and law. But the measure of success as a manager, no matter what the degrees or past experiences are, is how well one identifies goals and problems and then drives toward the realization of those goals and the resolution of those problems for the good of a company.

86 wam   Most of us have had occasion to write business letters from time to time whether to apply for a job, to comment on a product or service, or to place an order. Often it seems to be an easy task to sit and let our thoughts flow freely. In other cases we seem to struggle over the proper wording, trying to say what we want to say in just the right way. Writing is a skill that can come with practice and, most of all, with study. One can learn. There are many writing principles that must be studied to ensure good letters. Some of these principles are as follows: Use language in letters that you would be comfortable using face-to-face. Use words that are simple and direct. Choose words that will not offend others. Try to be positive. Emphasize the bright side of a situation when possible. Be kind. Write the way you would like people to talk.

88 wam   One of the most important areas for a business student to study is report writing. Many persons who are working in business organizations indicate that one of the areas they feel the least prepared for is report writing. Most people in college do not know that they probably will be asked to write reports on the job. However, most colleges are aware of this problem today and are striving to correct the situation. They are succeeding. There has been quite a large increase in the range of report writing courses in business curriculums in recent years. Reports may fall into categories such as horizontal, radial, and vertical. Horizontal reports move from person to person or from department to department and are informational. Radial reports may be publicized research. Vertical reports go up and down in the company and include status reports or policy statements.

90 wam   Almost everyone has experienced interviewing for a job during his or her life. For some persons, the interview is a traumatic time. But when a candidate adequately prepares for this interview, it doesn't have to be very frightening. A person should apply only for those jobs for which he or she is professionally prepared. Before an interview one should obtain detailed information about the company with which he or she is seeking employment. You should always learn the name of the person who will conduct the interview and use the name during the interview. It's also best to take a neat copy of your resume. It goes without saying that suitable business attire is required. As a candidate, you will be judged on personality, appearance, and poise as well as competence. At the finish of every interview, it would be prudent to stand up, shake hands, and address the interviewer by name.

92 wam   Are you an active listener? Listening is a skill that few people possess. It is one important way to bring about change in people. Listening is not a passive activity, and it is the most effective agent for personality development. Quality listening brings about change in people's attitudes toward themselves and others' values. People who have been listened to become more open to their experiences, less defensive, more fair, and less authoritative. Listening builds positive relationships and tends to constructively change the perspective of the listener. Active listening on the job is extremely important whether an employee is in the top levels of management or works at the lower end of the hierarchy. Every worker should try to analyze his or her listening habits to see whether some improvements in listening can be made. Pleasant human interaction will often bring about even more job satisfaction.

94 wam
Listening is a skill that is an essential component of the communication process. A great many experts have found that lack of good listening skills is a major cause for the breakdown in effective communications. In the first place, there must be understanding. If ideas given by a speaker are not completely understood, it is most likely that there will be problems. In addition, a listener must attempt to keep an open mind for any new, bright ideas which might be considered. A good listener must be active. Three steps should take place. Think about what the speaker is saying. The ideas and facts that you hear should be compared to information that you already know. Second, try to analyze what the person is saying, and try to read between the lines. Third, show empathy toward the speaker. This can be achieved by putting yourself in the speaker's place. You should make an attempt to establish a bond with the speaker.

96 wam
Speech is a major factor in the communication process. In evaluating the quality of your voice, you should analyze the four factors of pitch, tempo, tone, and volume in order to determine whether or not some improvements must be made. Pitch refers to the sound of a voice. A shrill voice would turn people off. If a voice has a very low pitch, it might be too dull or too hard to hear. The voice which is the most pleasing is the one which has a moderate pitch. The tone of a voice might help reveal the attitude and feelings of the speaker. You should hope to project a tone that is both cheerful and pleasant. You should always adapt the tone of your voice to the meaning of the words that you are speaking. Volume is also a critical factor in evaluating a voice. Your voice should carry to every person in a room. Using good breath control, you can enhance your ability to increase or decrease the volume of your speech to satisfy all audiences.

Supplementary Timings

SUPPLEMENTARY TIMING

Spacing: Double

Since the early settlers first came to this land, our   11
people have always had a strong interest in the actions of   23
our government. When you speak of our national, state, or   35
local government, you can be sure that a lively debate will   47
start. This is most true when election time comes and the   58
candidates speak to the issues. Media reports of debates   70
and of election issues tend to be quite broad and can serve   82
as a gauge of what voters seem to want.   90

Of course, economic issues are bound to start a major   101
debate on the part of those who pay taxes. Raising taxes   113
or changing the tax laws will often start a debate. One   124
other topic that causes much debate deals with our defense   136
plans. Many candidates have used this issue to put forth   147
their own campaign. If you look at the past history of our   159
nation, you will see that issues of defense will always be   171
a chief concern.   175

In addition to economic and defense issues, you will   185
be amazed at how quickly a lively debate can start over   197
social issues. For instance, crime, education, and privacy   209
are topics that have been of special interest in recent   220
years. There has also been a good deal of debate about the   232
environment, as well as many questions about our welfare   243
system. A lot of people have a profound interest in the   255
actions of our judicial groups and the way in which they   266
respond to social issues that face our nation. It is easy   278
to see that issues debated by government are sure to be of   290
concern in years to come. People must be concerned.   300

| 1 | 2 | 3 | 4 | 5 | 6 | 7 | 8 | 9 | 10 | 11 | 12

More and more people are retiring at a younger age as ⸝11

new retirement programs are being offered by business firms ⸝23

and by the government. A good number of the people who ⸝34

retire early may even be starting in a new career or a new ⸝46

job. This is happening at a time when the life expectancy ⸝58

for adults has been quickly rising in our changing society. ⸝70

With the increase in life expectancy and the early ⸝80

retirement plans, it can be seen that adults must be sure ⸝92

to plan carefully for their retirement years. If planning ⸝104

is not done, many people who are in good health could find ⸝115

themselves at this point in their lives with plenty of free ⸝127

time and not much to do. As one ages, it is important to ⸝139

look at the activities that one enjoys and to strengthen ⸝150

one's interest in those things. At the same time, it is ⸝162

important to find new interests and hobbies so that the ⸝173

time in retirement will be enjoyed to the very fullest. It ⸝185

should be noted that the financial part of retirement must ⸝197

also be planned in a careful way. One should be sure to ⸝208

check all investments. ⸝213

Of course, some retirees enjoy visiting with family ⸝223

and friends. Others plan to travel as much as they can to ⸝235

many parts of the country or of the world. Then one can ⸝247

find some retirees who pursue a hobby with intense zeal. ⸝258

Whatever one wants to do, the most critical factor is that ⸝270

planning must be done with care prior to the date one sets ⸝282

for retirement. In this way, one can be sure to have a ⸝293

retirement that brings much success. ⸝300

| 1 | 2 | 3 | 4 | 5 | 6 | 7 | 8 | 9 | 10 | 11 | 12

The value of team play and of team effort has been a 11
topic of great interest to many different people. There 22
are experts who look at the actions of people in a variety 34
of research studies in order to find out the impact of a 45
unified effort on how much the group is able to achieve. 57
The results are always the same. When a group of people 68
tries to meet a shared goal, it is quite likely that more 80
will be gained. This is true in many environments--office, 92
plant, home, school, or church. It is especially true when 104
one looks at the success of athletic teams. 113

Many business firms have now begun quality circles in 124
their offices and plants. The goal of these circles is to 136
encourage small groups of workers to meet on a periodic 147
basis to find out if any of the procedures or steps that 158
they follow in the jobs they do can be improved. The small 170
groups give each person in the unit a stake in the way the 182
unit functions as a whole. A quality circle recognizes the 194
benefits that can come from a team effort. 203

The concept of team effort is most evident when it 213
comes to athletic events. Each time that a study is made 225
of a championship team in any sport or event, many comments 237
can be made about the team play and the team spirit that 248
were observed. This point is often discussed after a big 260
game by sportswriters and the many fans of a team. A lot 271
of experts, in fact, would back the notion that team effort 283
is more important than the talents of any single player or 295
players on any one team. 300

| 1 | 2 | 3 | 4 | 5 | 6 | 7 | 8 | 9 | 10 | 11 | 12

Spacing: Double

For over three decades, firms have been trying, with 11
higher and higher levels of success, to harness information 23
technology. The role that top management has played has 34
often not been as useful as it could have been. Managers 46
have helped things happen rather than made them happen. 57
People today must know something about the technology that 69
helps them do their jobs. Telecommunications involves some 81
fairly simple concepts that quickly expand into complex 92
details. The jargon alone is often enough to numb the mind 104
and cause some concern. 109

It makes no sense for managers to try to learn the 119
nuts and bolts of the technology. The field is moving too 131
fast for experts to keep up their knowledge base. What 142
managers need is the same level of basic understanding that 154
a person involved in business has to have about accounting. 167
They should have a sense of the major sections and terms, 178
such as debits and credits. They must be able to interpret 190
a computer plan in the same way that they read a financial 202
statement. That level of knowledge in no way means they 213
are experts, but it enables them to take part in planning 225
and not be scared off because they don't know the topic. 236

When managers deal with technology, they often will be 247
dealing with change because it brings organizational and 259
business issues to the foreground of planning and action. 271
It pushes senior managers to take on a new relationship 282
with what has often been outside their scope. Ten years 293
ago, few executives would have defined an understanding of 305
technology as part of the profile of an effective manager. 317
If they don't do so now, they soon will. Change may be a 329
problem, but it also can bring new growth. Technology can 341
pave the way for new growth for all executives. 350

| 1 | 2 | 3 | 4 | 5 | 6 | 7 | 8 | 9 | 10 | 11 | 12

Pick up any newspaper or turn on any news program on 11
TV, and it seems you will hear yet another story about an 22
oil tanker that has spilled its cargo or a landfill that 34
has reached its limit. As more and more people are paying 46
heed to the environmental concerns, more and more companies 58
are following suit by setting environmental goals. 68

What are the reasons so many firms have a new stance 79
on these issues? First, and foremost, there appear to be 90
more simultaneous threats to our world today than at any 102
other time. Our federal government believes that four out 113
of ten Americans live in places where the air isn't healthy 125
to breathe. Other issues include ozone depletion, acid 137
rain, the fouling of thousands of rivers and lakes by raw 148
sewage and toxic wastes, destruction of rain forests, and 160
the greenhouse effect. 164

A second reason for the growing concern over these 175
issues in corporate America is a response to heightened 186
public awareness of the problem. Nine out of ten people 197
say they would be willing to make a special effort to buy 209
products that show concern for protecting the air, land, 220
and water. Membership in environmental groups is soaring. 232
There are now tens of thousands of conservation groups; 244
each town seems to have two or three doing anything from 255
trying to save a trout stream to questioning the building 267
of a shopping mall. 271

In recent decades over a dozen major environmental 281
laws have been passed. As a result, the overall pollution 293
levels have dropped. New regulations focus on the keeping 305
of records and seem to focus less on the ideal standards 316
that are set up for business firms to follow. While much 328
has been done, strong maintenance is the key to keeping our 340
air, water, and land clean and usable in the future. 350

| 1 | 2 | 3 | 4 | 5 | 6 | 7 | 8 | 9 | 10 | 11 | 12

Spacing: Double

The perception of time by human beings has grown out 11
of a natural series of rhythms which are linked to daily, 22
monthly, and yearly cycles. No matter how much we live by 34
our wristwatches, our bodies and our lives will always be 46
somewhat influenced by an internal clock. What is of even 58
greater interest, though, are the many uses and perceptions 70
of time based on individuals and their cultures. 79

Rhythm and tempo are ways we relate to time and are 90
distinguishing features of a culture. In some cultures, 101
folks move very slowly; in others, moving quickly is the 113
norm. Mixing the two types may bring about feelings of 124
discomfort. People may have trouble relating to each other 136
because they are not in synchrony. To be synchronized is 148
to move in union with another person; it is critical for a 159
strong and lengthy partnership. 166

In general Americans move at a fast tempo, although 177
there are regional differences. In meetings, they tend to 188
be impatient and want to get down to business right away. 200
They have been taught that it is best to come to the point 212
quickly and avoid vagueness. Because American business 223
works in a short time frame, prompt results are often of 234
more interest than the building of long-term relationships. 246

Time is also the basic organizing system for all of 257
life's events. Time is used for establishing priorities. 269
For example, lead time varies quite a bit from one culture 281
to the next. When you do business with people of other 292
cultures, it is crucial to know just how much lead time is 304
required for each event. For instance, numerous corporate 315
executives have their time scheduled for months in advance. 328
Last-minute requests by telephone are often viewed as poor 339
planning and may be perceived as insulting behavior. 350

| 1 | 2 | 3 | 4 | 5 | 6 | 7 | 8 | 9 | 10 | 11 | 12

Spacing: Double

All too often companies place too much importance on 11

the rational, logical side of the intellect and neglect the 23

creative, intuitive side. As creative thought occurs in 34

the mind, it cannot be seen and, therefore, is not easily 46

measured. Perhaps for this reason, there are only a few 57

socially accepted roles where it is okay to be creative, 69

try out new ideas, or seek different methods for reaching 80

goals. Even when managers claim to want creative ideas 91

from their employees, the fear of taking risks may squelch 103

all of these efforts. 108

As a result, creative people often find themselves on 119

the outside looking in as new ideas are analyzed over and 130

over again in an effort to minimize or eliminate the risk. 142

It may be next to impossible to start a new product which, 154

in the firm's early days, might have been launched quickly 166

without excessive controls and approvals. As a response to 178

this restraint on imagination, thousands of our businesses 190

are launched every year, many guided by former employees of 202

large companies who found their creativity and innovative 213

ideas stifled. 216

While some creative people leave the corporate world 227

to find their own niche by starting a small company, many 239

stay and try to teach their bosses how to better utilize 250

the talents found right in their own firm. Although some 262

experts think that creativity comes only from a few special 274

people placed in top jobs, most believe that creativity 285

can, and should, be sought from all employees. If given 296

the right support and enough time, nearly everyone has the 308

ability to find better systems, strategies, or products. 319

A part of the challenge of encouraging creativity, 330

though, is learning to manage creative people effectively, 342

which is not an easy task. They tend to question policies 353

rather than accept the way things are always done. Their 365

high energy levels may result in poor behavior and burnout. 377

Creative workers tend to be driven by the belief that they 389

can overcome sizable obstacles and bring about change. 400

| 1 | 2 | 3 | 4 | 5 | 6 | 7 | 8 | 9 | 10 | 11 | 12

Spacing: Double

There are a few essential items businesspeople today 11

should know about telecommunications in order to be up to 22

date in their field. Although it may seem confusing at 34

first, it is quite simple once you realize that there are 45

just four main components involved in almost all systems. 57

The first part is called transmission and includes all the 69

links along which the signals are sent and the techniques 80

for coding information. The medium may be cable, microwave 92

radio, satellite, fiber optics, or anything else that can 104

carry the data signal. 109

The next component is the switches. Switches are the 120

specialized equipment at set points of a communications 131

network. At these points the signals from transmission 142

links are processed in order to route them to the terminal 154

or computer, translate them from one message format to the 166

next format, improve the efficiency of transmission, or 177

handle other aspects of the network control. It is in this 189

area that the technology is moving fastest and is the most 201

unstable in terms of products, standards, and vendors. 212

Terminals, devices that access the computer network, 222

are the third area. Most of the time they are personal 234

computers linked to a distant computer for accessing data, 245

processing data, or communicating messages to some other 257

terminals. There are other possibilities, such as word 268

processors, telephones, central mainframe computers, and 279

even some types of workstations. 286

The final part is the network. This is a system of 297

switches and transmission links, as well as a listing of 308

the terminal points that can access them and thus contact 320

each other. The U.S. phone setup is one such network, with 332

the phone number providing the address. The same phone can 344

link itself into other countries' networks. Even though 355

these systems may use different transmission features and 367

conventions, special switches can translate the protocols. 379

In the same way, a single terminal may access many networks 391

which, in turn, can be linked through switches. 400

| 1 | 2 | 3 | 4 | 5 | 6 | 7 | 8 | 9 | 10 | 11 | 12

Spacing: Double

Employee recruitment has become both more demanding 11
and more urgent in recent years. In order to compete in 22
the global marketplace, many companies are giving their 33
workers duties that require greater levels of trust and 44
power. Finding people able to handle these added tasks is 56
a tall order for recruiters at a time when the typical pool 68
of recruits is shrinking and filled with many folks who are 80
not qualified or interested in taking responsibility for 92
additional tasks while on the job. 99

To meet this challenge, smart employers will do two 110
things: expand current recruiting methods and design new 122
ones. Expanding old methods, such as creatively using the 133
help-wanted section in the local paper, seems to be the 145
current plan of action for the majority of firms. While 156
adjusting current procedures may be helpful in the short 168
run, these new procedures may not be enough to meet future 179
challenges unless they are mixed with unique methods. 190

One way of designing a new recruiting method is to 201
work diligently to obtain a workforce that is diverse. 212
For instance, some companies make special arrangements to 224
match the needs of new recruits they are trying to target, 235
such as older people, students, or the handicapped. Then 247
they market these benefits with certain campaigns designed 259
just for those audiences. A second creative approach is to 271
hire more workers on a temporary basis. Such hires are no 283
longer support staff or unskilled workers but now include a 295
sizable number of high-level professionals. 304

All of these changes will require firms to be better 314
trained, less biased, and more holistic in their future 326
thinking on recruiting and hiring goals. They will need to 338
know the facts about what inspires people to join them. 349
Smart recruiters will take a long, careful look at hiring 361
strategies, including their recruiting materials and the 372
interview process. Since retention can no longer be taken 384
for granted, recruiters will also have to gather data on 395
why employees stay or leave. 400

| 1 | 2 | 3 | 4 | 5 | 6 | 7 | 8 | 9 | 10 | 11 | 12

Index